ROB ROSE

STEINHEIST

Markus Jooste, Steinhoff
and SA's biggest corporate fraud

TAFELBERG

Also by Rob Rose

The Grand Scam: How Barry Tannenbaum Conned
South Africa's Business Elite

Tafelberg, an imprint of NB Publishers,
a division of Media24 Boeke Pty (Ltd),
40 Heerengracht, Cape Town, South Africa
www.tafelberg.com

Set in 11 on 16 pt Chaparral
Cover and infographics by scarletstudio.net
Cover picture by Gallo Images/Financial Mail/Jeremy Glyn
Book design by Nazli Jacobs
Edited by Russell Martin
Proofread by Lisa Compton
Commissioning editor: Gill Moodie

Printed and bound by **novus print**, a Novus Holdings company

First edition, first impression 2018
Third impression 2019

ISBN: 978-0-624-0-8597-3
Epub: 978-0-624-0-8598-0
Mobi: 978-0-624-0-8599-7

Contents

Author's Note
and Acknowledgements

———

It is fair to say that Markus Jooste didn't much like me. Back in October 2011, I'd written about a court case in which the South African Revenue Service (SARS) had dragged him to court, demanding R207m in back taxes from him. What was interesting about that case was not the fact he was fighting with the tax authority – he'd been pushing the limit for many years. Rather, it exposed a side of Markus Jooste that nobody had ever seen: how he appeared to be making millions personally through side deals involving Steinhoff; deals that, notably, hadn't been disclosed as "related party" ones. In that case, the tax authority claimed he'd made hundreds of millions when his company bought the Thesen forests in Knysna for R11.9m in 2001, and then had flipped it onto Steinhoff for R159.7m a few years later – a handsome profit indeed. It was the sort of self-dealing that gives capitalism a bad name – an economic system already facing some-thing of a credibility crisis in a country where 37% of the adult population don't have a job.

The forestry deal was intriguing because it suggested that the CEO of this rapidly expanding retail company, who'd been described as charming and one of the hardest-working guys around, wasn't just in business for the shareholders. It seemed there might be another dimension to the Steinhoff story.

That newspaper article rankled with him. Often, he'd mention it to his colleagues, who'd tell me about it. Then in September 2017, he gave an interview to the *Financial Mail* in which he complained about the article, as it had come out "when I visited my mother for lunch". "I refused under that pressure and under SARS' threats . . . When [SARS] lost, six-nil in court with costs, do you think anybody wrote anything? Nothing – and that's the problem," he said.

In Markus Jooste's world, he's always been the victim of unfair publicity, an unfair vendetta by a former business partner in Austria, Andreas Seifert, and unfair criticism by analysts who just didn't truly understand what he was trying do. In that same interview, Jooste railed against the German criminal investigation into him and Steinhoff, which made headlines in 2015, days before the company's listing on the Frankfurt Stock Exchange. Journalists "twist it to make it sensational", he said. "At the end of the day, the authorities worldwide are looking for more tax . . . you must remember: it's a game for money." It was a revealing choice of words, even as he insisted that Steinhoff was a business built for the long term. "Our game is for long-term investors who want to invest in a business that will be there when all of us are gone. We plant a tree for every tree we cut. Why should I do that? The trees they're going to harvest being planted now, I'll be dead for 15 years before we cut them. It's about sustainability, it's about the long term," he said.

It turns out that it wasn't just trees that were being cut. Corners were being cut all over the place, but most especially in Europe, where a series of opaque companies were set up under the pretence that they were independent from Steinhoff, but whose real goal seems to have been to help burnish its accounts.

When late at night on Tuesday, 5 December 2017, Steinhoff announced that it had found "accounting irregularities" and that Jooste "has tendered his resignation with immediate effect", it wasn't just the fifty thousand individual investors in South Africa and overseas who felt the aftershock. South Africa's investment reputation took just as much of a hammering. As Shane Watkins, the founder of investment company All Weather Capital, put it, foreign investors from places like the US, Europe and Asia had invested in South Africa, despite the fact that its growth rate was relatively low, because it was seen as having some of the best-managed companies in the world. "Then we had Steinhoff, and other examples since, that reflect badly on us. I'm concerned that those who came here in the search for quality businesses will re-examine this rationale." Nicky Newton-King, who heads the continent's largest stock exchange, the JSE, agrees. "South Africa had pretty much an unblemished reputation among emerging markets for having the strongest management and ethical corporate standards. Now, after Steinhoff, it creates the impression that we're no longer first among equals – we're no different from other emerging markets where there are issues."

What has happened has challenged the view that the governance in South African companies is strong enough to stop these sorts of ethical breaches. More than that, there was a bracing realisation that the moral decay that had assumed grotesque forms under former President Jacob Zuma from 2009 until 2018 may not have been confined to venal politicians.

Craig Butters, a portfolio manager at Prudential Investment Managers, is someone who'd been sceptical about Markus Jooste and Steinhoff for more than a decade. Famously, he'd met Christo Wiese in 2009 to warn him off Steinhoff. "It has broader resonance. Everyone has been pointing fingers at government officials for their poor ethics. But we've shown them that we're not any better in the private sector." This may sound dramatic, but then Steinhoff *is* South Africa's Enron – one of the largest companies on the stock exchange that had, entirely unnoticed, been apparently corrupted for years.

Of the 1,651 pension funds registered in South Africa, 948 had exposure to Steinhoff – more than half of all retirement funds in the country. Consider that from its peak at R96.94 in April 2016, the stock had ebbed to R45.65 before Jooste's resignation. But, within two days it had lost 86% of its value. In the end, it reached a low of just R1.12 in June 2018 – a loss of 98% in just more than two years. This meant that, at last count, civil servants whose pensions were invested with Steinhoff had lost more than R21bn.

As Heather Sonn, who took over as Steinhoff's chair after Jooste's resignation in December 2017, puts it: "At Steinhoff, I believe there was purposeful deceit where certain people went to great lengths to misrepresent the financial statements, in collusion with others." In this way, she says, what happened is comparable to Enron. At least in the case of Enron – the Houston-based energy company that went bankrupt in 2001, after massive corruption was discovered, including off-balance sheet vehicles designed to hide losses – people went to jail. By contrast, as damning as the Steinhoff evidence appears to be, nobody is holding their breath that South Africa's Hawks – a supposed elite crime-fighting authority thoroughly gutted by the rotten years of Zuma – will be able to secure any convictions. They're more like buzzards with crooked wings than any sort of real bird of prey.

What we do know, and what you'll read in this book, is how Steinhoff bamboozled the country's wealthiest, most accomplished and most powerful business leaders.

In many places in the book, such as the first chapter, which recounts what happened behind the scenes in the week before Steinhoff's collapse, the narrative has been reconstructed and verified with a number of sources from within those meetings and boardrooms. (In the first chapter I did not use quotation marks to denote when the various characters are talking. This is deliberate and is meant to highlight the fact that it is a reconstruction – and that I was not there in person.)

You'll also read the story behind the Steinhoff leaks, written by the *Financial Mail*'s tenacious reporter Warren Thompson. Those emails, published here, are damning evidence in themselves.

To be able to tell the story of Steinhoff, I am deeply indebted to numerous people who were instrumental in this book being written. This includes Craig Butters, who first began talking to me about the "imminent collapse" of Steinhoff more than eight years ago; my colleague Warren Thompson and the brains trust at the *Financial Mail* who acted as the cliché police while I was writing; publisher Gill Moodie; and all the journalists who have done a fantastic job in telling this story for months – most particularly among them, my wife Janice. And, finally, the dozens of people I spoke to, both from within Steinhoff and from outside, who filled in the rough outlines of the story with luminous and arresting colour, giving life to the story of what I believe is South Africa's most epic fraud.

ROB ROSE
September 2018

1

The Unravelling

Wednesday, 29 November 2017

For the first time since the rumours started, Christo Wiese's blood ran cold. Until then, he'd largely written it off, the scurrilous talk of fraud, the endless drivel. That day, it all changed. It was Wednesday – almost a week before Steinhoff International, a company that had been moulded into the swaggering bullyboy of international retail by its bulldog chief executive, Markus Jooste, would announce its CEO was resigning amid an investigation.

At Wiese's office in Parow, a beige industrial region of Cape Town marked by car-washes, food trucks and formless, characterless warehouses owned by the likes of Pepsi, the atmosphere was chilling quickly, in contrast to the languid early summer heat outside. Years before, Wiese, one of Africa's three wealthiest men, had picked the unfashionable Parow as the head office for his clothing chain, Pep. It was a statement, as much as anything, of how in a business that sells T-shirts for as little as R44 and shoes for R79, Wiese wasn't willing to pay a cent more for the sort of unnecessary high-rises of many of his peers. Back in 2016, a profile of Wiese reported Shoprite's former boss Whitey Basson as describing him as "stingy". "He'll give me the nicest bottle of champagne as a present, and I'll open it up, and I'll see he forgot to take out the message. It's a bottle from Lord So-and-so. He's a re-gifter."[1] Basson, one of Wiese's good friends, would rib him about it often. But it was a cultural thing about not wasting cash,

Wiese would say. "If you've got a Persian carpet, don't put it on the floor of your shop, because your customer will know that *he* is paying for it." (It was, of course, totally different at Steinhoff, which was happy to blow a rumoured R60m to R80m on entertaining clients at the 2015 rugby World Cup in England.)

Wiese, with his gravelly, forthright manner, could also be intimidating. If your facts were slightly woolly, he'd cut right through your story in a heartbeat. This is perhaps why the bespectacled lawyers and twitchy accountants sitting in the boardroom of the third floor of the Pep HQ that summer's day were so visibly tense, shifting uncomfortably, as they considered how to break the awful news to him.

Joining Wiese in that boardroom that day was Dr Steve Booysen, the 55-year-old former accounting lecturer who, until a few years before, had been the CEO of South Africa's largest commercial bank, Absa. Booysen, irredeemably unpretentious, was the banker who you sensed would always rather have been sitting on the stoep of his farm with a glass of pinotage. He was rapier smart, too, and had been one of the central architects of South Africa's biggest deal at that stage, the 2005 purchase of Absa by British bank Barclays. Now he was chair of Steinhoff's audit committee – a curse that would soon assume the level of a technicolour horror movie.

Also in the room was Dr Karsten Randt, a specialist in criminal law as it related to tax, who'd also once been a lecturer at the University of Osnabrück on the subject but who was now a partner at the German law firm Flick Gocke Schaumburg (FGS). For months, Randt's company had been investigating claims that Steinhoff, and Jooste, might have broken the law, as police in the German town of Oldenburg believed. In three reports, FGS had found nothing wrong. It repeatedly said there were no sham transactions, as some believed, thereby entirely vindicating Jooste.

So, Wiese started the meeting: I believe you have a few things you need to discuss with me. I just want to make it clear, this discussion must be very frank and open. Don't pull punches because we are now only days away from finalising Steinhoff's year-end accounts. We can't pussyfoot around now. What's the problem?

Then, one of the auditors from Deloitte, one of the "big four" audit firms, which had been hired by Steinhoff to reassure the public that the accounts they published were accurate, stood up. Thank you for that, he said in his thick Dutch accent. (Since Steinhoff had shifted its headquarters to Amsterdam a few years ago, the Dutch were everywhere in the company.) Then he dropped a bombshell: we have reason to believe that Steinhoff's management have been defrauding the company for years. The balance sheet is highly inflated, and revenue has been significantly overstated.

The enormity of the words hit Wiese as if a wave of icy water had rolled up out of nowhere, and smacked into him.

He took a minute, then replied: Well, this comes as a huge shock, obviously. Why are you saying this? What do you know?

The Deloitte auditor handed him a document containing a list of Steinhoff's assets – about five items. These are the assets in terms of which we have concerns about their validity and the recoverability, he said. Or, to be blunt, Deloitte didn't believe that the accounts they'd been given by Jooste's executive team represented anything like the truth. We're only willing to sign the accounts on two conditions: firstly, we need all the cash flow and accounting audit trails (and all the supporting documents), and secondly, we want Steinhoff to commission a forensic investigation.

Though the list that Deloitte gave to Wiese was short, it was indisputably weighty: the total value of those questionable assets was no less than €6bn. Wiese stared at it. Firstly, Deloitte had red-flagged a bunch of properties that Steinhoff wanted to value at €1.2bn – properties it had acquired about five years before, when it bought the Austrian low-end supermarket chain Kika-Leiner for €452m.

Secondly, Deloitte was worried about several mist-encircled deals that had been taking place in Europe between Steinhoff and various obscure overseas companies, like Talgarth Capital (which was registered in the secretive tax haven of the British Virgin Islands). For one thing, these companies seemed to be run by people close to Jooste, yet the auditors and the board had never been told these were related parties – which would have required greater scrutiny.

Thirdly, the draft accounts included a $600m profit from a deal in the US, which Steinhoff's American albatross, Mattress Firm, had supposedly done with mattress company Serta Simmons. Jooste had claimed the deal had been finalised, and the $600m should be included in Steinhoff's revenue for the year – but the auditors doubted this. For one thing, they didn't have a shred of documentary evidence for this.

Also, Deloitte was worried about a line in Steinhoff's accounts in which Jooste had stated its cash and cash equivalents at a ludicrously high amount. The auditors worried that this cash number was being manipulated. (In Steinhoff's 2016 audited results, the only item that didn't have an explanatory note was its "cash and cash equivalents".)

The auditors asked Wiese: Do you trust Markus?

Are you kidding? he replied. Let me tell you the history, said Wiese. I did a R62bn deal with him based on just a handshake in 2014. We agreed that Steinhoff would take over my company Pepkor, and we shook on it. You don't do a R62bn deal based only on a *handshake* unless you trust someone entirely.

Wiese stared at the list again. He was sceptical of the auditors' conclusion. Hang on a minute, he said. On the issue of the cash, explain to me what the problem is here. Cash is cash. Surely, you just ask the bank what's in the bank account, and you'll know how much cash Steinhoff has?

Well, yes, said Deloitte, but cash equivalents are something else entirely. This is because in Germany there is the concept of a *wechsel*, which is pretty much the equivalent of an IOU – a written debt obligation. The thing about a *wechsel* is, if you have such a promise from somebody who owes you money, you can claim it as a cash equivalent asset in your accounts. In other words, it makes it seem like you have more money, based on a promise.

This point was critical. In general, investors and the public need to know how much cash a company has as a buffer in case disaster strikes. And for analysts, the flow of cash is often the most fundamental element of a company's accounts. After all, cash (which would include cash equivalents) is meant to be the one figure that even the smartest financial whizz can't cheat. So, if you can manipulate this number in the accounts to create the illusion of money in the bank, it's a masterstroke of a real conman.

But Wiese was just as dubious about Deloitte's other conclusions. On the properties, he said, surely that's just as easily resolved? Either those Kika-Leiner properties are worth €400m, or they're worth €1.2bn. How hard can it be to resolve that? And those properties, he pointed out, had been externally valued by an outside valuer. He told them how, just two weeks before, one of Germany's largest banks had come to Steinhoff with a plan to fold all the properties that belonged to Steinhoff and Shoprite (both companies in which, at that point, Wiese owned the largest individual share) into a massive fund, which would then be listed on international markets. And that German bank had apparently agreed with Jooste's valuation of the properties. But either way, he said, it can't be too difficult to agree on the valuations.

Wiese looked at the auditors: All these five items you've got here, weren't they all in the accounts in 2016, when you, Deloitte, signed them off? All except the $600m Serta Simmons deal, which is new. The thing is, Deloitte agreed on these points last year; so why are you raising them as obstacles this time round, demanding a forensic investigation? Does this mean last year's accounts, which you signed, are wrong?

Deloitte's auditors replied: Well, yes – probably.

At this point, FGS's Karsten Randt chimed in: You don't need another forensic – we've done all the work. Here's our forensic report, he said, pointing to the bound volumes on the table from FGS.

We can't use that, said Deloitte. We don't think you're properly independent of Markus Jooste's management team, so we can't make use of your report.

Randt was incensed: How can that be? We've never worked for Steinhoff before this. We're a highly regarded professional firm.

Yes, the Deloitte auditors replied, but you're in "defence mode".

Wiese chimed in: But nobody has been charged for anything. How can you say that FGS are in "defence mode" when nobody has been charged?

Technically, this was true. Two years previously, in December 2015, police in the sleepy town of Oldenburg had raided Steinhoff's offices in Europe, as well as the offices of its founder, Bruno Steinhoff. They'd suspected tax fraud. Then for months – nothing. Until in late August 2017, a German publication called *Manager Magazin* had published an article, impeccably sourced, that said the German prosecutors had zeroed in on Jooste and a few others as the main suspects in a probe into allegations of accounting fraud. Steinhoff hotly denied these "allegations of dishonesty". It said that "no evidence exists" that Jooste, or anyone else, had done anything wrong.

Evidently, however, Deloitte had become skittish. This angered Wiese, as Steinhoff was meant to publish its full-year accounts for the year to September the very next week – but Deloitte was now refusing to sign the financials until they were "comfortable".

Wiese turned on the auditors: Have you discussed any of these issues with Markus?

The Deloitte auditors shook their head. (In reality, Deloitte had been asking Jooste for the documents numerous times in the previous few weeks. But he bluntly ignored them.)

Wiese told Deloitte: So why are you coming here and asking me, a guy who's only been the chairman for a year, about all this? Let's just get Markus in to clear it all up. It's an easy thing – let's fix it. So, Wiese picked up his iPhone, and summoned Jooste, who was in Stellenbosch.

Jooste sounded impatient, hot-tempered and cranky: But I've given Deloitte all the bloody information, he said. I gave them a memory stick with many gigabytes of information. And I've given it to them plenty of times.

OK, said Wiese, well then, can you just come over here and speak to them about it. They've got a list of documents they say they haven't been given and they're demanding a forensic.

Jooste grumbled, but he climbed in his car and drove to Pepkor's office in Parow to "tell them what's what". About forty minutes later, he walked into the boardroom and met a wall of solemn accountants and lawyers, alongside Wiese and Booysen.

Wiese said to him: Markus, I want to tell you, we're all talking very frankly here, and you must now respond equally frankly. Here are the allegations we've got. I want you to respond to each of these in turn, because to me it seems very simple.

Jooste, characteristically smooth and ice-calm, didn't blink. No problem, I understand it totally, he said. Do you guys honestly think I don't know how a *wechsel* works? he asked. It's all above board. You guys are panicking for nothing.

Calmly, and without raising his voice, Jooste gave a compelling explanation for each of the five points. He named people, he gave dates, he mentioned the specific documents that demonstrated how it was all just one big unnecessary mix-up. Simple, he said.

To which Deloitte replied: OK, fine. But, look, we just need those documents, to substantiate what you've just said.

Jooste fixed the auditors with his penetrating brown eyes and icy tone: it's absolutely no problem – I'm pretty sure I've already given all of them to you, but to make you lot calmer, I'll go and get them, he said. I'll get them *again*.

Then the Deloitte auditors asked if they could have some privacy to consult among themselves. They went to the room next door and for over an hour were locked in intense deliberations. An impatient Jooste, meanwhile, had climbed in his car and driven back to Stellenbosch.

Finally, the auditors emerged. We have good news, they announced. We're happy to say we're putting our requirement for a forensic investigation on ice and, instead, we'll focus on getting the accounts out the next week.

Wiese remembers their demeanour flipping 180 degrees from a few hours earlier. They were less edgy, less braced for confrontation. Jooste's magic and well-reputed charm, it seemed, had worked on Deloitte.

Well, said Wiese, that's a helluva relief. He phoned Jooste and told him that all that needed to happen was that he must get the documents to give to Deloitte. Fingers crossed, he said, we can still get Steinhoff's year-end accounts out within a week.

Jooste seemed mighty relieved. Thank God, he told Wiese.

The crisis, Wiese believed, had passed. The accounts would be signed off, once Markus had gone through the formality of fetching the documents that proved his case. Dark phrases like "accounting fraud" wouldn't be uttered again in his Parow office.

Thursday, 30 November 2017

The next day, just after midday, Wiese got another call from Deloitte. We're very sorry, they said, but we've reconsidered. For us to sign off the accounts, we *will* need that forensic investigation, as well as all the documents we asked for.

This upset Wiese. He knew that the odds of getting Steinhoff's audit finished in time so as to release the accounts the following week had just been torpedoed. There was no way that, even if they received the documents, they could work through them within a few days.

So tell me, what information did you get between yesterday and today that made you decide you now need the forensic again? he asked. This just isn't good enough. Come talk to me, face to face, he demanded.

So, the auditors hauled themselves off to Steinhoff's office in Stellenbosch. Here they got a hostile reception from Wiese. But Deloitte explained that when they got back to their office, and went through what they needed from Jooste, the list was far more extensive than they'd realised. Code red, again. With that, Wiese summoned Steinhoff's top brass to an urgent meeting, including Jooste and Booysen, and told them of Deloitte's latest demand.

It was at this meeting that Jooste floated a convenient theory for the first time: that Deloitte were "biased" because they'd been representing one of Steinhoff's sworn enemies in Austria, Andreas Seifert. Seifert had poisoned them, Jooste suggested. To understand his argument, you'll need some background.

The reclusive Seifert, a cantankerous 62-year-old Austrian businessman who refuses to allow any photographs taken of him, is perhaps more to be thanked for blowing apart Jooste's apparent mythmaking than anyone else.[2] The story is that in the 1970s Seifert and his brother Richard took the struggling XXXLutz, a small regional furniture company in Austria, and turned it into a pan-continental powerhouse, the second-largest chain in Europe. As it happened, Seifert's quest for *lebensraum* coincided with Steinhoff's expansion into Europe, too, and initially Jooste and Seifert got on fabulously. Then in 2007, Steinhoff bought 50% of the German discount chain Poco from its founder, Peter Pohlmann, a chain which has 123 stores and which clocked up €1.6bn in sales in 2017. Jooste and Seifert were so keen to work together – to take on Europe's largest furniture company, Ikea – that they began scheming of ways to make this happen.

But the problems began in 2014 when Seifert bought the other 50% of Poco – and the battle for control took a poisonous turn. Within months, Steinhoff and Seifert were jousting publicly, both claiming they'd found various "breaches" that entitled them to boot out the other partner and take full control of Poco. Remarkably, Jooste behaved as if Steinhoff already had full control of Poco, going so far as to claim 100% of the chain's assets in its accounts in 2015. An outraged Seifert approached prosecutors in Germany to investigate Jooste.[3] And in doing so, Seifert threw open Pandora's box.

Reports in *Manager Magazin* in August 2017 said that when Seifert was questioned in July 2016 by police inspectors at Osnabruck in the course of the Steinhoff investigation, he was asked to explain certain documents containing his signature. They included a contract from 2012, in which he promised a company close to Steinhoff "exclusive use of his brand Möbelix in Europe".[4] Seifert's response was: "I have never seen these papers and did not sign them."

It was all starting to look rather serious: allegations of forgery, self-dealing, accounting fraud. It's the kind of thing that tends to make auditors wake up sweating at four in the morning.

So, back to that day in November 2017 at Steinhoff's Stellenbosch HQ. Jooste's argument was that since Deloitte's Austrian office had acted as advisers to Seifert in his court battle with Steinhoff, the audit firm was "biased against us". Deloitte's independence has been compromised, Jooste said, so maybe we need to get rid of Deloitte anyway, and find new auditors. Wiese hadn't known about this Seifert link, so he called Deloitte to ask them. And it turned out that Deloitte's Dutch auditors had no clue about the link either, given that it was Deloitte's Austrian office that had worked for Seifert.

Either way, Steve Booysen argued, we can't get rid of Deloitte at this stage. He told Markus: If we get rid of Deloitte, there's a good chance we won't be able to find any new auditors to replace them. And even if a new auditor does accept the job, they'll have to start from scratch and there will have to be full disclosure of what happened with Deloitte. Which means they'll probably ask for a forensic investigation, too.

But at this stage Deloitte wasn't budging: We still need a forensic audit, they said, as a non-negotiable starting point. So Wiese called another of the large audit firms, PwC, and asked if they'd be willing to perform the forensic audit that Deloitte wanted.

Nonetheless, Jooste had thrown enough dust into the air to shift the discussion from the "missing documents" to "auditing malpractice". Steinhoff's board began debating whether they needed to fire Deloitte, given the "conflict of interest" over Seifert. It looked as if Jooste's rabbit-and-hat trick had worked, at least as far as Steinhoff was concerned.

Friday, 1 December 2017

By now, the boardroom at Steinhoff's offices in Stellenbosch had become a war room, where squadrons of lawyers and accountants had decamped. Neither Booysen, who lives in the picturesque farmland of Irene near Pretoria, nor the lawyers had any real idea when they'd be able to go home.

But Jooste had a plan. At about 5 pm, he picked up his car keys and said he planned to drive straight to the airport to catch a flight to Germany and retrieve all the documents that Deloitte needed. Also, he said, he'd organised to meet the American lawyers dealing with the $600m Serta Simmons deal in Germany. They'd give him all the documents that Deloitte wanted. Don't panic: I'll be back on Monday morning with everything we need.

This comforted the increasingly gun-shy Wiese: if Markus just fetched all those documents, the whole misunderstanding could be cleared up. Booysen was less certain. The former banker's suspicion of Jooste had been growing over the previous few days. At this point, Booysen thought, I'll believe it when I see it.

As for Wiese, he was still struggling to reconcile what was going on. At one point, when he was alone with Deloitte's auditors, he turned to them and said: You can accuse Markus of many things, but you can't accuse him of being stupid. If he did everything you say he did, he'd have to be bloody stupid.

The auditors replied: No, Christo, you're wrong. If he did *all of this* stuff, then he'd have to be bloody smart.

Earlier that day, Wiese and Booysen also called in Ben la Grange, Steinhoff's young, ultra-slick chief financial officer. They showed him Deloitte's five points.

Ben, what do you think of this? Can it be true?

La Grange flipped through the list, and shook his head. Look, I have no idea about this stuff, but I can't see how it *can* be true. You'll have to ask Markus.

Christo replied: But Ben, *if it is true*, how could you *not* know about these things?

Ben replied: Well, I've always trusted Markus's bona fides. Markus is the CEO of the European business, after all, and I trust what he tells me. There's no reason to doubt him. It was a reasonable enough answer, Wiese and Booysen believed.

PwC called Wiese back: We've assembled a big team to make the forensic investigation happen, and we can do it quickly. Go ahead, said Wiese.

This was also good news. It made Wiese believe that, despite new landmines exploding every few hours, maybe Steinhoff could still put out audited financials within a few days after all. So, he climbed into his Lexus SUV, and headed home for the weekend.

Sunday, 3 December 2017

Wiese hadn't slept particularly well. He woke up early and called Jooste in Germany.

How's it going? he asked. Have you gathered everything we need?

It's going great, Markus replied. I've already met the Americans and I'm gathering all the documents together too. It's all under control – I'm getting ready to fly home tonight, and I'll see you Monday morning. We'll sort this all out, he said.

Conspicuously, however, Jooste hadn't told Wiese why he was really in Germany in the first place. The truth is, he didn't fly there to "sort out the Deloitte problems", as he'd implied. Rather, he'd been invited to the 80th birthday party of Steinhoff's founder, Bruno Steinhoff, in Westerstede, on that Saturday night. Jooste had even been asked to give a speech at the party – one in which, when he stood up, he emphasised to Bruno's guests just how fundamental the value of *trust* had been in building up this mighty retail conglomerate over the previous five decades. It was an odd thing *not* to mention such an occasion.

As it turned out, the Serta Simmons officials did actually meet Jooste in Germany that weekend – but they just never got round to discussing the $600m deal.

That night, back in South Africa, Steinhoff's audit committee had another crisis meeting. Late on Friday, Steinhoff had put out an announcement saying that even though it hadn't obtained Deloitte's signature, it still planned to release "unaudited results" the coming Tuesday. It told investors that Deloitte had "not yet finalized their review of certain matters" which had arisen in the Germany criminal investigation.

Not everyone agreed. Booysen, for one, didn't believe that putting out unaudited results was the right way to go. What happens if those unaudited results change dramatically, he said – it'll ruin the board's credibility. Rather, let's wait and see what Markus can give us when he arrives back tomorrow.

Monday, 4 December 2017

At 8.40 am, Jooste left a message on Wiese's mobile phone. Christo, I've landed from Germany, and I've got all the documents that Deloitte needs.

Dirk Schreiber is with me too. I'm just going home for a shower, so you can line up all the auditors. I'll see you at the Steinhoff office at 11 am. (Dirk Schreiber, a dour East German, was the finance chief of Steinhoff Europe at the time, and a critical cog in Jooste's machinery.)

At which, Wiese summoned the auditors, the lawyers and the rest of the crisis committee to the war room. And then they waited.

An hour later, at 9.48 am, Steve Booysen got an SMS in Afrikaans from Jooste. Steve, I'm just finalising the last two documents, but I think you'll appreciate that, given the seriousness of the allegations, I'll have to take legal advice. It was in that instant that the shot went off inside Booysen's head, when weeks of woolly concerns coalesced into certainty. He put the phone down, and looked at his colleagues, the veteran accounting guru Len Konar and the former banker Theunie Lategan. He's getting *legal advice*, Booysen told them. We all know what *that* means. You don't get legal advice if you've done nothing wrong.

Over the next few hours, Booysen got a number of other SMS's from Jooste, saying he was on his way, he was just putting together the files, he was sorting out the documents. But these messages were all in English – a sign he'd probably crafted them with his lawyer.

Elsewhere in that office, Wiese was waiting, still hoping that Jooste would come through. But 11 am came and went; so did 12 pm and 1 pm, with no word from Jooste. Perhaps Jooste was simply still organising all the documents at home, thought Wiese. By his reckoning, there certainly were enough documents for him to need to order them.

By this stage, from the trading desks inside Joburg's big banks to the money managers in Cape Town, investors had begun to smell blood. Something was going dangerously awry in Steinhoff's kitchen, they figured. It almost never happens that a company is forced to put out "unaudited" accounts. So, the panic selling began: the price of Steinhoff's shares on Johannesburg's stock exchange, the JSE, began to deflate rapidly. By the end of Monday, the stock had lost 9.9%, tumbling from R55.81 per share to R50.25. In round numbers, Steinhoff's total value had dropped by R23.9bn that day, from R236bn.

Meanwhile, in Stellenbosch, Wiese was still clinging to hope, a little naively. He still believed "unaudited results" were the way to go. After all, Jooste had assured him that any "unaudited" accounts would still pretty much reflect the same reality as any "audited accounts" signed off later. Sure, it wasn't ideal, he thought, but it wouldn't be an utter disaster.

Finally, at 5 pm, one of the FGS lawyers called Wiese: Christo, are you at the office? he asked. Stay there. I'm on the way with "a message". Then Wiese knew.

After about twenty minutes, the lawyer walked into Steinhoff's offices, where he was greeted by dozens of unblinking eyes in the boardroom. The news he conveyed was sensational: Markus is at the wine farm Lanzerac, and he's a mess. Unshaven, sobbing uncontrollably, Markus is tearing his hair out, saying he screwed up. The lawyer told Wiese: Markus has asked me to give you this message: he is offering his resignation, and you must decide whether to accept it. It's up to you.

It was the ice-water-down-the-spine moment that Wiese had always feared. The worst-case scenario had come about, and there was no way round it. A board meeting was scheduled for the next morning. Wiese and Booysen prepared themselves to break the bad news.

Tuesday, 5 December 2017

That Tuesday morning, Bruno Steinhoff and his daughter Angela landed at Cape Town International Airport to attend the board meeting. On the way to Steinhoff's offices, Wiese told them the whole story. They were shaken. Just three days before, they'd seen Markus in Germany, and he hadn't breathed a word of how, back in South Africa, the company was burning.

The board meeting was to be held at Steinhoff's headquarters in Stellenbosch, a sprawling university town about an hour from Cape Town. While some of South Africa's most successful businessmen have gravitated towards the town, including Johann Rupert, GT Ferreira and Jannie Mouton, Steinhoff had become *the* dominant corporate presence in Stellenbosch. The town had been soaked in Steinhoff's familiar burgundy colours, with the university's cricket fields and the Danie Craven rugby field draped in Steinhoff branding.

As Steinhoff's directors began to drift into the boardroom at De Wagenweg Office Park, none of them, at that point, had any idea just how appalling the news really was. Heather Sonn, a feisty 45-year-old and the retailer's youngest director, walked in and saw the solemn faces. She turned to Theunie Lategan and said in Afrikaans: "En nou? Wat gaan hier aan? Dit lyk soos 'n begrafnis."

Lategan looked at her gravely. It pretty much *is* a funeral, he said.

* * *

Over the next few months, Sonn would play a vital role in trying to save the company. But on that day in December, she had no clue of what she was about to confront.

Wiese and Steve Booysen kicked off the board meeting by relating the entire story of the previous week, as well as Markus's offer to resign. We have to make an important decision right now, Wiese said. But my feeling is that we should refuse to accept his resignation: after all, he's the only guy who knows what happened here and what he did. We need him to help us fix it.

After two hours of haggling – not everyone thought it wise to keep a compromised CEO on the board – there was a broad consensus around the need to ask Jooste for help. So, Wiese stepped out of the meeting and called Jooste on his cellphone.

Where are you? Wiese asked.

I'm at my lawyer's office in Cape Town, Jooste replied.

Wiese continued: Look, what you'd done, you've done. There's no turning back on that. But at least come and help us sort out the mess so that Steinhoff can publish its accounts. Because, without its accounts, it may not even survive. Are you prepared to do that?

Jooste responded: Yes, I will. I'll see you in two to three hours.

Jooste hung up – and that was the last time Wiese heard from him. Just as before, he didn't arrive. This time, however, he didn't even bother sending a message. Instead, he simply melted away into infamy. His final interaction with most of those directors was, appropriately, a lie.

Inside Steinhoff's offices, the company's 150-odd staff figured that something was up, given the number of earnest men in suits, with lever-arch files precariously balanced in their hands, half jogging in and out of the building. Then a message popped into some of their inboxes. It was from Markus Jooste. "Hi there. Firstly, I would like to apologise for all the bad publicity I caused the Steinhoff company the last couple of months," it read. "Now I have caused the company further damage by not being able to finalise the year-end audited numbers, and I made some big mistakes and have now caused financial loss to many innocent people. It is time for me to move on and take the consequences of my behaviour like a man. Sorry that I have disappointed all of you and I never meant to cause any of you any harm. Please continue to live the Steinhoff dream and I must make it very clear none of Danie, Ben, Stehan and Mariza had anything to do with any of my mistakes. I enjoyed working with you and wish you all the best for the future. Best regards, Markus."

The people he referred to formed his inner circle: Danie van der Merwe, Steinhoff's chief operating officer; Ben la Grange, its finance director; Stehan Grobler, its group executive for finance; and Mariza Nel, the corporate services executive.

It's unclear why Jooste sent that admission. Perhaps he was trying to pre-empt fingers being pointed at the others, or perhaps it was written for him by someone he trusted. Whatever the reason, at the Stellenbosch HQ, when it became clear that Jooste wasn't coming, Steinhoff's board prepared to tell the country what had happened.

At 8.44 pm in Germany, Steinhoff issued an announcement to the world bearing the grim headline: "Steinhoff announces investigation into account-ing irregularities and resignation of CEO". It was just ten words, but it was to precipitate bloodshed across the stock market. In an abbreviated series of staccato sentences, Steinhoff declared stiffly that "new information has come to light today which relates to accounting irregularities requiring further investigation". It added that Jooste "has today tendered his resig-nation with immediate effect and the Board has accepted the resignation". The earlier promise of imminent financials had also been retracted. Instead,

Steinhoff said, helplessly, that it would publish its full-year results "when it is in a position to do so". Wiese would be acting as "executive chairman", it said, and he would be assisted by Pepkor's former chief executive, Pieter Erasmus.

As if to somehow mitigate the crushing blow, Steinhoff added that it still had "a number of high quality profitable businesses around the world". It was parlous consolation.

Wednesday, 6 December 2017

As the stock market opened, the slaughter began. The reaction was carnivorous: Steinhoff's share price went into freefall, cartwheeling 61% from R45.65 to R17.61 per share. Within 24 hours, R120bn in value had vanished, as traders at the banks flooded their Bloomberg screens with frantic "sell" orders. Most investors, even the veterans who'd been around during the Asian crisis of 1997, had never seen such a rapid loss in value. It is hard to imagine what a R120bn loss looks like: after all, this amount that went up in smoke in hours is roughly double the $4.4bn GDP that Swaziland makes in a year, and four times what Lesotho makes ($2bn).

Paul Theron, the sharp-tongued 51-year-old managing director of asset manager Vestact, remembers the carnage. "There was an immediate sense of horror, that maybe all those stories you'd heard for years about Markus's shenanigans, which you'd discounted, might actually be true," he said. "A lot of the guys were panicked, but trying to comfort themselves by saying the share price drop was too severe, and that Steinhoff was still worth R25 to R17 anyway. The truth was, nobody knew what to think."[5]

For Theron, a trained engineer who launched South Africa's first internet-based stockbroker called Tradek in 1996, the revelation undermined what he had hitherto considered a reliable instinct for detecting scoundrels. With a street fighter's nose for trouble, Theron had once locked horns with an oleaginous rogue called Brett Kebble, who also happened to be the CEO of three large mining companies, years before. His instinct was that Kebble was hopelessly crooked. And he was right. Facing the prospect of his wide-scale larceny being exposed, Kebble hired hitmen to assassinate him on a bridge in Joburg in 2005. But with Jooste, Theron's instinct may have failed him.

Theron says he'd been one of those who'd bought Jooste's story, hook, line and sinker. "I was in the camp that believed that they had a world-class team of auditors behind them. I bought Jooste's story and I was taken in. But then, I suppose, all of us were taken in to some extent," he says.

Greg Davies, the head of private client trading at the small boutique investment company Cratos Capital, remembers the drumbeat of tension that morning when he got into his office in Joburg's forested suburb of Dunkeld. "I've been in this game for more than two decades, and I've never seen anything like it. Everywhere, there was fear, anxiety and shock. It was the sort of emotional ride you have when you find out someone close to you has died. You can't believe it can be true," he says.[6]

The way it works on the stock market is that every day there is an "opening auction" of company shares, which sets the mood for the market. Stockbrokers put in orders for their clients, and make an assessment of the sort of price a stock is likely to trade for. Usually, it's just a couple of percentage points away from the previous day's price. But that morning, all bets were off when it came to Steinhoff's shares.

Davies says: "The computerised trading system gives you an 'indicated price' of what you can expect to buy or sell those shares for. That morning, the computers were saying the 'indicative price' was 10c. Now, that was totally crazy, because Steinhoff's share price had ended the previous day at R45. So, it was clear this was serious."

The price yo-yoed violently, before opening at about R20 – half the level of the previous night, but still many leagues better than the 10c Davies expected. On the trading desks, the phones hadn't stopped ringing. Stuttering clients were frantically trying to reach their brokers, almost too scared to ask how much they'd lost. Should we sell the rest now? Or wait for it to recover? How can this even be right?

Anchor Capital, a small investment house run by Peter Armitage, a barrel-chested former rugby player who still looks the part, immediately fired off a letter to all his clients. Anchor announced it had taken an "in-principle decision to exit our holdings" as "there are clearly more unknowns than known information". "Fraud remains a distinct possibility," he added. Armitage, a man who was famously born in a caravan park (well, the truth is, his family *owned* the caravan park), says the ordeal was "very painful and traumatic at the time". "We'd had a fifteen-year history with the Steinhoff guys. I'd been overseas with them and I must have attended twenty results presentations. Afterwards, I'd often sit down with Markus and have a drink and talk about what was happening. So, at the time, in early December, we were actually quite excited about what we thought would happen with the company,"[7] he says.

On the day the news broke, Anchor Capital had to make a knee-jerk call. Luckily, for Anchor, its exposure was only about R200m – which wasn't in the league of the money managers who were in it for billions, like Coronation or Investec – so it was easier to dump the stock. "Over the previous few months, there'd been a number of shocks, like Brexit, so we knew we had to move fast," says Armitage. "And one thing we do know is that when a CEO resigns with immediate effect before a company's results are released, that means there's a big, big problem."

Many other investors froze. Greg Davies says that among many of the more brash analysts, there was a visceral sense of denial. The whole thing has been blown out of proportion, they said. Just wait, Steinhoff's share price would soon be back at nearly R50, and the panic sellers would all look silly. "Many of us were laughing at Anchor Capital at the time, reckoning they were overreacting by selling everything. Well, it turns out they were far smarter than we were," he says.

It was also a salutary lesson in how, despite the dogma that the best investors ought to strip out all emotion when making their decisions, the primordial reaction to seeing your savings vaporise is an instinctively emotional one. "It was unprecedented," says Davies. "It's hard to properly describe the shock you feel in that moment. So, I had to call those clients and explain what was happening. Most people had already heard it on the news, but I can tell you, those were tough calls to make."

As Steinhoff melted away, a number of other companies on the stock exchange also began to bleed. Shares in PSG, the Stellenbosch-based investment company that had given birth to banking group Capitec and schools outfit Curro, tumbled 6.9% (wiping out R4.86bn). Steinhoff Africa Retail (STAR), which had split off from its parent company only three months before to hold Steinhoff's African assets, plunged 22% (erasing R19.3bn). It was carnage that few stockbrokers had ever seen in their careers. "You have to realise just how rare this was," says Armitage. "It really was a once-in-a-lifetime investment event. At the time, Steinhoff was in the top ten largest companies on the JSE, and for this to happen, you'd have to have an epic failure at so many levels."

The inevitable comparison was with Enron, the Houston-based energy company that shot itself to pieces in 2001. Enron is the Olympic Gold of corporate fraud. Fuelled by the lip-smacking ambition of Ken Lay and Jeff Skilling, Enron had grown to become the third-largest electricity wholesaler across the US by the turn of the century. Investors drooled over it, journalists amplified the myth, and its executives were feted as all-conquering heroes who'd hit on a new formula that beat the market. Only, Enron's accounts were a fiction. It had found a way to magic profit from its assets, and when it came time to reconcile its accounts, it would simply shift debts to another company which it didn't show to investors. In other words, it lied about its assets. As one banker put it at the time, Enron were "black belts in structured finance".[8] Worse still, Enron's auditor, Arthur Andersen, helped it deceive the world. When shards of reality began slicing through the myth, Andersen hired a shredding truck from a company called Shred-it to destroy the masses of evidence.

The similarities between Enron and Steinhoff were eerie. Both companies were in the top ten largest companies on their stock exchanges when they imploded. Both were led by bullying, egotistical CEOs whom nobody dared challenge, but who had created indecipherable companies in the shadows designed to present a rosy picture of what was going. And, as Wiese would later say, "both companies had audit problems that slipped past the auditors".

"Consider the quantum of the fraud at Enron," says Armitage. "In rand terms, Enron lost R693bn in its last year, $67bn, while Steinhoff at its peak was R350bn. This makes Steinhoff the largest corporate fraud, globally, of the last two decades."

So, if that's where it ended up, how did it get there?

2

Farm to Table

—

In the beginning, there was war. The Steinhoff story begins in November 1937, in a small town about an hour outside Münster in northern Germany called Herzebrock. It was there that Bruno Steinhoff was born, one of five boys in what was, for a short time at least, an idyllic life on the farm. At the time, only the eldest boy got to inherit the family farm. The others were left an inheritance which they were meant to use, in the German tradition, as seed capital for their own farms. This milieu is freeze-framed in a watercolour painting of the farm, as it was in the misty years before Adolf Hitler laid Germany to waste, that hangs outside Bruno Steinhoff's fourth-floor office in Westerstede, next to the towering Steinhoff warehouse. In that painting, horses graze absent-mindedly next to a rambling double-storey farmhouse, with only the odd farm implement nearby to imply any technological context. The Steinhoff farm was the pre-war incarnation of that modern corporate cliché: an end-to-end solution. It did everything – cows, maize, potatoes, hogs, whatever you needed. That was mostly the way it worked in the rural areas of Germany in the early twentieth century.

Then came Hitler, the Third Reich and the grainy years of mud and war. Bruno Steinhoff, now 80 years old, remembers it as a time of grim attrition. "I was very young, but I remember how terrible it was. I remember seeing the fighting, I remember seeing planes get shot down," he says, recalling those early years from his office in Westerstede.[1]

What would ultimately shape Steinhoff's future was Hitler's miscalculation in Operation Barbarossa, when he invaded Joseph Stalin's Russia in June 1941. Ultimately, Hitler's hypothermic Nazi soldiers failed to take Moscow, but as the offensive was continuing, the Germans took five and a half million Russian prisoners. This proved a headache for the Nazis: while they had 23 *Russenlager* prisoner-of-war camps and 12 concentration camps, they were all bursting at the seams. So, Hitler ordered that more than 130,000 Russians be repurposed as "forced labour" on German farms.

When the Russian prisoners first arrived at Steinhoff's farm, Bruno was only 5 years old. It would be a formative experience for the youngster and instrumental in shaping a furniture empire that would straddle the Iron Curtain. But, as Bruno tells it, it was also an experience that taught the Steinhoff boys about fairness and how to treat others. "My parents insisted everyone got the same treatment," he says. "Every day, the Russian prisoners ate with us, and we all got the same food. During the day, they worked on the farm." It would have been one of the more benign experiences for Russian prisoners of war in Germany. In what is widely credited today as one of the forgotten atrocities of a war that was renowned for its casual brutality, 3.5m of the 5.7m Russian prisoners died in Germany – 6,000 a day in some cases.[2] A witness at one of the camps recorded: "The hunger is so terrible that a mile away, they can be heard groaning and shouting 'food'. They eat grass. Dozens die from starvation."[3]

But at Steinhoff's farm, the prisoners not only survived but also began teaching Bruno their language. He was a quick learner too, picking up phrases and conventions that would come in useful later. Not that there was much else to do with his time. The nearest school had been converted into a Red Cross nursing station for wounded soldiers. "When the war ended, many of the Russian soldiers didn't go back home. They'd seen another life and that we weren't the crocodiles they'd been told about. And at home, Stalin was a dictator and they knew it," he says. "Our Russian soldiers, the ones who'd lived on our farm, begged us to be safe when they left. My parents had been nice to them."

After the war ended in 1945, Germany was just a husk. Rural Germany had been hollowed out even more, as the weary procession of troops across the shelled countryside had sunk their nails into whatever they could from the farms as they hauled their way back to the bombed-out cities.

The Steinhoffs wanted to send their children back to school, but they couldn't. "At that stage, all the German families wanted to send their children to schools to learn ... but for nearly a year going to school was not possible," he says. There were too many children looking for schools, and far too few schools in total.

Within a few years, Bruno Steinhoff took an internship at a factory near Münster, about thirty kilometres from his parents' house, which made upholstered furniture. "For many years after the war, there were no jobs, nothing. We were hungry, and just wanted to survive – nothing more, nothing less. So that factory was where I did my learning," says Bruno today. But while the factories began churning out furniture, there weren't many people who could afford to buy their products.

After he'd finished his internship, Bruno Steinhoff did a basic business course. Then, with a short CV consisting of his furniture experience, the young man made his way to Berlin. "There, I was able to get a job at a large furniture retailer, where I learnt retail. But this retailer, it had an import company, which was bringing furniture from the east. One of the jobs I had was to negotiate how to sell that furniture," he explains.

Berlin, at the time, was the fulcrum of a wider geopolitical split in ideology. To the east, you had Stalin's Soviet Union expanding its tentacles to encompass everything under the rubric of communism; to the west, you had countries aligned to the United States, governed typically by free-market democratic ideals. Berlin was split down the middle, with a 3.6-metre-high wall that stretched for 66 miles as a tangible symbol of the divide.

Bruno Steinhoff straddled both worlds. He'd arrived in Berlin before the wall was built, almost overnight, in 1961. But over the three years he worked in the divided city, he developed an enviable black book of contacts from both sides of this ideological wall.

From Berlin, he went to Bavaria, where he took the position of sales manager at the largest upholstery furniture producer in Germany. "I soon realised that I could do this all myself," he says. "The East Germans knew me well, and they said to me, 'Oh Bruno, welcome'. I know how to produce furniture, and I know how to do the marketing. The East Germans said, 'Oh, this is better now with Bruno.'"

This is how the Steinhoff enterprise, the one that would meet its reckoning in a boardroom in Cape Town more than five decades later, was born in July 1964.

*   *   *

At first, Bruno Steinhoff Möbelvertretungen und -vertrieb was simply an importer. It didn't make any furniture, but it was able to arbitrage through the Iron Curtain, buying a smorgasbord of products from East Germany, and hawking it on to the West. Furniture, of course, was Bruno's first love, and would become the foundation on which Steinhoff's fortunes were built. But back in 1964, he imported everything. Chances are, if you saw an advert for an umbrella or a clock in the pages of *Die Welt*, Steinhoff had imported it. "The first wristwatch that was advertised in Germany for 9.99 Deutschmarks was from me. I sold millions at the time. I was well known at the time," he says.

In faded black-and-white photographs of Steinhoff at the time, he appears as the exemplar of the post-war German trader, with impeccably slicked-back hair, double-knotted tie, crisp and piercing brown eyes. It helped that for the thoroughly modern German entrepreneur, politics were considered to be something indulged in by people with too much time on their hands.

And, philosophically, it was clear there was no common water between him and the communist states, as he remained the embodiment of the hard-nosed, unrelenting capitalist. "I always had a rule: unless you're going to make money, you won't achieve anything. There's no reason to get out of bed in the morning if you're not going to turn a profit that day." While this notion of individual incentives may have been antithetical to the East Germans, their country had teetered on bankruptcy from day one, so it needed the cash.

Where Steinhoff had the advantage over any prospective rivals was that he could speak Russian, thanks to the tutorials he'd received from the prisoners on his family's farm. It provided a trade bridge for Steinhoff between the eastern and western bloc that not many people could hope to emulate. "At the time, the German companies had been too anxious about going to these crazy areas in Russia, and across the eastern bloc. Nobody wanted to do it. So, I was able to build great relationships with the government officials, who needed Deutschmarks."

Initially, Steinhoff had the exclusive rights to import East German goods into only two states in the western part of Germany – Lower Saxony and Hesse. But the business began to thrive. Perhaps the major slice of luck that put Steinhoff on the map was a single piece of furniture: the Gabi chair. The Gabi, with a rounded cup back and thin tapering legs, had a strong, mid-century Scandinavian influence. If it was in dusty pink or mint green, you could imagine it being quite a drawcard, even today. Typically sold in red, and upholstered without armrests, it might well be the unobtrusive seat of an arch-villain, waiting in his minimalist underground lair to welcome a shackled Sean Connery.

But, back then, its patented design flew off the shelves faster than Steinhoff could get it shipped to his warehouse. Even today, Steinhoff attributes much of his early success to the Gabi. If you visit his office, next to his desk you'll see a miniature model of the Gabi. "I saw this chair on one of my trips. The [East German] government couldn't sell it, even though they had huge amounts in stock. So, I told them: 'Give me the contract, I'll do it.' And I did. I became very famous in East Germany for it, and after a year the government gave me a contract to sell all the upholstered furniture they made," he says.

Soon after, the East Germans approached Steinhoff and asked him if he'd help them develop their factories across the eastern bloc. "I said, 'Sure'." So, Steinhoff hit the road, travelling to Hungary, Romania, the old Yugoslavia and Bulgaria, building factories in those countries and swapping prized Deutschmarks for furniture made behind the Iron Curtain.

At the time, as a 27-year-old, Bruno built a head office for his new, expanding furniture enterprise in Westerstede, a sleepy German country-side town, criss-crossed by horse trails and bike tracks. It wasn't exactly an obvious place as the base for a rapidly expanding European furniture empire, but Bruno was drawn to it, as much for the nearby lake, Zwischenahner Meer, where he could use the boat he'd bought, as for the fact that he'd made close friends nearby. It was the sort of place you could bring up children. His company, too, was a strictly family affair. His mother, who had spent decades working on the farm, took up the role of her son's secretary. "I started with nothing. We built the warehouses from scratch, we built the logistics arms from scratch," he says.

Most of the time, Bruno was on the road, if not doing deals, then staying up late drinking vodka and whisky with his business partners in smoky rooms in Sofia, Budapest or Moscow. He'd got married in 1970 and a few years later had two daughters, whom he rarely saw. Often, he'd land from one gruelling overseas trip, only to pick up his boarding pass for the next. "My wife accepted it, the fact that I was not much at home. But there was no choice for me. I was the frontman: if there was a problem, I went to settle it."

Financially, the business provided Bruno with a windfall. The year before he started Bruno Steinhoff Möbelvertretungen und -vertrieb, he'd taken home a salary of 10,000 Deutschmarks a year. But in its first year his company made 500,000 Deutschmarks.

Bruno Steinhoff was also uncompromisingly strict. If a factory did not perform, Bruno was unsentimental about chopping it. "Obviously, I bought shit businesses. It is normal to make mistakes, even though you forget this when you look back. But the people who always go on about the mistakes forever – they're not business people, they're teachers. So, what I did was, I sold those shit businesses. You learn the first time when the bankers knock on your door not to wait around. You act fast."

But Steinhoff's ambition didn't stop at Europe. In 1974 he decided to take his flirtation with communist commerce a step further and travelled to Mao Tse-tung's China. There, he painstakingly built up a new network of traders. "I went to China, Thailand, the Philippines and I bought everything from the east: cane furniture, watches – everything. I imported whatever I could because these people here, in the west, they had too much money and were lazy, and were too anxious about dealing with foreign countries after the Second World War. So, I had no competition doing this," he says.

Simultaneously, about twelve hundred kilometres north, there was another furniture company that had also been slowly expanding its way across various borders. Started in 1943 in Sweden, it took its name from the first initials of its founder, Ingvar Kamprad as well as those of the farm on which he grew up, Elmtaryd, and his home town, Agunnaryd: in a word, Ikea. Ikea would become the yardstick by which all Steinhoff's victories were measured. It would be the Coca-Cola to Bruno's Pepsi, the Nike to his Reebok. And it was Ikea that ultimately would push Bruno Steinhoff into doing business in South Africa.

The story is that in 1974 Ikea opened its doors in West Germany, sparking a craze for natural wood furniture that gained pace over the next decade. "Over the next few years, everyone wanted pine furniture," says Steinhoff. "Of course, there are different qualities of pine, but I did some research and found that the best place to find really quick-growing pine was South Africa. So, I went to South Africa for the first time." It was a decision that would entwine his company's fate with a country thousands of kilometres away, at a point when most foreign businesses in South Africa were padlocking their shop doors and fleeing the country. It was 1985. The townships in South Africa, where black people were confined, were burning; Nelson Mandela, the putative leader of the African National Congress (ANC), had already been imprisoned on Robben Island for 23 years; and the ruling National Party had suspended what few rights existed in that country under a "state of emergency". The year 1985 would be the singular turning point for grand apartheid.

President PW Botha, the brutish enforcer of the security state known as the "Groot Krokodil", as much for his curled snarkish bottom lip as for his white-hot rage, had signalled in August that year that big changes were imminent, that the country was about to "cross the Rubicon". *Time* magazine, in anticipation of the event, had even described the speech that Botha was expected to give as the "most important announcement since the Dutch settlers arrived in South Africa 300 years ago".

Instead, people across the world watched Botha give a speech that flatly rejected reform and stubbornly recommitted the country to apartheid. And the prospects for commerce fell apart. "The rand fell sharply, capital flight accelerated and markets closed. South Africa faced an escalation of sanctions," says Hermann Giliomee in his book *The Last Afrikaner Leaders*. "In late August 1985, the United States Congress passed the Comprehensive Anti-Apartheid Act, which banned new investment and loans, withdrew landing rights and severely curbed imports of coal, uranium, iron and steel. The European Community and the Commonwealth imposed a variety of milder sanctions."[4]

But, as executives from multinationals like Barclays, General Motors and IBM were crowding aboard the packed Boeings at Joburg's Jan Smuts Airport, Steinhoff was stepping off the plane for the first time. "South Africa was a very strong country then, and I was sometimes the biggest buyer there during apartheid," says Steinhoff. "I was in all the factories here in 1985, so I got to know South Africa very well. I bought lots of furniture here."

Culturally, Steinhoff felt good chemistry with South Africa. "There were other countries I went to, where I decided I'd never go again: people there, they'd steal your money." But it still took no small amount of gumption to set up shop in a country that, at the time, had become the world's number one pariah. It was this blindness for politics that mirrored Bruno Steinhoff's earlier decision to cosy up to the communists. "Politics, I don't notice," he says. "Business has nothing to do with politics. I've always gone where no one wants to go and then it's easy: you have no competitors. It's wonderful actually."

Still, Steinhoff's early South African venture wasn't exactly a huge success. From the beginning, Steinhoff was attracted to the country's thick-growing pine – *Pinus radiata* – which is similar to the pine you get in Chile and Brazil. However, while the pine that Ikea sold was clear white pine from Scandinavia, the South African pine was yellow – and the colour only deepened over time. "It was a big mistake. In the shops, people were ready to buy the Scandinavian pine at double the price and more, so I had to stop this business with South Africa."

Then, a moment of global serendipity in South Africa and in Eastern Europe: *glasnost* and *perestroika* in Russia saw iron-fisted regimes in Poland, Hungary, Bulgaria and Czechoslovakia tumble. In 1989 the Germans began to chip away at the Berlin Wall. And in South Africa, FW de Klerk, a former hardliner, took over as president from the twitchy PW Botha. By Christmas, he'd decided "we'd have to make a 180-degree turn", and so, on 2 February 1990, he told the white Parliament he was unbanning the ANC and releasing Mandela.

This synchronized unravelling of both totalitarian regimes, the Soviet Union and South Africa, was marvellous for millions of people. For Steinhoff, however, it was an utter disaster. "When the Iron Curtain came down, my business went down too," Steinhoff says. The closeted business model of buying furniture cheaply in tinpot dictatorships and flogging it to the cash-flush West had run its course. "I had to make a change," he says. "I couldn't continue to import furniture, so I took a decision to build my own factories, or buy them from my suppliers. So, we bought factories across the world, even in South Africa." Steinhoff snapped up eight struggling factories in East Germany, owned by the government, built others in Hungary and Poland, and bought two existing manufacturers in the Ukraine. The company was no longer mainly an importer: it was going to make what it sold.

In all fundamental respects, this step marked the genesis of Steinhoff International.

*   *   *

Bruno Steinhoff's second venture into South Africa was far more successful. It all happened thanks to a close friend of his, a textile mogul who'd begun his career as a tax lawyer named Claas Daun, who lived a short distance away in a town called Rastede. Both men, Bruno Steinhoff and

Claas Daun, were the kings of their respective towns, the big swinging dicks of rural northern Germany. "Claas had become a director of one of my companies a few years before," says Steinhoff. "The banks insisted. They said they'd lend me money, as much as I needed, but I had to put in place a proper board in case I got sick or whatever. So, we became good friends. He's a clever man."

Daun, speaking in an as-yet-unreleased tape recorded in 2013 to celebrate Steinhoff's fifteen years on the JSE, described how he'd first decided to invest in South Africa, setting in motion the Steinhoff journey.[5] During the oppressive 1980s, he said, he visited South Africa and felt an overwhelming sense of the country's potential – despite apartheid. "I was travelling this country, and every time I was there, I said: why is this world so negative? The country is far better and even black people I met at that time were friendly and were optimistic; the country was wonderful and I saw a gap between the perception of the world and my own experience travelling."[6] So, in the late 1980s, Daun bought a house in Cape Town. Thanks to the recent invention of the fax machine, he ran many of his German businesses remotely from the Cape. He was there, he said, when the Berlin Wall collapsed – something he never saw coming. "For me, being with my family in South Africa – being at heart a capitalist, an entrepreneur – I said: that's paradise for South Africa that these communist systems have proven that they're not working."

Things moved quickly after that. In February 1990, when Mandela was released, Daun commented, "I was one of the very few white faces on the Parade in Cape Town. I don't know how many – fifty thousand [people] or whatever. The excitement was there." Daun says it was after hearing Mandela speak that day that he decided "now is the time to start. A few weeks later, I bought the Morkels chain from Federale – 75% or 76% of the shares." Morkels had been a household name in South Africa, founded in the early part of the twentieth century by Philip William Morkel, who, famously, got the money to seed his early stores from a man he was chatting to at a pub, who took Morkel's only form of security: his car. Daun not only bought the hundred Morkels furniture shops, he also got

50 Totalsports stores for less than 10 million Deutschmarks. "A comparable group of stores in Germany would be ten times or more," he said.

After that, he travelled around the country to visit the stores, where he spoke to many South Africans who thought he was insane to be investing when "the blacks" would be taking over. "They had indoctrinated all of the white South Africans who'd heard all their lives about the *swart gevaar*. They were pessimistic . . . [but] I was getting more optimistic," he says.

Daun hauled out the chequebook once more. In 1994, his company Daun & Cie bought a relatively anonymous furniture company situated south of Joburg near the township of Soweto called Victoria Lewis – which made its name building and selling discount bedroom suites to what was coyly described as "the mass market".

But it was the following year that Daun made the decision that would lift him onto the road to the modern-day Steinhoff. In 1995, one of Daun's colleagues came to him and told him about a commercially minded young accountant named Markus Jooste. "There's an entrepreneurial guy, an Afrikaner. Young guy with a huge factory in Gomma Gomma," this colleague said. In the landscape of the furniture industry at the time, Gomma Gomma was nowhere. It was just a speck, making unremarkable couches and lounge furniture from its base in Ga-Rankuwa, a dusty rural nowhereland north of Pretoria renowned for absolutely zero. Telling the story, Daun said at the time that he was understandably reluctant. Nonetheless, he went to meet Jooste for the first time in Joburg's Carlton Hotel – then the tallest building in Africa, and the site where Mandela, in 1994, declared South Africa to be "free at last".

It was late on a Sunday afternoon, but they chatted casually at the bar, with Daun stand-offish at first. "I was a little bit cautious, but then we set up a second meeting in May 1995. Beforehand, Markus had sent me figures and a balance sheet, and I remember, in this meeting, he showed me the factory in a photograph. It was massive – huge."

Jooste told Daun he was having trouble with his bank, Absa, and needed an investor. Daun was hesitant, in part because "it was a big amount of money at that stage – I had to pay R20m in cash to the bank". But over three or so meetings, Jooste sold him on the rationale. "In the end, I said: 'Markus – handshake, you are my man. We'll work together.' It was a decision from my gut feeling, and I was not always right in my life – I got other experience very badly [wrong]. But with Markus, it was a very lucky and good decision."

For Jooste, what stuck with him was the fact that Daun had done the deal – agreeing to repay the banks and settle the debt – based entirely on a handshake. In retrospect, a few years down the line, Daun would be justified in feeling less unambiguously positive about that decision. But in 1995 it seemed like a good idea.

Today, Bruno Steinhoff says his initial decision to invest in Gomma Gomma came after he got a call from Daun, asking him to help save his South African factories, which were all struggling to turn a profit after interest rates had spiked to 25%. "Claas phoned me and said, 'Bruno, I need your help, because all my factories, my supplier has gone bankrupt.' He said, 'I now have to buy these factories from bankruptcy, otherwise I have no suppliers.' So, I said, 'Claas, it is possible, but I'll have to invest a lot of time.' So, he said, 'Let's make this Steinhoff in Africa – and you'll get half the shares in it.'" So in 1997 Bruno Steinhoff bought 35% of Gomma Gomma, and this became the foundation for the modern Steinhoff.

Already, Daun had been leaning heavily on Bruno's expertise. He would regularly send his best furniture buyers over to Westerstede, to speak to Steinhoff about design and the new technology used to make furniture. "What Markus was lacking in Gomma Gomma was the latest technology in furniture production. And Bruno, with his factories, invested huge amounts of money into new equipment and technology . . . I said to Markus: 'We must bring this together, try to form a partnership.'"

So one day in October 1995, a confident, good-looking man walked into Steinhoff's Westerstede office as an emissary from Daun's team in South Africa. Good afternoon, he told Bruno, I'm from Gomma Gomma – my name is Markus Jooste.

*   *   *

Today, it would seem an exaggeration, but not altogether untrue, to say that Bruno Steinhoff has been irretrievably shattered by what happened to the company that carries his name. But it's clear the episode has clobbered him pretty badly. You sense he is not as certain as he once was, when he talks about certain deals Steinhoff made. At times, he seems to carry the hesitant humility of the recently divorced. Yet there is still that fierce competitiveness in his eyes that helped his company prosper. When trying to make a point, he doesn't break eye contact or stare off into the distance. Steinhoff was all about attention to detail. "I am very ashamed of what has happened now, after my 80th birthday. All this also wounded me deeply and I am still not in a positive spirit," he says.

It hasn't helped that the volcano erupted around the weeks when Bruno Steinhoff was toasting his endurance. At the end of November 2017, he had travelled to South Africa for what was meant to be a triumphant 80th birthday party at Lanzerac. His 80th was an aptly lavish affair. The Stellenbosch City Orchestra played alongside guest soloists André Terblanche, Janel Speelman, Niel Rademan and Charity Leburu. An exorbitantly priced glass marquee was set up and the champagne flowed. Steinhoff revelled in it. A few days later, he returned to Westerstede, where he held his "German party" for his 80th – the event at which Markus Jooste gave a speech, over that fevered weekend in December when all hell was breaking loose in South Africa.

It helped Bruno Steinhoff that he wasn't as involved in the business as he'd once been. In 2008, just after his 70th birthday, he'd resigned as Steinhoff's chairman, and given up most of his executive duties. He remained a non-executive director at Steinhoff until February 2018, but he spent most days in Westerstede rather than Cape Town.

Today, during the week, Steinhoff wakes up and drives the kilometre or so up the road from his gated estate in Westerstede to his office on the fourth floor of Steinhoff's European headquarters – adjacent to the immense 12-storey warehouse which squats over the town, branded Steinhoff Möbel. Outside that facebrick building, there are four flags that attest to the company's roots: the German flag, the South African, the European Union, and the one bearing the Steinhoff emblem.

Walk inside the door of that building, and you'll see it's a monument to the passion that drove Bruno Steinhoff for the last six decades: building furniture. The books on the shelves include the 1976 edition of *Möbel: Eine Stilgeschichte durch vier Jahrtausende – Mit über 1000 Abbildungen*, a history of trade in Westerstede over two hundred years, and a coffee-table book history of the furniture company. Perhaps incongruously, there's also *My Book*, the coffee-table book amalgamation of wildlife photography and "inspirational quotes" written by Brian Joffe, the founder of the industrial company Bidvest.

On one wall of his roomy office, on the fourth floor, there is a map of the world that Bruno Steinhoff is fond of using to illustrate Steinhoff's expansion, across Germany, across the Far East, and down to South Africa. It underscores how tactile a person he is, and why he would be wrong-footed by abstract and labyrinthine accounting shenanigans.

"I just look after the family business now," says Steinhoff. "It's nothing to do with furniture really. It's some property, some farms near where I grew up. Mostly, I come into the office to shout at Renata, and keep an eye on her boyfriend," he says, winking at his assistant of eleven years, and the immense, stuffed polar bear positioned awkwardly right next to his desk. Steinhoff has always been an enthusiastic hunter and the bear was shot 45 years ago in Alaska. It has boxing gloves – a gift, it seems, from the German middleweight champion Arthur Abraham – hanging over its paws. Behind his desk, there are pictures of him with Jooste, Christo Wiese and other South Africans on a hunting trip somewhere in South Africa.

You can see why Westerstede, with its laid-back small-town character, would be a perfect refuge for Bruno Steinhoff. It's a world away from the hysteria surrounding the company evident at the brasseries in Cape Town, the grillhouses of Sandton or the boutique art galleries of Stellenbosch. In Germany, you get the idea few people have any sense of the wildfire overseas linked to the Steinhoff name. Ask anyone in any of Westerstede's cottage stores, populated by the usual assortment of bicycles, carved wooden toys and picture books of rhododendrons, and they'll gush about how Steinhoff has done so fantastically well, and remains the biggest employer in the area. Few people know of the explosion in December

2017. "I'm still a hero here in Germany," says Steinhoff. "Here, nobody says shit about Bruno Steinhoff – they say I'm correct in what I did. I'm still an ambassador for Westerstede, and I'm very happy with that."

He's particularly proud of that accolade. Newspaper photographs in 2016 show a beaming Steinhoff, standing alongside Westerstede's mayor Klaus Groß, holding up the certificate that mandates him to act as an "ambassador" for Westerstede's business sector.[7] Groß gushed at the time: "We wanted to give Westerstede a face and find someone who represents the city to the outside."

Whether Bruno Steinhoff's presence today, as a representative of the small town, would induce the same sort of confidence that Groß wanted at the time is unclear. He hasn't been back to South Africa in months, though he says he plans to return soon with a small group of friends who together have become a crew of amateur cyclists. They plan to ride the Cape Argus tour, a 110-kilometre cycle event held in March each year. "Last year, I stopped because there was an awful storm. But my group of about ten people are all coming to do the Argus this year," he says. Cycling is now one of Bruno's big passions. In June 2018, his cycling crew rode more than 400 kilometres from Westerstede to the tiny island of Sylt in northern Germany, a stone's throw from Denmark.[8]

Today, months after Steinhoff's implosion, Bruno Steinhoff has made hardly any progress in understanding what had happened. In all his years, he says, he's never seen such a level of duplicity. "For me, it was a big surprise. I had no sense that this was possible. But even Christo, who is a good man, he lost most of his money. Me as well."

It is especially bruising since Steinhoff was perhaps the closest to Jooste of anyone outside Markus's family. "From the beginning, I found him to be a wonderful man. Markus would also tell people: 'This is my father.' And to me, I thought of myself as his father." Those close to Jooste say this is no misty-eyed exaggeration, softened by sentiment and time. "I've known them both for years," says one veteran of the company, "and Markus really was his adopted son. The relationship was *that* strong. So, what happened in the end, you can imagine what that was like for Bruno."

This is why the wound is so deep. Sitting in his office, where he'd spent many hours with Jooste, Steinhoff says, "I don't understand how Markus did that." But it probably helps that he's been stepping back from the company for years. "I'm out of the business now. For me, Steinhoff is history. I hope this company survives. I'm not happy with what happened, but I can do nothing. But my thing is, I'm looking forward without Steinhoff."

Perhaps, but it's been a bruising way for him to mark his fifth decade with the company that bears his name. So, he remains hesitant about returning to South Africa. "Now, with my name, I'm not so interested in going to South Africa. I *am* Steinhoff, so . . ." He trails off, but it's clear what he means.

3

The Cult of Markus

There was little to suggest, at least initially, that Markus Jooste, the polite and mild-mannered accounting whizz-kid who had introduced himself to Bruno Steinhoff that day in Westerstede, would become the central figure in what could turn out to be South Africa's greatest con.

Jooste had grown up in the country's capital, Pretoria, finishing school at the government-run Afrikaanse Hoër Seunskool, known as Affies, in 1978. In those days, there wasn't a huge amount of money in the Jooste household: his father worked as a civil servant for the Post Office in Bosman Street, in central Pretoria. It is clear that Jooste idolised his father, who, he said, would spend hours helping him with his homework. "He put his whole life into his children," he said during an interview in 2016. "He couldn't afford other things, so that probably helped a lot. He built that drive to be successful."[1]

Jooste's father, however, liked a flutter on the ponies apparently. In those days, there was a betting shop called Tattersalls next to the Post Office in Pretoria. So, on race days, Markus would go with his father to Tattersalls to take a punt. "The experience was totally different in those days. You listened to the commentary via radio. At the age of 12, I was what you call a runner – the guy who ran between bookmakers with tickets laying off their bets with each other."[2] It was exhilarating for the boy to see wads of money being won and lost in an instant, but the betting left a bad taste in his mouth. It stuck with Jooste, so much so that when he later bought racehorses himself, he'd proclaim that he never bet a single cent himself.

Allen Swiegers was one of Jooste's classmates at Affies, who went on to bigger things. Like Jooste, he studied accounting (though he went to the University of Pretoria, not Stellenbosch). Swiegers would spend much of his career at the auditing firm Deloitte. By the time he retired in 2016, he was Deloitte's chief operating officer in Africa. "Markus was a popular guy and very social, even though he wasn't part of the crowd of boys who played rugby seriously," says Swiegers today. "He was clearly very intelligent, though he wasn't one of those pupils who aimed to get seven distinctions. He wasn't top of the class, but he was clearly smart, and Affies took its academics very seriously."

At the time, Jooste was one of only a few of the Affies pupils to go on to study accounting. "Studying accounting wasn't sexy in those days," says Swiegers. (Sexy is perhaps not even a term you'd use too quickly to describe the profession even today.) "Kids became doctors and lawyers – it was what most of those 'seven distinction guys' went on to study. That's what your parents wanted. So Markus and I were outliers."

From Affies, Markus Jooste won a scholarship to Stellenbosch University. The bursary didn't pay for everything, so despite the vacation work he did at the small accounting firm of Theron van der Poel, he left university with a student loan debt of R100,000 (or so he claims). Never having had much money early on bred an intense desire to succeed, say those close to him. This drive was already evident early on in the legend that he obtained the highest mark in the country in his board exams.

By coincidence, Johann van Rooyen, the son of the Pep founder, Renier van Rooyen, also began studying at Stellenbosch in 1979, the same year as Jooste. They ended up in the same elite residence, Wilgenhof, as did Rian du Plessis, Markus Jooste's long-time family friend who'd later become CEO of the racing group Phumelela. "We were in different streams," says Van Rooyen today from Vancouver, where he now lives. "He was doing accounting, I was doing law. I was an avid supporter of the Progressive Federal Party (PFP) and I don't think we shared the same political philosophy, so we weren't close." Van Rooyen says Jooste had his own clique, often consisting of others from upcountry and especially Pretoria. "I remember him as the sort of person who aspired to be popular and part of the in-crowd."

Some say Jooste used to boast about his sporting prowess – how he'd played squash for Northern Transvaal. Which, of course, he hadn't. Others say he was initially unobtrusive: a *sluiper* – somebody who doesn't really participate in the sort of extra-curricular jollies you'd expect of students at universities. When he became more senior, he'd relish inflicting embarrassing initiation rites on first-year students – something for which Stellenbosch was notorious at the time. "If there was some fun to be had, such as catching and 'punishing' passing students who shouted 'bekfluitjie', you'd find Markus at the centre of the obligatory cold shower, or dunking a bucket of water over the offender's head," says Van Rooyen.

Thys du Toit, who later founded Coronation Fund Managers in 1993, was two years ahead of Jooste at Stellenbosch. "One businessman I knew had this saying: employ them poor, bright and with a deep desire to succeed. That was Markus to a T. He has an unbelievable drive to become successful, come what may," says Du Toit today.[3]

There were others who studied with Jooste who'd go on to make headlines too. Someone else who shared the same residence with Jooste was one of the best players ever to pull the national rugby jersey over his head, Carel du Plessis, who would play twelve times for the Springboks during the apartheid years. At the time, Wilgenhof was seen as the Petri dish for creating future Springbok rugby players. The housemaster at Wilgenhof was Danie Craven, the legendary and longest-serving president of the South African Rugby Board, from 1956 until 1993. Jooste was one of a minority at Wilgenhof who didn't play rugby, but he was still quite close to Du Plessis. Today, Du Plessis doesn't want to say much about Jooste. "He was a smart guy, a top student, but we didn't really stay in touch," he says.

The man who would ultimately take Craven's post as head of SA Rugby was also in Jooste's orbit: Rian Oberholzer, who as boss of the rugby federation presided over an infamous army-style training camp called Kamp Staaldraad. Contacted today, Oberholzer says he doesn't want to discuss Jooste at all: "I don't want to get involved in this."[4]

Jooste did his articles – the apprenticeship required of accountants and lawyers – at a Cape Town law firm called Greenwoods. Today, it is called Baker Tilly Greenwoods. In the evenings, he studied for his honours degree in accounting with the University of Cape Town. At the time, he shared a house in Cape Town with two people who'd remain trusted friends in Jooste's life and, later, became colleagues at Steinhoff: Jan van der Merwe and Frikkie Nel.

Jooste would describe their relationship as one of "full trust", saying that whenever a job came up, "we always looked for somebody within the circle who we could put in".

Fortuitously, on the first day of his articles with Greenwoods in 1982, Jooste was part of the audit team assigned to a company owned by Christo Wiese, called Octha Diamonds. Both Octha and Greenwoods shared office space in the old Trust Bank building in Cape Town. At that stage, Wiese was an entrepreneur who had a stake in the emerging low-cost clothing powerhouse Pepkor, but he hadn't yet taken control of the company. He wasn't then the rock-star businessman he'd later become.

Jooste, speaking about that first meeting years later, says that Wiese made an instant impression on him. "Christo impressed me – he built things, put deals together. I thought, I wanted to be like that."[5] Wiese says he remembers Jooste, but at the time he was one of many accountants coming through his business. "I noticed him as a bright young guy. I'm told he got the top mark in South Africa when he wrote his board exam, so he's clearly the sort of guy you'd notice."[6] Then Wiese bought control of Pep, and moved to his office in Parow. He lost touch with Jooste. "From time to time, I heard from friends of mine in Hermanus that this young Jooste guy is smart and is building a great business, but I didn't meet him again for years."

Jooste's ambitions in the 1980s went far beyond simply remaining an accountant, sentenced to a life of spreadsheet-constrained drudgery. As he said in one interview: "At 24, I left the auditing firm the day of finishing my articles because I knew that I had to do something for myself – the next morning I became a shareholder of my biggest client at the auditing firm. I think it's in your blood to want to have ownership."[7] Or perhaps, more accurately, to become wealthy. One of Jooste's mantras – one he would repeat to people he'd want to hire – was that you can't get rich by earning a salary. So, he'd liberally dose his executives with share options.

Jooste and Jan van der Merwe, his former housemate, were then conscripted to serve in the South African Defence Force in 1985, back up on the Highveld in Pretoria. At the time, "national service" was just the way it was for white men, who were forced to serve two years in the army. If you were lucky and had skills, you'd find yourself conscripted to somewhere relatively benign – a desk job perhaps – rather than wedged inside a Casspir army vehicle on any smoke-filled street in Soweto, firing a volley of teargas canisters to choke those rioters who'd dared demand the vote. So, with his accounting degrees, Jooste scored a job at the Receiver of Revenue, the tax authority, as a deputy director during his army years. The insight gained by working for the Receiver must have been invaluable training for a man who, later, seemed to be able to find every trick in the book – and some that weren't in any book – to reduce his tax burden.

Jooste was itching to run his own company, however. So, after the army, he began working for an older businessman named Michael Delport, who ran various companies in a desolate place in the sticks called Ga-Rankuwa. David Meades, a veteran stockbroker who was also a journalist for many years, knew Delport well. "Michael's family had large asparagus farms in the Northern Cape, but he'd decided to move to Brits, near Pretoria," says Meades, who has since retired to Somerset West.[8] "One day, I was visiting him, and he was gushing about how he'd hired this smart young accountant named Markus Jooste, who was probably only around 25 or 26 years old, but who was clearly going places."

To deem Ga-Rankuwa "unfashionable" is like suggesting China has a few quibbles with free speech. During the apartheid era, Ga-Rankuwa's barren, rust-red soil made it the ideal dumping ground to which the

National Party confined black people, declaring it part of the so-called independent homeland of Bophuthatswana. The people who were corralled into Ga-Rankuwa were largely labourers who worked on the motor vehicle plants outside Pretoria. Today, the industrial area Ga-Rankuwa is a knotted collection of rusted barbed wire, soulless warehouses, peeling walls where aspiring backyard panelbeaters have scrawled their numbers, and adverts for cheap beer by the case. There's hardly a blade of grass to be seen. This was hardly an auspicious place for the young Jooste to kick-start a dazzling career that would take him to the showrooms of France or the trading floor of the Frankfurt Stock Exchange.

Today, Michael Delport says that Markus Jooste first arrived at his door as an articled clerk, when Greenwoods came to audit various companies, which Delport owned. "I thought he was bright, and I needed a financial guy. He came to work for me, and was pleasant. I could see he was clever – he could think ten years ahead of me."[9] Delport said that eventually they parted ways. "I was probably not on a hunting trail to take over every other business – maybe I thought too small. I like to keep it simple and I don't want to go into a lot of debt." But Delport says he never saw anything shady with his company's finances. "I trusted the books and would have known if anything was wrong."

Quickly enough, Delport, who was fifteen years senior to Jooste, faded out of the picture. But official Companies Office records show that he and Jooste had a long association until the mid-1990s, both being joint directors of various companies, including Jurgens.[10] But Jooste was, in his bones, a dealmaker. So, when he and Delport were offered the chance to sell their business to the canning company Gants, they leapt at it. "We sold, got paid, and actually were without a job the next day. And for both of us, it was a thing that we didn't expect in the hype of doing a very good financial deal, in those early days," said Jooste in an in-house recording made in 2013.[11]

Then, a moment of remarkable serendipity broke. "We saw a sign opposite the street in Ga-Rankuwa, where our canning factory was, saying that on Saturday there's an auction, to auction off a building. So, on the

Saturday we went to the auction and we bought the building, for the simple reason that there was a separate little office park which was empty – and in the building Gomma Gomma was the tenant." It meant, at least, that he and Delport had a place to go on Monday morning. At the time, Gomma Gomma was largely owned by a man called Rafie Steel. But within three or four months, Steel ran short of cash, so he went to speak to Jooste and Delport. Jooste says: "We got involved, and we recapitalised the company Gomma Gomma and took control. And that's how we entered the furniture business. So, it was actually by total default. So, don't believe it's all a strategy that Steinhoff started many years ago."[12]

Jooste's belief was that the series of steps that led Gomma Gomma from the industrial wasteland of Ga-Rankuwa, to the Westerstede office of Bruno Steinhoff, and ultimately to the Frankfort Stock Exchange, were the result of luck and circumstance more than anything else. "Nobody is clever enough to think out all these things. They just happen, and you must follow your nose . . . I think the big difference in life is with the people who take those chances that get offered to them – that's really the difference." Fateful words, in the light of what would happen to him two decades later.

Soon, Markus began repaying his earlier loyalties. Frikkie Nel, discussing Steinhoff's origins in 2013, says that in the mid-1980s, "I got a phone call from Markus one day, and he said he was joining with Michael Delport, and they were looking for an accountant. I then decided to join them at Gomma Gomma."[13] Jan van der Merwe, who also joined, described it as a tough time. "It was a couple of us . . . getting into the furniture business: Markus running the company, doing the sales, Frikkie the financial director, Iwan looking at all the debtors and the creditors, and myself busy in the factory planning and loading trucks and doing the buying. There wasn't place for all the accountants to do the financial work."[14]

Gomma Gomma wasn't exactly flush with cash, and it owed a small fortune to its bankers, Absa. Legend has it that cash flow was so tight that when people trudged the short distance from the office to the furniture factory, they'd pick up paper clips from the floor for fear of wasting resources. It sounds apocryphal, but you get the picture.

One thing it had going for it, however, was the fact that during the apartheid years the governing National Party had given plenty of tax breaks to companies to set up their businesses in the "independent home-lands" like Bophuthatswana. But then, for the first time in 1994, all South Africans got to vote for a new government and the winner was the African National Congress, led by Nelson Mandela. For Gomma Gomma, which was already on the breadline, the new regime presented an immense risk. Terence Craig joined investment company Allan Gray as an analyst the week of that landmark vote. A few weeks later, he and a colleague went to visit Gomma Gomma's factory in Ga-Rankuwa, as Allan Gray had an indirect investment in it. "The first guy who walked up to me when I got there was Markus Jooste," says Craig today. "Markus came across as very slick, in his Doc Martens shoes and his very polished manner, and he gave us a tour of the factory."[15] Craig was impressed. But as he was leaving, he posed one last question to Jooste: the reason you located Gomma Gomma in Ga-Rankuwa was because of the tax breaks from the apartheid government. But now that democracy is here, this tax break will surely fall away. What will happen to Gomma Gomma – will it be profitable then? "Markus's answer stuck with me until today," he says. "No, we wouldn't be profitable in that case, he said, but we'll always find a tax break some-where."

It is now more than twenty years later, but Craig says he has thought about Jooste's answer plenty of times since the revelations of his she-nanigans first emerged.

* * *

Back in those early days, the furniture that Gomma Gomma churned out wasn't especially memorable. For the most part, it consisted of run-of-the-mill upholstered lounge suites – as many as 150 on some days – as well as a range of coffee tables. But, apart from its massive upholstery and show-wood factory, the company did have one major asset that would in time attract the interest of potential investors: Markus Jooste.

In those early days, Jooste worked harder than anyone, regularly pulling

16-hour days. Often, he would stay up drinking brandy and whisky with his staff till 1 am or later, after a tough day. But he'd also be the first one up at 8 am, impeccably dressed, chipper and keen to get cracking. "He never really slept a lot," says one person who knew him well. "It helped him get a lot done, while everyone else wondered how he found the time for what he did."[16] This never changed, even though Jooste later reached the sort of position where he could afford to take his foot off the accelerator. "He was the hardest-working guy I've ever encountered," says someone with whom Jooste once did a deal. "I once flew to London on the same flight as Markus, and he worked the entire flight. He was going through a balance sheet, and he'd first mark it with a black pen, then a blue pen, then a red pen. When we landed I asked him, 'Markus, did you sleep?' He replied: 'Ek het 'n uurtjie gevat.'"[17]

Throughout the years, Jooste would cultivate a reputation as a tough-as-nails *boytjie*. "Markus liked to party hard – staying up late and drinking with the boys. He was never far away from a double Johnnie Walker Black," says one former businessman who spent plenty of time with him. Famously, Markus could out-drink many people.

Early on, one of the companies that Gomma Gomma bought was a furniture maker called Bakker & Steyger, based in Epping in Cape Town, which churned out dining-room suites, coffee tables, wall units and other timber products. Christopher Rutledge, who was a director at Bakker & Steyger in those days, says it was clear that Jooste valued loyalty above all. "He had his lieutenants, Frikkie Nel and Jan van der Merwe, who did everything for him. Every decision that was made would pass through them on the way to Markus. It was all about the old Stellenbosch club."[18]

In those early days, Rutledge says the culture was rigidly homogeneous: uncompromisingly macho, Afrikaans and steadfastly patriarchal. Everyone deferred to Markus. "Even then, it was a red flag. The fact that he had this close group around him who weren't prepared to challenge his decisions, who'd all come from the same place and wanted to preserve that hierarchy, was worrying. Markus was untouchable." Rutledge recounted a story, which he's also written about for a news website, that provides an insightful example of how Jooste operated. One Friday night, after 8 pm, Bakker & Steyger's executives got an SMS from Markus, ordering them to be at the factory in Cape Town the next morning at 8 am sharp.[19] When they got to the meeting the next morning, Jooste was in "full battle cry". "He dragged the MD and the rest of the management team on a tour of the factory, pointing out pallets that were incorrectly stacked or unevenly packed, dust on the floor and any small infraction that could serve as fuel for his indignation and disgust at the quality of the management he was about to fire." Eventually, after running out of steam, Jooste turned to the MD: "Get out of my fucking factory," he told him. It's a tale that illustrates the single defining characteristic about which many people agree: Markus was an epic bully.

Speaking about him today, Christo Wiese concurs Jooste was a male chauvinist, uncompromising and not shy to intimidate people. But he says that these were not red flags in themselves. If anything, they were a commendation. "That was his assertive style. But I can say I'm not aware of any of the CEOs of my companies, bar maybe one or two, who *don't* have that sort of streak. It's their way or the highway." This is why Wiese says he has some sympathy for the executives now being blamed for not having detected Jooste's shady goings-on. "I know how he operated – how he could intimidate people."[20]

Wiese is certainly right that Jooste is far from the only exponent of strong-arm tactics in the mahogany row. One of the more famous recent examples was the pugnacious, thick-jawed Travis Kalanick, who was fired as CEO of Uber, but who had thrown his weight around to stifle all his critics.[21] Dr Mary Lamia, a clinical psychologist and professor at the Wright Institute in California, says while people think bullies have low self-esteem, their behaviour is usually a response to internalised shame. "Although some people who live with shame have low self-esteem, those who behave like bullies tend to have high self-esteem and hubristic pride. They attack others to take away their shame."[22]

The stories of Jooste's swagger are legendary. Insiders say he would routinely tell his executives where they should be buying a house, what brand of whisky they should be drinking, and if any of them dared sell any of their Steinhoff shares, he'd be knocking on their door that night, asking what unfortunate event had prompted their display of disloyalty. When it came to property, for example, some of Jooste's senior staff followed him to Val de Vie – the uber-wealthy estate nestled in Paarl in the Cape Winelands, about a forty-minute drive from Stellenbosch. Val de Vie is one of those few absurdly ostentatious places that outdo the brochures. A three-bedroom home at the estate goes for around R6m a pop, and even vacant land sells for more than R2m. But, then, perhaps that's what you expect when your estate has its own wine cellar, coffee roastery, a Jack Nicklaus Signature Golf Course and a swimming school run by an Olympic gold medallist, Ryk Neethling. It bills itself as South Africa's only "residential polo estate", which tells you pretty much all you need to know.

Jooste himself had bought land – a large stand next to a bridge over the Berg River – at Val de Vie in December 2015 that set him back R10.5m. (In the wake of Steinhoff's collapse, he sold it for R13m, paying transfer fees of R1.7m.) But other Steinhoff executives also bought into Val de Vie, bonding themselves to the hilt, some using their Steinhoff shares as collateral. Those stories ended unhappily, when Steinhoff's share price plunged 97%, and the banks came knocking.

Socially, Jooste was never shy of belittling even his senior executives. One person relates just such a tale: "There was this dinner party, attended by all Markus's executives. As you do, everyone brought a bottle of wine, and one of his friends bought a bottle of average MCC champagne." (MCC, which is shorthand for Méthode Cap Classique, is pretty much the South African equivalent of bottle-fermented champagne from France. But, unlike champagne, which goes for upwards of R500, you can pick up a reasonable bottle of MCC for around R120.) "Markus immediately held the bottle up and, in a booming voice, told the other guests: 'Nou wat se kak is dit? Wie het dit gebring?'" Only, Jooste knew exactly who brought it – the act was designed to humiliate.

Often, even at public events, he'd have no qualms about deriding people, often within earshot. "He'd point at someone nearby, and say 'Daardie een is 'n poes'. He didn't seem to care that people could hear him," said another former colleague.

Christo Wiese insisted he'd never seen Markus bully people like this. "That never would have washed well with me." But other former colleagues say Jooste would revel in deliberately shaming others – be it a board meeting or a casual dinner. "He would go out of his way to make other people feel stupid," said Christopher Rutledge. "Maybe that played a part in what happened later, and why people were too scared to challenge him."[23] Rutledge says that behind his back, those who worked with Jooste called him "the seagull" because "he would fly in, shit all over his executives and then fly out". This contrast – between the charming, easy-going ladies' man and the bruiser with the short temper – ensured Jooste remained enigmatic even to those close to him. Insiders speak of his split personality, and his remarkable ability to shift from Jekyll to Hyde.

"A lot of people at Steinhoff were scared of Markus," says one senior person who worked with him for years. "He could treat people who reported to him really badly, so many people just didn't want to approach him for anything." But, conversely, if Jooste needed something from you, he would flip the switch and turn on the charm. So, for example, if you were an analyst covering his company from whom he wanted a good recommendation, or someone with whom he was making a deal, or his superior, he'd treat you like a king. "In that case, he'd really roll out the red carpet. I think, in retrospect, that's why those guys he treated so well just can't believe he's the guy who did all this. They couldn't reconcile it."

But for those who reported to Jooste, he could be a tyrant. His own executives often didn't have the stomach to challenge him, fearing the ferocity of his ridicule. "Some people say Markus was a good leader," says a former colleague, "but I don't think that's true. If your staff are too scared to tell you what's going on, how can that make you a good leader?"

The cult of Markus was kept alive, in part, by a culture of fear. But at the time his empire was expanding, and his cohorts were making money. Everyone was making money, in fact. And so, he could get away with it.

* * *

On 23 September 1998, Markus Jooste blew the horn to begin Steinhoff's era as a public company listed on the JSE in Sandton. It was the culmination of his and Claas Daun's plan to stitch together Gomma Gomma and Bruno Steinhoff's European furniture manufacturing assets under one roof. The sales pitch was that investors could now buy shares in a company that made most of its money in Europe, 82% of it actually, right from their desks in Joburg.

Jooste had finally made the big show. For the first time, the public was able to buy into his company, and the ticker symbol would appear in the stock pages of the *Business Day* newspaper every day. It also meant that for the first time, a wide array of South African pension funds were exposed to Steinhoff. But it nearly didn't happen.

Ironically, listing on Johannesburg's stock market was not the first place Steinhoff's brains trust considered as an option to raise cash. At the time, in early 1998, Jooste was looking to buy a mattress supplier, but wasn't sure where to get the money. So they bounced around the idea of listing Steinhoff in Frankfurt. The catch here, one to which Jooste was utterly allergic, was the requirement of having to dedicate half the seats on the boards to the trade unions. "It was unthinkable," he said.[24] They settled on Joburg instead. As a result, people would get the combined might of Victoria Lewis, Gomma Gomma, Bakker & Steyger, its recently purchased logistics company, Roadway, and a network of companies inside Steinhoff Europe, such as "young-style" sofa maker Poco and "country-style" upholstered furniture maker Conforta.

A stock exchange listing was a novel idea for Bruno Steinhoff, who, for 34 years, had never taken public money. "To go to the stock market was absolutely new for me," he says. "I never learned that – I was never in a high school, I was always in my personal high school, learning everything by doing."[25] So, Steinhoff published a prospectus to woo investors. In it, the company billed itself as an "integrated lifestyle supplier that manufactures, warehouses and distributes furniture, bedding and case goods". Steinhoff's central competitive advantage, it said, was running its 43 factories in low-cost emerging countries, and then selling furniture into the wealthier developed world. Pretty much Bruno's modus operandi.

With Africa's largest bank, Standard Bank, in charge of running the show, there was some interest from the pension fund managers who liked the idea of earning "hard currencies" like the soon-to-be floated euro. That August, Jooste and his executives went on a roadshow with potential investors to Europe. The plan was to hire a bus, and drive fund managers and analysts around Eastern Europe, showing them the factories in Poland and the distribution warehouses in Germany. It was atrocious timing. That month, Russia's economy cratered, after months of being under siege from currency speculators. On 13 August 1998, its stock market collapsed, the yields on its ruble-denominated bonds spiked to more than 200%, and its currency collapsed.[26] "Russian officials were left with little choice. On August 17th, the government . . . devalued the ruble, defaulted on its domestic debt, halted payment on ruble-denominated debt, and declared a 90-day moratorium on payments by commercial banks to foreign creditors."[27] The problem for Steinhoff was that all emerging markets, particularly Brazil and Mexico, had been sucked into the Russian slipstream. In the space of a few weeks between June and August, the rand fell by 20% against the US dollar.[28] As the rand bled, skittish New York investment firms dumped any shares they had in emerging markets like South Africa, causing share prices to tumble. As the icing on this disaster, by early September, two weeks before Steinhoff's planned JSE debut, South African interest rates hit 25.5% – the highest they'd been since before democracy.

On that European roadshow, the analysts were on the phone the whole time to their HQs: should we ditch the trip and fly home? Should we cancel the commitments we've made to these Steinhoff guys? One of Steinhoff's executives on the bus got word from back home: "There's blood on the streets – don't even think about it."

When Jooste got back to South Africa, some of the funds that had agreed to put in money did indeed renege on their plans to invest. Jooste asked Claas Daun what he reckoned they should do. "Listen, if you're ready, go for it. Now is as good a time as any," he replied.[29] So, Jooste's team gritted their teeth, and kept going. It was the sort of *kragdadigheid* – set-jawed bloody-mindedness – that became synonymous with Steinhoff.

Some concessions were inevitable, though, given what had happened in Russia. Initially, Jooste had wanted to list Steinhoff's shares at R5 apiece. But the bankers cut this back to R4 a share. In the end, Steinhoff listed 650m shares, which began trading at R4 a share that morning. By the time the company's top brass went for a bang-up self-congratulatory lunch at Sandton's Michelangelo Hotel, the price had hit R5. "It was a huge mind-shift," says someone who worked there at the time. "It was exciting. We were going to be a name that was going to appear in the paper every day. Suddenly, a lot of people knew who Steinhoff was, and it was a proud moment." The listing was a success, raising R520m – even if it fell short of the promises made.

In the prospectus, Steinhoff set out some optimistic forecasts for its following year. It projected it would make total sales of R2.79bn and profit of R199m. This was a little too starry-eyed: for that year, it actually clocked up sales of R2.75bn and profit of R182m.[30]

One of the more interesting insights from this first prospectus is that it's clear that, right from the beginning, Steinhoff had set its stall to pay as little tax as it could get away with. For example, it boasted of how "the tax rate and investor-friendly tax policy currently available in Poland is one of the major reasons for Steinhoff's expansion into that country". Jooste, as one of the smartest guys in the room, with some experience of working in the bowels of the Revenue Service, wasn't going to let the taxman take more than he was due.

* * *

Nothing did more to fuel the cult of Markus Jooste than a series of fortuitous events in 1999 that led to Steinhoff's first major deal: the stealthy takeover of Pat Cornick for an absolute steal. This is the story. In 1997, the 800-pound gorilla of the local business sector was South African Breweries (SAB), which had tentacles everywhere, from hotels (through Southern Sun) to food (in OK Bazaars) and fashion (Edgars). It also had interests in the furniture sector, through a company called Afcol, which was worth R2bn and which controlled about 40% of its market. At the time, Afcol was an impressive beast, containing the Transvaal Mattress Company (which produced the first Sealy Posturepedic mattress in the country in 1967), Edblo, Grafton Everest and others. But SAB was trying to slim down, so it put Afcol up for auction. Steinhoff put together a bid, delivering an offer for Afcol of R17.25 a share in a sealed envelope. As it turned out, that wasn't rich enough for SAB, as a rival furniture company called Pat Cornick pitched up with an offer of R17.50 per share for Afcol. Everyone expected a knock-down punch-up for Afcol. But to everyone's surprise, Steinhoff threw in the towel. "Claus Daun said that's too much, and we walked away," said Jooste later.

For Pat Cornick, it appeared to be a coup. With Afcol in its stable, Cornick instantly became the largest furniture manufacturer in the southern hemisphere. But Afcol, it turns out, was the straw Cornick shouldn't have clutched at. For one thing, its American buyers stopped paying for the goods they were getting, leaving Afcol with R20m in bad debts. This meant that without any money coming in, the R158m that Cornick had borrowed to do the deal – which now had to be repaid – broke the camel's back.

So, a year after his failed bid for Afcol, Jooste sensed blood in the water. Steinhoff swooped in, ostensibly as a white knight, offering R3.82 per share for all of Pat Cornick, plus Afcol. It was an offer of some chutzpah – less than a quarter of what Pat Cornick had paid just a few months before – but Jooste knew that Cornick had run out of options. Graham Theobald, who was the executive chairman of Cornick at the time, recounts how the well-connected head of a chain of retail stores, David Sussman, suggested he approach Markus about doing some kind of deal to save the company.[31] "I met with Bruno Steinhoff and Claas Daun, and we agreed on a rough template for a merger: we'd get two shares for every one we'd put in," he says. "Steinhoff was quite small in South Africa in those days, whereas Cornick was pretty big, so this would have given them the scale they needed."

Sussman, who'd acted as the intermediary, was a big shot in the furniture industry back then. A tall and blunt hard-nosed retailer, he'd started in the furniture industry as a warehouse clerk at the Joshua Doore chain of stores. Joshua Doore's slogan was "You've got an uncle in the furniture business", and Sussman would end up as that uncle. In 1983, he founded JD Group when he opened two Price 'n Pride stores. But within a few years, Sussman had worked his way into opening plenty more brands and 600 stores. His network, by the late 1990s, included discount stores Bradlows, Russells and, somewhat ironically considering it's where he got his start, Joshua Doore. The point is that the JD Group was, at the time, Cornick's biggest buyer. But Sussman's loyalties were divided, as he was also an enthusiastic supporter of Markus Jooste. Sussman would later describe his relationship with Markus in this way: "From day one, it was a very close relationship, and of course, we wanted him to succeed – over and above that personal relationship and that chemistry."

In 2007, Steinhoff first tried to merge with JD Group, but that failed. There were then a series of deals, which led to Steinhoff taking control of JD Group. It seemed predestined. But back in 1997, what happened is that at the last minute, Steinhoff altered the ratio, so that Cornick would only get one share, in exchange for every share they put in. All of a sudden, at the eleventh hour, it turned out that they'd be getting 50% less than they'd expected. "I tried to get out of it after they changed the terms, but it was too late – they'd already sold it to the shareholders," says Theobald. "The idea was that I'd take over as CEO of the local business, but the way they'd changed the deal left such a bad taste that on the day I was meant to move into their offices, I resigned and left."[32]

In every sense, the Cornick takeover was a typical Markus deal: the purchase of a struggling business, done on the fly with just a handshake, the price paid for by not using cash, but rather Steinhoff's shares. Significantly, there was hardly a due diligence or thousand-page lawyer's document in sight. Jooste had done it on the basis of his instinct. "The top entrepreneurs are all successful today, because they do move quickly," said Jooste. "I think, if you've lived and worked with a guy like Claas, who set this example of listening, thinking and making decisions – and not wanting a due diligence and big books by auditors and big reports, to basically cover your arse."[33]

More than anything else, this deal was the making of the Markus myth.

Jooste would crow, accurately: "That bit of luck made us a powerhouse in South Africa, it triggered the escalation of Steinhoff." Daun also characterised the Cornick decision as "the most important event in the development of Steinhoff". "A year later, a lot of problems came out from [inside] Afcol: losses, bad business from the United States . . . we were lucky to reject this," said Daun.

The Cornick deal would be a template for the "Steinhoff way", which other executives would cite admiringly as evidence of Jooste's ability to wring a good deal out of any scenario. Danie van der Merwe, a logistics expert who linked up with Jooste when Steinhoff bought his logistics company, Roadway, as a better means to transport furniture, remembers that Afcol deal well. He reckoned it was the "wise old men" of the business who had tempered the impetuous younger Steinhoff executives, who might otherwise have got into a bidding war over Afcol the year before.[34] "Claas said: 'You never pay too much for a business. You must never want it too badly, because otherwise you're going to overpay. And once you've overpaid, you never get that money back.' And Bruno said: 'We are all hunters. You must load your gun and wait. The animal will come. You must be patient.'"

Danie van der Merwe would become a fundamental cog in Markus's machine. The relationship had first warmed back in 1997 over one of their shared passions: rugby. "I gave him four seats in our box at Ellis Park [the rugby stadium south of Johannesburg], he gave me four seats at Loftus [the stadium in Pretoria] and that's how we started communicating," he said. But Van der Merwe would end up as one of the big losers from Steinhoff's implosion in December 2017. His family had owned 6.1m shares in Steinhoff, which, at their peak, would have made him fabulously wealthy with a fortune of R550m. By September 2018, those shares would have fetched barely R15m.

When Jooste quit overnight, it was Danie whom the board asked to step into the role of CEO – much to the surprise of those who'd seen their close relationship deepen for decades.

* * *

The Cornick coup changed Steinhoff in more ways than one. Firstly, and most obviously, up to that point the early Steinhoff was a relatively inconspicuous furniture maker in South Africa. Sure, it had the Gomma Gomma factory, Bakker & Steyger making case goods, and a few businesses that made lounge foam, but it wasn't a big deal. It didn't have much clout when it came to getting its product into the big stores. "All of a sudden, we had all the brands," says one insider. "We became the dominant player in South Africa, all of a sudden. We had the manufacturing sewn up, and we could really go into negotiations with retailers and be someone."

But the second shift was more intriguing. While the Cornick takeover was indeed a dramatic catalyst, the intense desire to make it work and show the rest of the industry how smart Steinhoff was raised other sharp questions. Christopher Rutledge says that already there were some blinking red lights. What happened after the deal, he says, "was a shock for all of us". Initially, he says, there was no sense that Jooste would permit any corners to be cut. Rutledge tells the story of how, early on, it emerged that one of the managers was cooking the books. "It seemed that this person wasn't passing along the credit notes, in which we acknowledged we owed somebody for something, to the accounting guys. This would obviously have meant it wasn't accounted for as a liability, so it would have made our profits look too good. But when Markus heard about, he lost his nut." At that stage, he says, Jooste appeared to stand for clean governance.

This is how many of Jooste's advisers saw him at the time. In the words of one of Jooste's long-term bankers, who'd known him for years and had often gone to dinner with him and his wife: "I'd never have suspected this in a million years. I always saw him do everything by the book. He was conservative, smart. He never once asked us to do anything we felt compromised by doing." [35]

Allen Swiegers, who'd gone to school with Jooste, said he'd often bump into Markus Jooste from time to time. Swiegers, by that time, was climbing the ranks at Deloitte, which audited Gomma Gomma's accounts and, later, Steinhoff's. While Swiegers wasn't involved in those audits, he'd see Jooste a few times a year at client events. "He was still the same Markus I knew at school: very confident, pleasant and entrepreneurial. He wasn't shy of speaking his mind – if something was wrong, he'd tell someone to fix it, in very direct language. But never in my wildest dreams would I have suspected him of the things currently alleged in the media."[36]

But as the years went on, and Jooste's prestige and wealth expanded, it seems he began to believe the myth of his own grandiosity – that his presence somehow *demanded* grovelling respect. There is one story that deftly illustrates this point.[37]

Veteran journalist and radio presenter David O'Sullivan emceed a few Steinhoff events for Jooste. They knew each other, in other words. So, one day, at Cape Town's airport, O'Sullivan bumped into Jooste. "Hey, Markus, how you doing?" he asked, making conversation.

At that point, Jooste's wife Ingrid stepped between them and glared at O'Sullivan. "How dare you speak to my husband like that," she spat. "It's *Mr Jooste* to you."

Behind her, Markus Jooste stared at O'Sullivan with cold, lifeless eyes, saying nothing.

Well, screw *you*, thought O'Sullivan. Who does this guy think he is?

It's an interesting question. The answer, most likely, is that Markus Jooste thought he was corporate royalty, in the presence of whom others should display unbroken fealty.

But many businessmen found Jooste suave and charming – even if their wives, in many cases, didn't agree. Over dinner, he'd dish out aphorisms that were the sort of pearls that could, perhaps one day, be collected into a *Rough Guide to Business by the Rough*. In one case, an executive was describing how his company was being rationalised, which meant job cuts and departments shrinking. Jooste leant into him and whispered knowingly: "Hey, be careful you don't cut yourself to bankruptcy." Which is sound advice.

But with the Cornick deal, some felt a discernible, if subtle, shift. Says Rutledge: "Cornick was losing money hand over fist. Yet shortly afterwards, Steinhoff claimed it was showing profits from those assets. We knew that company well, and we just couldn't see where they were getting that profit.

Our suspicion was always that the finance guys were shifting around assets to manufacture a profit."[38]

Whether anyone who might have been doing this saw it as crooked is, however, uncertain. Those who knew the company at the time say there was a sense that Steinhoff would use every accounting trick it could to make its figures look better than they were. But this wasn't seen as blunt crookery; rather, it was just being smart, and moulding the system to suit one's purposes. "The guys working there, like me, understood that the business would be run on the basis of 'smoke and mirrors'. All the focus was on the accounting, and how to present something," says Rutledge. "We'd know, for example, how one of the companies was struggling, yet then we'd read in the annual report how well it was doing. It was astonishing." This, he says, is the essence of the discomfort he felt around Pat Cornick.

It was never obvious enough that people felt compelled to say something, but, intuitively, they sensed that something felt wrong. It was hard to put your finger on it. But every time it came to publishing financials, the Steinhoff accounting boffins had found some way to capitalise some expense or other, or discontinue some business, so it wouldn't reflect in a way that looked bad. This magic – the ability to transform companies that looked sickly into models of corporate vigour – burnished the legend of Markus Jooste. It would become his trademark.

Another manager who was there at the time says he left the group precisely because he spotted certain "accounting tricks" that he wasn't happy with. "Right from the beginning, I believed that companies were being set up – special purpose vehicles – specifically to hide certain losses, and make it seem like the profits were much better than they were. It made me feel uncomfortable. I didn't want to be part of it."

Of course, hiding losses in companies that don't reflect in your accounts – an "off-balance sheet company", in accounting terms – is one of the oldest tricks in the journal. This is ultimately what felled Enron, when it emerged that it owed far more debt than it had let on. It is ironic that those adrenalised early years at Steinhoff coincided with the last few years of Enron's life, when these sorts of accounting high jinks had become something of an open secret.

For Steinhoff, there would have been a number of benefits to doing this, besides simply boosting profit. For one thing, Jooste's preferred currency for paying for new companies that he bought was Steinhoff's own shares. So, by making the shares appear more valuable than they really were, he was able to boost Steinhoff's negotiating firepower.

Rutledge reckons that after Cornick, the finance whizzes at Steinhoff believed they could do anything, applying lipstick to pretty much any porcine figure that staggered through the door. It may have started innocently enough, but it placed pressure on the pencil jockeys to repeat the trick with every deal after that. And the one thing you didn't want to do was disappoint Markus . . .

4

Looking after Number One

In the few years after Steinhoff went public, the scrappy furniture company vacuumed up pretty much anything in its path. In 2002, it boosted its stake in the trucking and logistics company Unitrans to 26%, acquired 34.9% of timber company PG Bison, bought into the 150-year-old British mattress company Relyon, and formed a joint venture in Australia with the Freedom Group. In 2004, it bought the rest of PG Bison, and by 2005 it had added British furniture chain Homestyle (R1.06bn) and taken control of Unitrans. The next year, it bought 27% of manufacturing company KAP (R316m) and Australian furniture firm Bravoscar (R515m).

The pace was becoming increasingly frantic. It was all happening so fast, in fact, that nobody noticed how, in the shadows, Markus Jooste may already have been bending the rules. Quite how this was happening only emerged years later when, in 2011, the South African Revenue Service (SARS) went to court to retrieve R207m in back taxes from Jooste, dating back to the very early years. It was an eyebrow-raising revelation partly because – as was well known in Steinhoff circles – Jooste hadn't sold any of his shares in the company. Nor was his salary at the time, as the head of a middling furniture company, anything to write home about. So where would Markus Jooste have got anything like the sort of money to warrant a R207m tax bill?

It was a critical question that goes to the heart of the eventual *schlenter* at Steinhoff. As one former Steinhoff executive put it in 2018: "I'd always assumed the sting happened after 2015, in the later years. Now it turns out it was happening right from the beginning." This is the unavoidable implication of a trail of court documents, which suggest that Jooste was looking to cut corners from the very beginning: before the deals to swallow JD Group (2009), Conforama (2011) and Pepkor (2014), and before listing on the Frankfurt Stock Exchange. And, in doing so, Jooste made himself a fabulously wealthy man.

*   *   *

The most glaring instance of self-dealing can be traced back to Knysna, a seaside town on the Cape Garden Route, built around a natural lagoon and set on the edge of a vast forest. Knysna's miles of indigenous forests have made it the main source for South African timber since the 1700s. It's no coincidence that the name of the town itself, it turns out, comes from the Khoisan word meaning "place of wood".[1]

The story begins in 2001, when Barloworld, one of the largest industrial companies on the stock market, decided it wanted to sell the sprawling forestry plantation it owned in Knysna. Steinhoff was keen. After all, it needed timber for the furniture it made, and it could also then export part of the wood to Europe, for use in Bruno Steinhoff's factories. So, in May 2001, Steinhoff signed a deal with Barloworld to buy the forests for R45m, as well as the sawmill and plywood factory on Thesen Island in the lagoon. Press releases were issued, backs were slapped, and Steinhoff director Danie van der Merwe was even quoted as talking of how Steinhoff would export pine products to Europe, the UK and America. It's a "perfect fit for our strategy", he said.[2]

But at the last minute, the deal flopped. Later, in court, Van der Merwe said Steinhoff's top brass had vetoed the deal because "it did not wish to own fixed property in South Africa".[3] It's a curious explanation, considering that at the time the value of Steinhoff's "land and buildings" actually increased during the 2002 financial year to R1.5bn, from R955m. Nor is there any mention in the 2002 annual report of such a switch in strategy.[4]

Anyway, Van der Merwe said that while Steinhoff didn't want to buy property, it still wanted to "have access to the plantation". The trick, he said, was to "find somebody to own the land".[5] So, Van der Merwe chatted to Alan Evans – an Englishman and one of the long-term Steinhoff insiders – who was working for an obscure company called Fihag Finanz und Handels AG, registered in Zurich, Switzerland, in 1997. Quite who owned Fihag is clouded in mystery. Initial records show that it belonged to Bruno Steinhoff, but it seems it was sold later in 2003. Either way, it was in every sense a "related party".

Apparently, Steinhoff structured a deal in which Fihag created a new shelf company, called Kluh Investments, to buy the forests from Barloworld, but then let Steinhoff use those plantations. And it was all done through an "oral agreement", which meant that, conveniently, there were few documents to record what was happening. Court records show that Fihag paid R29.5m for the forests, partly using a R10m "loan" it got from Steinhoff. It then sold off part of what it bought, so that, in effect, the mysterious Swiss company paid R11.5m for the forests.

(Pause for a second and consider the poverty of the rationale for the deal: if, supposedly, Steinhoff wasn't interested in owning land in South Africa, why would it be willing to lend R10m to its own insiders to buy land? It means that Steinhoff was still, essentially, carrying the risk for land in South Africa it apparently didn't want.)

The arrangement would seem to be a classic fronting deal. The land would belong to Kluh, but Steinhoff ran the plantation: it harvested the trees, owned the equipment and paid the salaries of those who worked there, and it also paid more than R1m every year to insure the trees. By contrast, Kluh had no equipment, and no staff – just an incredibly valuable piece of property.

Evans, of course, knew nothing about running a plantation. He'd only been told by his masters at Fihag that owning the forest was "strategically advantageous".[6] For Kluh, "advantageous" was no small understatement.

Within two years, Steinhoff's board had a surprising change of heart. Now, Steinhoff decided, it actually did want to buy the plantation after all, supposedly because of "escalating timber prices and the scarcity of plantation resources".[7] (This seems another awful fib. Forestry South Africa numbers show that between 1992 and 2002 the value of solid wood exports soared, from R379m to R3.78bn. But over the next few years, during which Steinhoff decided it now wanted to buy plantations because of "escalating prices", South African exports of solid wood actually fell back to R3bn.)[8]

Anyway, within two years of having pushed Kluh into the deal as a middleman, Steinhoff's in-house lawyer drew up agreements to buy the plantations from it. In 2003, the deal was struck: Steinhoff would pay Kluh R159.7m – more than eight times what Kluh paid months before. As Judge Owen Rogers would later wryly point out, "It is not surprising that Kluh agreed to sell."[9]

So, who owns Kluh? Who would have benefited from this windfall? Well, thanks to SARS, we now know: Markus Jooste, the company's CEO who insisted on Kluh getting interposed as a middleman. Predictably, establishing Jooste's ownership wasn't easy. Fihag was registered in Zurich, after all, and one of the reasons people register companies in Switzerland is its secrecy provisions. The only Swiss records available show that Fihag was set up for the "acquisition and permanent management of investments in domestic and foreign companies" and also to "acquire and dispose of patents, licences [and] securities".[10] But SARS, eager to discover who made a fortune from the Knysna forests, dug deeper.

Investigator for the tax service Pretisha Khoosal said in court affidavits that initially "Kluh was ultimately controlled by Fihag, a company in turn controlled by Bruno Steinhoff, who at the time was the executive chairman of Steinhoff".[11] Khoosal then recorded that Jooste's company Mayfair (which he owns through the Markus Jooste Kindertrust) bought Kluh from Bruno Steinhoff. Reports from Bloomberg show that Fihag transferred control of Kluh to Mayfair for no money – even though Kluh had assets of R644m. Khoosal then followed the trail of money, establishing that part of the R159.7m windfall was "ultimately used to settle a portion of a loan due to Capstone" – another company associated with Jooste. In other words, Jooste personally benefited from the forestry deal, even though he sat on both sides of the fence: his company Kluh was the seller of the forestry assets, and he was also the pivotal figure at the buyer, Steinhoff.

In accounting terms, if you have somebody on both sides of a deal like this, it is considered a "related party" transaction. Company law says you must declare these "related party" deals to your shareholders, so they can check to see they're not paying far too much to enrich the bosses. In some cases, the company must even get an external independent party, such as a lawyer, to provide a written opinion about whether this deal is "fair and reasonable" for investors. Steinhoff did none of this. We're left to guess what an independent person might have said, because Jooste didn't declare this to anyone as a "related party" deal.

In 2011, when SARS took Jooste to court to demand R63m from Kluh for the profits he had made on the forests, the case made headlines in the *Sunday Times*. At the time, I asked Stehan Grobler, a Steinhoff director and head of its treasury, why this wasn't declared as a related party deal. His answer: "They both said to us they weren't related parties, and we independently checked that. If [Jooste and Bruno Steinhoff] were involved, it definitely would have raised issues, but that's why we took steps to verify that they weren't."[12]

An unlikely story. Had Grobler checked who actually owned Kluh, his inquiry would have led him to Fihag, at which Bruno Steinhoff's daughter Angela was one of the registered offices from the beginning. How did SARS trace the trail back to Jooste, yet Steinhoff, in whose offices Jooste sat, couldn't? The whole affair smacks of complicity, considering that Steinhoff's fingerprints were all over Kluh, and that its own CEO made a mint from the deal. It's the sort of insidious self-dealing that gives free-market capitalism a bad name.

In 2009, Jooste's son-in-law, Stefanus Potgieter, became a director of Kluh. In an affidavit he signed for the court case with SARS, Potgieter claimed "all transactions between the various entities occurred on an arm's length basis". Then, Potgieter added the twist: he says SARS's argument is "far-fetched" and it now "seems SARS seeks to embarrass [Jooste and Bruno Steinhoff] and this forms part of their ulterior motive". Quite what this "ulterior motive" is, he doesn't elaborate.

The irony is that nobody would have been any the wiser about the machinations over the forests had Jooste not fought to keep his tax bill as low as possible. This is because SARS is obliged to keep all taxpayer information "confidential". In this case, the sordid machinations only came to light because Kluh filed tax returns, claiming that it should only be taxed 10% of the capital gains from the property deal – in other words, the profit it made from the sale over those two years. SARS saw things differently. It argued that by owning the plantations, Kluh had conducted a "farming enterprise", so the sale of its forests was in the normal course of doing business. The bottom line was this: the taxman wanted income tax (around 35% of profits) rather than capital gains tax of 10%. This is why SARS slapped Jooste with a R63m bill.

Initially, in the court battle, the Tax Appeal Court agreed with SARS. This was partly because Judge Dennis Davis didn't find Steinhoff's witnesses "persuasive". Davis said: "When the evidence of Danie van der Merwe . . . and Alan Evans is tested against the documentary evidence, the probabilities cannot be said to favour [Kluh's] version." Kluh then appealed this case to the High Court, which found in its favour. Judge Owen Rogers said that just because Kluh owned plantations, it didn't necessarily make it the actual farmer. The ruling was that Kluh could pay the lower capital gains tax.

In the end, Jooste had won the battle, but he'd lost the war. The public revelations of his self-dealing with the forests had been splashed all over the Sunday papers, under such pull-out quotes as "SARS reckons R200m is due in unpaid taxes by top businessman's companies".[13]

For people in the horseracing industry, who'd been wondering how Jooste was funding his voracious appetite for wheeling and dealing on the turf, the court case was an eye-opener. "At the very least, the [Kluh tax battle] starts to explain how some of the funding may have been created," wrote one of Jooste's critics on a racing website.[14] He added: "If this turns nasty, the ripple effect could be severely detrimental for all local racing."

Some legal pundits were surprised that the judges hadn't delved further into Kluh's motives for doing the forestry deal in the first place. Could it just have been a fancy scheme designed to enrich the Steinhoff CEO? Tax lawyer David Clegg, who has written seven books on tax, seemed entirely sceptical of Steinhoff's argument, as well as of the High Court ruling. Writing in the journal *Tax Talk*, Clegg said he found aspects of the case "distinctly unusual". He singled out "the oral agreement between supposedly arm's-length companies, one of which is a 'special purpose vehicle' whose purpose remained unexplained, granting the indefinite use of valuable property for no consideration".[15] As a result, he said, "I find the readiness of both the High Court and the Supreme Court of Appeal to fully accept the evidence of the witnesses somewhat surprising."

If the forestry deal was the only instance of self-dealing, you could argue, perhaps, that it was just a coincidence. It wasn't. It was, after all, just one leg of the gargantuan R207m claim that the taxman lodged against Jooste. The other was a R144m claim, relating to another company controlled by Jooste, called Capstone 556. In that case, Jooste did make a quick buck personally – but it was far less blatant than Kluh.

The background is this. In 2001, a company listed on the JSE called Profurn – which owned seven chains, including furniture chain Morkels and Africa's largest audio-visual retailer, HiFi Corporation – hit the skids. Profurn owed R900m to banking group FirstRand and R70m to Steinhoff. It seemed destined for the chopping block. So, Jooste met JD Group's chairman, David Sussman, and together they hatched a plan that would ultimately lead to Profurn getting a cash injection, before being merged into JD Group. This merger was vital, Jooste believed, "to stabilize the furniture industry". The deal was complicated, but, essentially, a consortium led by Claas Daun, including Jooste's company Capstone, would invest R600m to buy 16.7% of the new merged entity: this worked out to around R18 a share.

Weeks before the deal was struck, in November 2003, Jooste was chatting to Citigroup's former South African head, Nick Pagden, at a coffee shop in San Francisco. Jooste suggested that Citigroup lead a "book building" for the JD Group shares – essentially, a programme designed to drive up demand for the JD Group shares, which should lead to the price rising.

Citigroup's book building was a fantastic success. Everyone, it seemed, wanted a piece of the "new JD Group". This was good news for Jooste: his company Capstone managed to offload the shares, for which it had paid R18 apiece just a few months before, for R42.50. Jooste made a mint in the process, and SARS reckoned that because the shares were sold so quickly, at such a profit, it was almost like a "trading profit". In other words, the taxman wanted to tax Capstone's profit as income (at around 35%), rather than as a capital gain (just 10%).

As with Kluh, Jooste disagreed, and the dispute ended up in court. As with Kluh, SARS won the initial rounds in the tax court, but Capstone appealed and Jooste prevailed in the high courts.

*   *   *

So, what do these two stories – of Kluh and Capstone – tell us? After all, it's not illegal for an executive to flip assets in this way, even if it's seen by many as beyond the pale. "If shareholders knew what was happening, it would have changed everything," says someone who has known Jooste for thirty years. "It would have been seen as the CEO enriching himself at the expense of his shareholders, and it would have been seen as poor governance."

However, what is required, from an accounting perspective, is that all deals between "related parties" must be declared to the board and reflected in the company's financials. But this didn't happen. You won't find a word in any of Steinhoff's annual reports about either Kluh Investments or Capstone. Was there a Steinhoff code of *omertà* that stopped people from breathing a word of such things?

These two cases are also significant for a number of reasons. Firstly, they show that Jooste was always on the lookout for how to make a quick buck for himself. And in the case of the forests and JD Group, he did this with steel-focused precision. Secondly, they raise other uncomfortable questions about his personal behaviour. This is because, in its court papers, SARS claimed that neither Capstone nor Kluh had bothered to file financial statements for years.

Had Steinhoff investors known about these side deals, red flags would certainly have been raised. One lawyer with inside knowledge of the case said Jooste spent two days testifying in court during the Capstone case – and it was illuminating. "I can't imagine that too many people in that court believed what he was saying. The thing that stuck with me, that I found so fascinating, was his ability to rationalise what he was saying. He would get asked a question, then get caught out, but he'd always find an answer that he, at least, seemed to believe." The lawyer uses the word "sociopathic" to describe the testimony. He concludes: "Markus Jooste got away with murder."

*   *   *

There was another kickback deal, too. During Steinhoff's fledgling years in 1999, it bought Unitrans from Murray & Roberts. This was a big deal, giving Steinhoff greater control over its supply chain, as it now owned a company that could cart its furniture around the country and into the wider region – to countries like Zimbabwe and Zambia.

Discussing the deal at the time, Jooste said: "To bring a lounge suite or mattress from anywhere in the world to the consumer's doorstep – that's the trick. Logistics, distribution and access is probably about 90% of our challenge."[16] Danie van der Merwe said it was part of Steinhoff's plan to control all three arms of the furniture business: manufacturing, logistics and retail. "Unitrans, without a doubt in our minds, was the number one player in South Africa. And to get the economy of scale – to get the right tyre prices, the right fuel prices, the right prices for trucks, and to get the expertise of a team that know distribution . . . – that was our idea."[17]

The marriage only happened because other companies began stalking Unitrans. Jo Grove, who ended up running Unitrans for Steinhoff, said he'd only just joined the company in 1998, when one of its competitors made a hostile approach. So, he went to Dave Brink, who chaired Unitrans' 56% owner, Murray & Roberts, at the time. "I was very upset about it – I hadn't gone to Unitrans to sell the business. I went to see Dave and he said: 'Find a partner.' To sell the business to the opposition wasn't an option for us. We wanted a strong, strategic shareholder. We had a really good relationship with Danie and Markus that went back many, many years."[18]

Steinhoff liked the idea a lot. In fact, the degree to which Jooste was salivating over the prospect of owning Unitrans took Brink a little by surprise. "I couldn't figure it out really. Of course, now I've learned why – because of the importance of logistics to Steinhoff."[19]

Brink said that from the beginning, Jooste had "a lot of fairly high-flying ideas about what could be done with the business, and there was some scepticism around". In the end, Steinhoff struck an incremental deal: it first took 10% of Unitrans in 1998, before increasing its stake to 26%, then 60.8%, and finally 100% by 2007.

It wasn't always an easy relationship, say insiders, since the Murray & Roberts CEO, Brian Bruce, apparently didn't like Jooste one bit. As Steinhoff dugs its claws in deeper, tensions flared to the extent that Murray & Roberts even reported Steinhoff to the financial regulator, the Financial Services Board (FSB). But as Brink said: "We got over that, and the deal was done."

It proved a good deal for Steinhoff. Arguably, it was even better for Markus Jooste, thanks to a complicated "restructuring" that passed entirely unnoticed. Steve Keys, who headed Unitrans' automotive division at the time, explains that in the early 2000s Unitrans' freight division (which shipped everything for large companies, from sugar to boxes of biscuits) was expanding aggressively. It needed cash to finance this growth. "Unitrans didn't necessarily want to go on a capital-raising exercise through a rights issue at the time, but what we *did* have was land and buildings, so Gensec structured a 'sale and leaseback' deal for us that saw us sell the properties to this vehicle, Clidet 386, then lease it back." In other words, the deal allowed Unitrans to take the properties off their own balance sheet, still keep the secured tenure at those properties through the lease, and also get cash to expand. There didn't seem to be much downside. "This would give the freight division the money they needed to expand," says Keys.

Gensec, at the time, was a hotshot financier of structured deals exactly like this. If there was some novel scheme to raise debt for a transaction, or some new fancy tax-structuring plan, Gensec would be your first port of call. At the time, it was owned by life insurance giant Sanlam, and would later be absorbed entirely into the wider Sanlam business.

Back in 2002, Steven de Bruyn was Gensec's executive in charge of debt-structuring deals, exactly like the one Unitrans wanted. So, he went to speak to Markus Jooste. De Bruyn says Steinhoff asked him to put in place a run-of-the-mill deal "to take their property portfolio off their balance sheet, through a conventional sale and leaseback".[20] The Gensec deal worked like this: 37 properties, on which Unitrans's vehicle dealerships were located, were whisked out of the company and sold to Clidet 386 – a new company bought "off the shelf" to be used as a vehicle for these sorts of deals. A group of banks would then "lend" money to Clidet to buy the properties, and they'd use the properties as security for that lending. Clidet would then collect rent from Unitrans, which they'd use to repay the banks.

In those days, it wasn't an unusual deal. Financiers like Gensec would often create these kinds of structures, which would allow companies to shift assets off their balance sheet by selling them to an outside party. It meant they'd get a big chunk of cash for the properties upfront, which they'd use (for expansion, in the case of Unitrans), and still get to rent the properties. It also looks good in the accounts: the windfall of cash boosts profits in the first year, while the rentals can usually be included in the (tax-deductible) cost of sales; and because you're shifting clunky properties off your balance sheet, the ratios that investors and credit agencies like to look at, such as return on assets, are improved.

Many companies follow this route. Petroleum giant BP, for example, used this strategy to sell its Alaskan headquarters, Singapore Airlines did it for its jumbo jets, and South Africa's state-owned transport company Transnet did the same with its properties. In many cases, the company selling the asset also has an "option" to buy back the assets at some later stage.

So, in the case of Unitrans, documents obtained by the author show how Unitrans signed just such a sale and leaseback agreement on 16 May 2002, to sell a portfolio of properties to Clidet 386 for R72.7m. According to a separate 28-page agreement, Clidet was said to have "purchased the properties" and "let the properties to Gensec", which then agreed to "sub-let" them back to Unitrans.

To raise the R72.7m, Clidet 386 borrowed R45.6m from Gensec itself, and R27.2m from Sanlam. It was a soft deal, of course: Clidet only had to repay the money "as and when [it] is in a financial position to do so". From Unitrans' position, it was able to claim "revenue" of R72.7m upfront, which would show up in its profits, and then it had to pay rentals on these properties of R8.6m per year from 2003. The rentals would, however, increase annually.

"It was a pretty conventional deal at the time," says De Bruyn. "It helped Unitrans raise finance, based on its property portfolios." But if this was standard, what would *not* have been usual was for any of Steinhoff's executives to have any stake in the special vehicle – and then to benefit if those properties were sold back.

In 2007, almost as soon as Steinhoff had obtained 100% of Unitrans, it immediately bought back all those properties from Clidet. The price it paid wasn't disclosed in its accounts. But, through a laborious process of sifting through the Deeds Office for each of the 37 properties, it is possible to arrive at the amount that Steinhoff would have paid. The answer? More than R501.6m. This is the total listed as the "transfer values" for those 37 properties when they were bought back by Steinhoff. So, in a nutshell: Steinhoff's logistics arm Unitrans sold all those properties in 2002, only to buy them back five years later for 580% more than they paid.

Again, the question becomes: who scored from this "revaluation"? Who, in fact, owned Clidet 386? Many insiders say that at the time they simply assumed Gensec or the banks owned the shelf company, as usually happens in leasebacks deals. But nobody checked. And Steinhoff's financials did not record that any "related parties" were involved. To be fair, anyone who was intent on following the money would have had to spend hours tracing Clidet's true owners through a head-scratching maze of opaque transactions, curious "transfers" and name changes. What happens first is that in 2005 Clidet 386 renamed itself Erfvest. Another document I've since been leaked, which is marked "strictly confidential", is dated October 2005 and signed by Sanlam and Erfvest. It records that another company called Business Venture Investments 338 "holds the entire issued share capital of Erfvest". Tellingly, BVI 338's only director was Jooste's son-in-law Stefan Potgieter. Then in June 2007 Erfvest transferred R316.5m to Kluh Investments – the company that would later, according to SARS's investigators, end up being owned by Markus Jooste. In other words, the man who benefits from the massive Unitrans revaluation is Markus Jooste. Again, there is not a peep about "related party" deals in any of Steinhoff's reports. As with the forestry deal, the evidence suggests that Jooste found a way to make another buck for himself on the side, rather than to help Steinhoff shareholders. All with zero disclosure to investors.

Speaking today, Steven de Bruyn says Gensec would definitely have rejected any deal structured in a way that allowed Steinhoff's executives to have any stake in that special purpose vehicle, and then to benefit if those properties were sold back.[21] "We wouldn't have been comfortable putting together a structure in which the executives had a personal interest, somewhere along the line. It wouldn't have been acceptable to us, or our board." So, had Jooste, or any other Steinhoff executive, had a share in Clidet, Gensec would have demanded this be disclosed. "It is, of course, possible that an executive could hide something from us, but typically we'd do quite a thorough due diligence before agreeing to put together such a structure for a company."

Unitrans executives, speaking today, are outraged at the prospect of Jooste having engineered the property transactions so as to take a cut. "We knew nothing about any side deals," says one of the former executives, who would only speak to me anonymously. "At the time, Unitrans wanted to improve the strength of its balance sheet, but there was never any suggestion that Markus would be getting a cut from it."[22] He says nobody would have suspected Jooste was looking for a kickback. "I always thought he was a bit of an arsehole, but he was hard working and, I believed, as honest as the day is long. Now it turns out nothing could be further from the truth."

Steve Keys, for one, says he had no clue that anyone from within Steinhoff would have benefited from the transaction – least of all Jooste. "I believed this was a simple capital-raising exercise, and that the properties would be returned to Unitrans when the lease expired."

Another banker who worked with Steinhoff during their early days was equally startled. "I am flabbergasted," he says. "It's a mystery to me how Markus could manipulate it to benefit like that, especially since they had a credible board. But if you know Markus, you'll know he's a domineering guy. So if he told the others that this is the way it is, no one would challenge him." He went on to say that this does, at least, answer one question that bothered many in the Stellenbosch clique for years. "We could never understand how Jooste seemed to be accumulating wealth faster than anyone – the racehorses, the properties in Hermanus, and everything. Yet he never sold his shares. Now we know."

*　*　*

After 2007, once Steinhoff had bought back control of the Unitrans properties, other strange things began happening. Steve Keys says that at that stage the properties were sharply revalued upwards. "I went to the guys [at Steinhoff] and asked them why the properties were being revalued – it happened twice within a short period of time. Their argument was that this was permissible because the rentals we were getting were going up." Sharply hiking the values of the properties would have been a shortcut to boosting Steinhoff's assets in its balance sheet, to present a better picture to investors.

Keys says it would have been fine to have increased the values of the properties, provided the company was getting high enough rent to justify it – in other words, if the "yield" on those properties stayed high. "But this didn't happen. The yields dropped to around half of market-related yields on similar properties in the open market. To me, that suggested those properties had been valued too high." This provides some intriguing insight into the accounting machinations taking place inside the Steinhoff kitchen, at its various subsidiaries. It also sheds new light on why

Unitrans might have been far more valuable to Jooste than a causal glance suggests.

At around the time of the shadowy property transfers, in 2007, the brokerage firm JP Morgan questioned why Steinhoff continued to own Unitrans anyway. "We question if Steinhoff's investment in Unitrans makes strategic sense," it wrote. "Only a third of Unitrans' business is aligned with Steinhoff's core business. The bulk of Unitrans has very little in common with Steinhoff's core competencies – 48% of Unitrans' operating profit consists of retail and rental of vehicles."

It was a good point. But if it allowed Steinhoff's top brass to take a kickback or use it as an avenue to dress up the balance sheet, well then, perhaps Unitrans was an invaluable asset.

*   *   *

Steinhoff's top brass weren't shy of gratuitously enriching themselves, either. Back in December 2003, Steinhoff put forward a new "share incentive plan", which saw it issue 18,903,653 "share options" to twenty of its executives at 0.5 cents apiece. At the time, Steinhoff's share price was R6.80 per share.

Now, share options are a complicated thing, which is why investors usually gloss over these sorts of announcements. But in this case, the enrichment was glaring: it meant that Steinhoff's top layer of management could pay less than 1c for options worth R6.80. Even then, it was an unusual "incentive plan". The way the scheme normally works in the corporate world is that if a company's share price is R10, their executives are given an "option" to buy shares at R10 a share, so if the price rises to R20, say, they can get the benefit of the upside. Essentially, you want your management to share in any "upside" but not be rewarded if the share price drops, or goes nowhere.

In Steinhoff's case, however, it was an undisguised gimme. Provided those executives met certain, not particularly difficult targets, they'd get millions of shares (almost) free.

So, Jooste himself was handed shares worth R31.1m, at a cost to himself of R22,933. Finance director Frikkie Nel got shares worth R5.1m for just R3,763; Danie van der Merwe got shares worth R12.9m for R9,512; Jan van der Merwe got shares worth R14.9m for R10,975; Stehan Grobler got shares worth R5.4m for just R4,037; and Siegmar Schmidt got shares worth R4.2m for R3,096. In total, these directors got shares worth R128m for a princely sum of less than R100,000. Which is, you'll admit, nice work if you can get it.

Investors in Steinhoff, not typically being the most critically minded group at the time, pitched up at Steinhoff's AGM and voted overwhelmingly to approve this incentive scheme. But not everyone was so complacent. In particular, Steinhoff's scheme rankled with Terence Craig, from Element Investment Managers (known as Frater Asset Management at the time). (Craig, you may remember, had first met Markus Jooste in 1994 at Gomma Gomma, where he was told there'd always be a tax break "somewhere" for the company to use. So, perhaps you could say he was more alert to what might be happening on the margin.) In 2007, Craig was invited to speak at a conference for financial advisers at the Spier wine estate in Stellenbosch. His presentation centred on the poor governance of certain JSE-listed companies – and one of the examples he chose to highlight was Steinhoff.

"I spoke about that 2003 share incentive scheme, which was one of the worst cases of governance I've ever seen," says Craig. "Effectively, they were just giving themselves money, for no risk. I asked how Steinhoff's shareholders could have voted for this."

Nobody from Steinhoff was at the presentation, but nevertheless, two days later, Craig received a letter. "It was from Steinhoff. They said they disagreed, and wanted to speak to me about where I'd gone wrong. I told them of my calculations, and told them I stood by my figures." It was clear Craig wasn't going to back down. But Steinhoff, nonetheless, told him he was wrong, and wanted to meet to explain his mistake. He resisted.

But to Craig, the debacle of the share scheme spoke of a disturbing willingness on the part of Steinhoff's executives to make money for themselves in ways that neither accorded with proper governance principles nor seemed intuitively fair.

* * *

While the Unitrans and the Knysna forest deals hinted darkly at self-dealing, there were a number of other deals that also didn't look kosher – though it would take some time for the truth to emerge. Right at the top of this list is a strange entity, loftily called 'Hemisphere'. Ultimately, Hemisphere would deal out a great deal of pain to Steinhoff's shareholders.

What happened is that in June 2008 Jooste "sold" Steinhoff's properties in Germany, Poland and Hungary to a new company registered in Holland, which he called Hemisphere. Why Holland, you might ask? The answer is: tax breaks, plenty of them. While not considered an outright tax haven (like Cyprus, Mauritius or the British Virgin Islands), the Netherlands still offered enough incentives to be rated third on Oxfam's list of the fifteen top corporate tax havens. (It lost the title to Bermuda and the Cayman Islands, but beat Switzerland, Ireland and the Bahamas.)[23] The Netherlands has low tax rates for "dividends" from other countries (such as retailers that pay rent to a Dutch company) and also has a few special tax innovations, like an "innovation box", which allows companies that make profits on patented products to pay a lower tax rate. This made the Netherlands the top destination for American foreign investment by 2013. "The laws in Netherlands shield a variety of profits from taxation, making it attractive for big multinational companies like Starbucks, Google and IBM to set up offices," said the *New York Times*. "Even rock stars like the Rolling Stones and U2 have taken advantage of Dutch tax shelters."[24]

Usually, Holland's tax rules work best when it's the middleman for a multinational. Take Google: it first books its European advertising revenues in Dublin, then declares its "royalties" to a Dutch company, before shifting the "profit" to a subsidiary in Bermuda.[25] Steinhoff, with Jooste at the helm, was never one to ignore an ascendant tax fad. Asked in 2016 why they'd shifted to the Netherlands, Jooste explained that "the double tax agreement between the Netherlands and South Africa is a very favourable and fair way of distributing tax between the two countries".[26] He said shifting headquarters to Amsterdam had to be done in such a way that shareholders could swap their shares in a South African company to a Dutch company and not be hit with capital gains tax.

So, Hemisphere was registered in Holland and, in return for injecting its European properties, Steinhoff got 45% of the new company. The other 55% was held by an anonymous company, registered in Germany, called Dolus Grundstücksverwaltungs, a shelf company created for this deal. The new company would have properties worth R4.68bn and liabilities of R2.7bn – which included a strange item entitled "intercompany payables" of R1.68bn. The way it was meant to work was that Hemisphere would then lease all the properties it owned to Steinhoff Europe, collect rent, and split the profits with its owners.

Right from the beginning, the arrangement caused analysts' antennae to twitch. "It seemed an odd deal from the beginning," says Craig Butters, who was a manager at hedge-fund firm Brait at the time. "But what made it a lot worse was their poor disclosure around it, and who was really benefiting. Of course, later we found out . . ."

Why, for example, should Dolus Grundstücksverwaltungs get 55% of Steinhoff's properties without putting in anything? And who even owned Dolus? As with Unitrans, the immediate thought was that the banks owned it. In a presentation that Steinhoff's head of treasury, Stehan Grobler, gave in Germany in 2010, he explained that Hemisphere was funded by a consortium of banks, led by the Norwegian bank HSH Nordbank, and including Investec, HSBC and HypoVereinsbank (UniCredit).[27] Then, the flip. A year later, in 2009, Steinhoff bought back the other 55% of Hemisphere, ostensibly paying Dolus Grundstücksverwaltungs R1.16bn for their stake. It didn't pay any actual cash – Jooste hardly ever did – but Steinhoff issued 72m shares to the Germany company.

What was the point of this, do you imagine? After all, Steinhoff had owned all those properties two years before – why fork over shares worth R1.16bn to buy them back? Certainly, this doesn't seem part of some great strategic shift. Two years earlier, before it had even sold its properties to Hemisphere, Steinhoff bragged in its annual report that "property plays a key part in our strategic retail offering and during the year we strengthened our position by purchasing a number of leasehold retail properties situated in central continental Europe".[28]

So why do this? Well, in answering this question, it's helpful to follow the money. In other words, who got those 72m Steinhoff shares? Though you won't find this disclosed in any official documents, the Steinhoff share register at 31 August 2009 revealed a sizeable shareholder who just happened to have come into 72.1m shares. Its name: Fihag Finanz und Handels AG. Yes, the same company which passed through the hands of Bruno Steinhoff, before it "gave" Kluh Investments to Markus Jooste without charging a cent.

The unavoidable implication, then, is that the Hemisphere "transaction" was just an avenue to suck R1.16bn out of Steinhoff, to enrich insiders close to Jooste.

* * *

There is, of course, another reason for flipping properties out to Hemisphere, then effectively buying them back a year later. These deals allow the buyer to "revalue" those properties. And, as was pretty clear with the Unitrans properties, Steinhoff was never shy of adding a few zeros to the value of its properties.

In 2009, almost as soon as the Hemisphere repurchase was done, it faded from view. Steinhoff didn't disclose the value of Hemisphere's properties separately, nor what warehouses, stores, land or factories it was merrily injecting into the company. By the end of 2017, right before Jooste's unmasking, we now know that Hemisphere owned 138 properties throughout Europe. Most of those, 101 of them, were leased to stores in the group – including the UK's Bensons for Beds, the French retail chain Conforama, Pepkor Europe, the Austrian chain Poco and British discounter Poundland. In Eastern Europe, more than half its properties were leased to the struggling Austrian chain Kika-Leiner.

With so many of these deals taking place in-house, there was plenty of potential for the property values to be radically skewed. The talk inside Steinhoff certainly suggested this: many insiders believed the Hemisphere portfolio was, if not rotten, certainly overvalued. It was only at the end of 2017, after Jooste scarpered, that the forensic auditors waded into Hemisphere's accounts, and found out just how skew they were. They found that Hemisphere claimed its 138 properties were worth €2.2bn, while it owed €938m to various banks.

But under Jooste's leadership, these properties had evidently been constantly revalued to reach that €2.2bn value. So, Steinhoff hired the world's largest real estate company, the Los Angeles-based CBRE, to divine Hemisphere's true value. In April 2018, CBRE came back with the bad news: Hemisphere's properties were valued at roughly double what they should be. The real value of Hemisphere's portfolio was €1.1bn, once you stripped out all the "inter-company" deals within Steinhoff.[29] In other words, Jooste and his property executives had applied so much lipstick and mascara to Steinhoff's property assets that they had presented an entirely distorted picture of just how strong the company's balance sheet really was. The reality was that those €1.1bn worth of properties barely covered the €938m in debt that Hemisphere owed. With some understatement, Steinhoff said that considering this news, "it is likely that the net book value of the Hemisphere portfolio will be materially lower than the €2.2bn".

Today, you'd be hard-pressed not to believe the entire Hemisphere structure was just one immense three-card monte. Shareholders were duped into forking over 72m Steinhoff shares to entities connected to Jooste and, then, as if that wasn't bad enough, they were duped into believing a fairytale about the actual properties held by Hemisphere. If the whole saga hadn't been so brazen, it would almost be impressive.

* * *

It mystifies many outside the group that such a volume of purple deals took place, without anyone inside Steinhoff blinking an eye – despite the squadrons of executives, directors and advisers who had all those fancy-sounding duties to ensure this didn't happen. Insiders say this is because the culture was, in many cases, similar to the Mafia.

The one unyielding ingredient for thriving at Steinhoff over the decades, one seen as definitive of the business, from the warehouse manager to the executives who flew on the company jet to Poland, was "trust". Speaking in 2013, Danie van der Merwe said that when he got involved in Steinhoff in the late 1990s, "I sold our family business into Steinhoff, and I still don't have a signed document as I sit here. That is how we trusted each other." The essence of it, Van der Merwe said, was to "never go back on your word". "Even if it doesn't work for you as you want it, you stick to your word. And I think that's what we did over many years. Whatever we agreed to upfront, we stuck to. And I think that, in the end, is where the trust comes in."

One accountant, who worked for Jooste in the early days, said the culture "consists of people who trust each other blind . . . we think alike, we operate alike, we respect alike, and we like alike".

Gavin van der Merwe, who was one of the executives at PG Bison, which Steinhoff bought in 2001, says the deal to buy the timber company was struck entirely on a handshake. "I remember getting this one-page contract to sign over our entire wealth, and I thought: Hang on. Up till now, every bank I've dealt with I've got a telephone directory for. So, I've got to go on trust – handshake-sign my entire wealth, sell my shares to Steinhoff." And the locus of this trust was Jooste. If it had been the Mob, who could imagine that it would be the Don himself, selling out the family?

As Danie van der Merwe explained: "We were confident in Markus's ability to do deals, and we had the team to back that, and the team to support what he was doing overseas." Jooste's inner circle prided themselves on the lack of paperwork, the fact that a handshake alone could clinch a deal – that destinies could be decided over a bottle of Merlot. To people outside the company, it seems unfathomable. But it was a culture that laid the table for what appears to have been an immense fraud, facilitated by other executives who had no clue this was happening.

Ben la Grange, Steinhoff's former chief financial officer, is the most obvious example of someone who may have trusted Jooste too much. But there were others before him, like Jan van der Merwe, who was Steinhoff's chief financial officer between 2003 and 2009.

Andrew Cuffe, the former head of research at brokerage JP Morgan, tells a story of how his analyst, Sean Holmes, had contacted Van der Merwe to ask for specific information about transfer pricing across different countries before 2009. "His response to us was 'Ask Markus'. That's just unacceptable for the financial director either not to know what was going on, or to let the CEO run his portfolio. Jan was responsible for the company's finances," says Cuffe.[30]

But nothing changed when others took over the post. In particular, when Ben la Grange took over as Steinhoff's finance boss, he was just as deferential to Markus Jooste. Many Steinhoff executives, to this day, believe La Grange knew nothing of the alleged fraud taking place. Says one: "Ben is a nice man, who wasn't involved in any shenanigans. But the obvious question is, how as the financial director could he *not* know? Surely he *had* to know." The answer to that, the executive says, is that La Grange would never challenge Jooste. "Ben would never ask the hard questions, and when he did, Markus had a good argument for why something was a certain way. Because Markus was a very clever guy, who could think on his feet and rationalise anything," she says.

The truth is that Ben la Grange entirely trusted Jooste. At least, La Grange can reply that most of the apparent fraud happened in Steinhoff Europe, which reported to Jooste directly. But still, it was evident to those who saw the two of them together that La Grange understood the way it worked: loyalty to Markus was everything. He'd repay that loyalty too. Every Christmas, Jooste would send a box of wine to people he'd done business with. It was a tradition going back years, since long before he'd even owned the wine farm Klein Gustrouw. In those early days, he'd send wine from other estates, like Rustenberg.

In 2016, one businessman who'd got the box of wine, called the office Jooste had hired to send the packages. "Look, I don't really need the wine. I don't know why Markus is sending it to me – I haven't done business with him for more than a decade." Relax, said the person who'd sent it to him: Markus has given us a list of 380 people to send the wine to. You can't give it back – nobody has ever done that.

You don't just leave the Mob, it turns out.

5

The Minority Report

On a summer's morning in December 2009, a lanky, soft-spoken investment manager sat down for breakfast in a discreet corner of Reuben's restaurant at Cape Town's One & Only Hotel, overlooking the city's waterfront. Craig Butters was there to meet Christo Wiese and try to convince the chairman of Africa's largest grocery chain, Shoprite, to steer well clear of Steinhoff. Butters believed that if Steinhoff wasn't an outright Ponzi scheme, it was pretty damn close. And Steinhoff's brawny CEO, Markus Jooste, was a man who oozed insincerity, Butters believed.

Though Wiese was already one of South Africa's wealthiest men (with an estimated fortune then of R5.1bn), he had no stake in Steinhoff at the time. But what he did have was an 8% stake in another Stellenbosch company, PSG, which was chaired by Jooste's good friend Jannie Mouton. And it was pretty clear that Jooste wanted Wiese at Steinhoff. It seemed only a matter of time – unless someone warned him off.

Butters had prepared a 40-page presentation to show to Wiese. The slides – which contained phrases like "opaque businesses", "tax risk", "weak balance sheet", "poor disclosure", "significant transactions with unknown private entities" and "extremely poor" quality of earnings – would leave nobody in any doubt about the utter disregard he had for Steinhoff. The picture Butters would paint for Wiese was of a rubbish business that had been cooking the books for years – even by 2009.

With a runner's physique, an acerbic sense of humour and a finely tuned bullshit detector, Butters was nobody's fool. Unusually for a stock market analyst, his first degree at the University of Cape Town in 1986 was in statistics, which he'd followed up with a postgraduate finance qualification. After university, he managed investments at companies like Prodigy and RMB Asset Management. At the time of his meeting with Wiese, Butters was running a hedge fund for Brait Specialised Funds, whose parent company had a long-established relationship with the billionaire. Two years later, in 2011, Wiese would buy 33% of Brait.

Together with his Brait colleague Bruce Mommsen, Butters put together a pack of slides to show Wiese. "At a previous firm, Bruce had independently arrived at a similar conclusion on 'The Hoff' as we used to call it", says Butters.

Butters reckoned much of his conviction on Steinhoff's shady behaviour was due to Mommsen's in-depth analysis.

"Christo was extremely polite, grateful, and he listened intently," recalls Butters. "Throughout the presentation, which took about an hour and a half, he asked thoughtful questions. Afterwards, I really felt like he'd got it."[1]

Even though Butters was at Brait at the time, those forty slides weren't in the format that investment managers there typically use. "I was really concerned that this presentation would end up in Markus's hands," he says today. Butters's suspicion of Steinhoff dated back to 1999, shortly after the furniture retailer had listed on the JSE, when he'd attended a meeting with Jooste and Bruno Steinhoff. "At the time, I knew pretty much nothing about Steinhoff, but the way Markus behaved there left me feeling very uneasy," he says. "He had such unnatural confidence. He would forecast, for example, that Steinhoff's margins would get to 8.2% *exactly*. Just the sheer precision of what he said made me think – be very careful."

Butters knows a thing or two about slippery characters. He has a fascination with spiders and reptiles, and describes himself as "reasonably comfortable handling venomous snakes", including the variety that psychologists Paul Babiak and Robert Hare describe in their 2006 book called *Snakes in Suits* (more of this later).

After that first meeting, Butters wouldn't look at Steinhoff again for about four years, until he began managing hedge funds at Brait. "Then I took a far deeper look, and it was astonishing: the numbers just didn't remotely add up. Not only was the company overstating its profits, it was overstating its cash flows. Investors always say you can overstate profits, but not cash. But the reality was that Steinhoff was doing this while generating almost no cash." Those forty slides that Butters showed to Wiese crisply illustrated this. Seen from today's vantage point, Butters's argument was also jaw-droppingly prescient. Nearly a decade later, in 2018, forensic investigators from PwC would uncover many of the same issues that Butters had flagged years before. For example, in a slide entitled "opaque business", Butters asked how it was that many of the largest European economies were "under strain, yet Steinhoff's business was thriving – all while its competitors were failing". He also flagged "significant transactions with unknown private entities", which became all the more sinister thanks to "poor disclosure" of who all these mysterious people were that were doing deals with Markus Jooste. Another red flag: when some of the divisions began making a loss, Steinhoff would simply stop revealing how that arm of the business made its money. For example, the "manufacturing and sourcing" division was just one big black box.

The most alarming fact that Butters calculated was that an astounding R4.5bn of Steinhoff's profit since 2005 – 41% of all its earnings – had come not from proper sales that produced actual cash you could put in the bank, but from fancy accounting tricks instead. These sorts of tricks were dotted all over Steinhoff's accounts. Take the forests that Steinhoff owned all over the country, particularly in the Eastern Cape, which it used to make its wooden furniture. Between 2004 and 2009, Steinhoff had "revalued" these forests upwards by nearly R1bn – or R977m, to be specific. What Steinhoff would then do was include the difference between the "old" and the "new" value of those forests in its profits for the year. This made it seem like Steinhoff was performing fantastically well every year. The truth, however, was these were only ever "paper profits", as there was never any cash changing hands.

And the trickery was becoming more blatant every year. In 2009, for example, no less than 12% of Steinhoff's entire pre-tax profit had come from these "forestry revaluations". While the accounting didn't contravene any accounting standards, the vast amounts were a concern – particularly seen in the light of other disturbing issues.

Forestry revaluations (in rands) as a percentage of Steinhoff's pre-tax profit

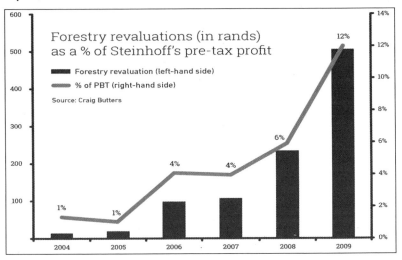

Butters flagged several other sources of "paper profits" too. For example, since Steinhoff did business in several countries and earned money in euros, Australian dollars and other currencies, it would then have to convert these back into rands before presenting its financials to its shareholders. But because the rand yo-yoed, the "foreign currency" movements had to be accounted for. Now these sorts of foreign currency fluctuations are quite common in the accounts of multinational companies. What *wasn't* common, however, was that these "currency translations" *always* seemed to boost Steinhoff's profit – no matter if the rand fell one year, then climbed the next. Over a five-year spell, from 2004 to 2009, Butters showed how these "foreign currency translations" led to an increase in profit every single year: R121m the first year, R167m the next, R206m in 2007, followed by R238m in 2008 and R302m in 2009. In short, Steinhoff's profits had benefited from a R1bn currency bump over five years.

There were so many other mysterious sources of profit, you could almost throw a dart at the financial statements and hit one. For instance, Stein-hoff included a vast chunk of "interest" and "profit participation" that it got every year from unnamed companies to which it had lent money. Only, quite who they were Steinhoff didn't say.

Speaking today, Butters says it seems that loans were being made to "off-balance sheet companies" – companies it secretly controlled, but which didn't appear in its accounts – and, later, these companies would be bought by Steinhoff to make it all disappear. "Interest and profit participation was capitalised to the loans, and recorded as income – despite not being received in cash," he says. Then, when Steinhoff bought these "off-balance sheet companies", those inflated loans would just disappear in the wash and be written off as part of the cost of doing the deal. Even back in 2009, Stein-hoff was a serial buyer of other companies. So, a few smaller acquisitions were hardly ever noticed.

Mix all these factors together, and you have what analysts call "low quality earnings", because those profits don't come from a reliable flow that you can predict every year. Instead, there were always "once-off adjust-ments" that helped Jooste pull a rabbit out of the hat. And Butters's complaint was that Steinhoff would never show you what was in that hat. But the bottom line was this: nearly half Steinhoff's profits every year came from "revaluing" its existing assets and other fancy tricks that didn't amount to real cash.

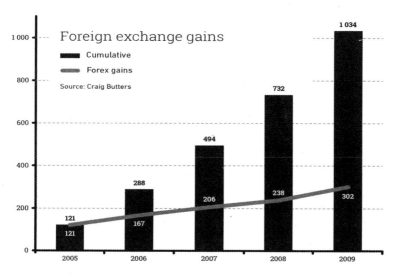

Among his slides, Butters also raised other issues, including:

• *Truly awful cash flow.* In finance terms, the real action happens in a company's "cash flow statement". It's like your bank account, showing you what actual money is flowing in and out. This is why it's the one figure that can't be manipulated. (Jooste would later prove this theory to be false, but that's a story for later.) So, when you compare Steinhoff's cash flow with that of Shoprite, you can see that, contrary to the story of prosperity pitched to its investors, Steinhoff was burning through cash as if it was the only fuel source in a blizzard. Every year, Steinhoff's cash flow from its actual business (its operating cash flow) was being sucked up entirely by the amount of cash it "invested" elsewhere, partly due to its shenanigans in the "loans" it had made to closely related companies. In 2009, for example, its "net" cash flow was a negative R2.13bn, and the year before it had been a negative R1.39bn. This was a nasty contrast to Shoprite, where the grocery chain's "net cash flow" was a positive R89m in 2009 and a positive R1.1bn the year previously. Put plainly, Shoprite was actually generating real cash, whereas Steinhoff was guzzling through it like an alcoholic eyeing closing time. Butters pointed out to Wiese that the overstated operating cash

Bad company: Steinhoff generates negative cash flows every year . . .

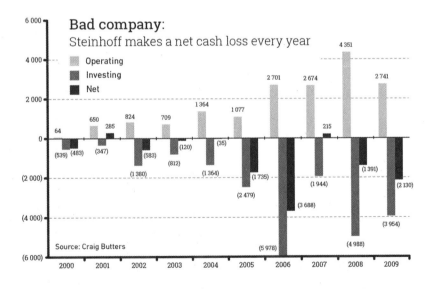

Bad company:
Steinhoff makes a net cash loss every year

Source: Craig Butters

94

flow was being offset by similarly overstated investing cash outflows, largely due to the "income" recognised from those loans. "You only had to look at the extraordinarily low cash dividends Steinhoff paid," Butters said. "This was a major red flag on its own."

*... **Good company: Shoprite generates positive cash flows every year***

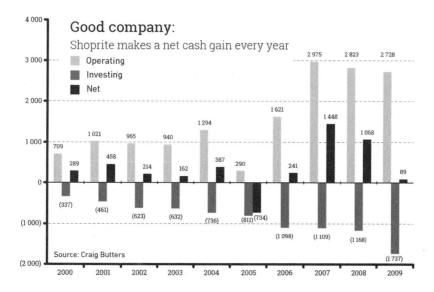

Good company:
Shoprite makes a net cash gain every year

Source: Craig Butters

- *Inflated assets.* Right from the time of its listing, Steinhoff had been buying anything that wasn't nailed down. But when you buy a company, you don't just get its physical assets, you're also buying the fluffy "intangible assets" like its brands, trademarks and its "goodwill". But because there's so much guesswork involved in valuing brands or intellectual property, the scope for accounting shenanigans here is immense. In Steinhoff's case, Butters calculated that if you stripped out all these fluffy items, and looked only at the company's "tangible net asset value" – in other words, its assets that were underpinned by something physical – you'd see that this number had been falling steadily since 2004. In other words, this gave the lie to the notion that all these deals were making it a stronger company. Moreover, the banks were increasingly funding these intangible assets, which meant the financial risk in the company was steadily growing.

By 2004, for every Steinhoff share you owned, R5.36 was the value of its "tangible net assets" – but by 2009 "tangible assets" accounted for just R1.68 per share (having actually turned *negative* in 2008, a trend that would later continue). The frenzied acquisition spree, often snapping up shoddy companies, had masked this true picture. Again, a comparison with Shoprite is illuminating: between 2004 and 2009, Shoprite's tangible net asset value more than doubled, while Steinhoff's went backwards.

Comparing Steinhoff's (SHF) tangible value with that of Shoprite (SHP)

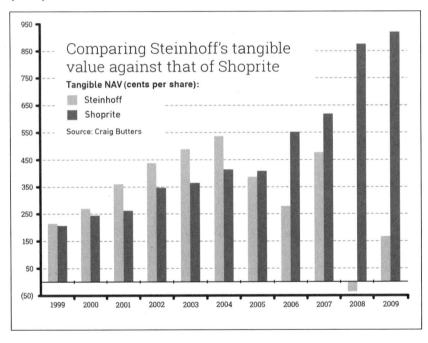

- *Suspiciously low tax rate.* How long could Steinhoff keep its tax rate at just 14% of profit? Butters asked. This didn't look sustainable, considering that company's tax in South Africa, for example, was 28% at the time. Instead, Steinhoff's use of "tax structuring" and shifting businesses to low-tax countries like Switzerland smacked of an almost obsessive desire to pay as little as possible. The question was: Was this because Steinhoff was inflating its income but not recognising the tax on those magicked-up numbers? And could this continue, or would the taxman come knocking?

- **Shoddy acquisitions.** Butters pointed out that in many years Steinhoff's growth in profit was often due to some or other company it had bought that year. Butters believed Steinhoff almost *had* to do a deal every year, to boost its earnings – which sounds eerily similar to a Ponzi scheme. There were other curiosities, too. For example, Steinhoff would often *buy* its own "struggling customers to whom loans have been advanced". This had a number of advantages: firstly, before it bought that company, Steinhoff could include "interest" supposedly accrued to it from those loans in its profits. Secondly, after buying those companies, the debt disappeared, as it was "consolidated" into Steinhoff's accounts. The implication was that Steinhoff's top brass "lent" money to companies run by friends, so it could include the (theoretical) interest repayments in its profits. But those companies were never likely to repay the debt, and therefore Steinhoff had to find a way of making the loans vanish from its balance sheet.

- **Awful disclosure.** "Steinhoff is the *only* JSE top forty company that does not take questions at results presentations," Butters said. And the disclosure in its financial statements was unacceptably poor.

- **Smoke-and-mirrors property deals.** Butters also flagged the curious 2008 property deal with Hemisphere (discussed in the previous chapter). What was the rationale in selling your property assets to this new company registered in Holland, only to buy it all back later? Unless, of course, it was a way to boost your profits and overstate your assets, all the while issuing shares to a friendly party (like Fihag) in the process.

- **Most anonymous auditors in the world.** Another red flag was that Steinhoff Europe's auditors were an unknown outfit called Commerzial Treuhand (CT), with just five offices in Germany. Later, it would emerge just how Markus Jooste had managed to pull the wool over CT's eyes.

These were just some of the highlights of Butters' presentation to Wiese. Many of these matters anticipated the allegations that the German prosecutors would later investigate in 2015, though the German investigation would be far wider in scope and use the word "criminal" and "fraud" a lot, Steinhoff's protestations notwithstanding. Still, there in the forty-slide presentation that Butters gave to Wiese were all the elements of the underhand tactics that would later fell Steinhoff: secret third parties helping to hide costs, suspect tax treatment, an unhealthy reliance on paper money, and perpetual "revaluations".

As the breakfast wound up, Wiese thanked him. He said he'd found the presentation informative. Butters never heard from him again. Yet three years later, in March 2012, he'd learn that Wiese had taken ownership of his first stash of shares in Steinhoff, thanks to a complicated deal in which he sold his wine farm Lanzerac to a consortium headed by Jooste. Today, Butters still finds that decision baffling. "I'm still surprised that Christo went ahead, after I'd shown him all of this. It was after this that he went and put R59bn of his own money into Steinhoff. He'd been warned, and yet he still did it. I still can't make sense of it."

Wiese, today, says he remembers Butters's presentation well.

"Look, if anything, what Craig Butters told me gave me pause. After that, I waited another two years before committing to anything." But Wiese says he looked at how the banks and the wider investment community painted Steinhoff as something of a darling. "During those two years, I watched how things were presented and how many audit functions were being performed within the group. So, I concluded that Butters's criticism wasn't well founded."

Today, Butters has since moved to Prudential Investment Managers, based in the leafy Cape Town suburb of Claremont, where he runs the investment house's Dividend Maximiser and Core Value funds. "Look, I feel for the innocent guys who lost money from Steinhoff's collapse, but there is some satisfaction, I must say, having been vindicated in my analysis. To be honest, I wasn't sure when they'd get caught out, but it had to come at some stage. I spoke to analysts, audit partners at Deloitte, bankers and anyone else who cared to listen."

Craig Butters's story is a critical point in the Steinhoff tale. It demonstrates the poverty of the myth that nobody could have suspected Jooste to be a scoundrel. It also illustrates that if somebody doesn't want to hear anything that contradicts their worldview, they won't hear it. Back in 2009, there were numerous analysts and fund managers who fell into this camp, guilelessly cheering on Jooste and toasting every new deal he did. But while Butters may have been in a minority, he wasn't the sole voice of dissent on Steinhoff.

*   *   *

In April 2007, Sean Holmes, a young analyst at the local arm of American bank JP Morgan, published a savage 56-page research report that methodically deconstructed Steinhoff's flaky business model.[2] It was two years before Craig Butters's meeting with Wiese, and Holmes's report set the stage for other critics to break their silence.

At the time, JP Morgan's head of research was Andrew Cuffe. Today, Cuffe says Holmes's report was especially brave, since many shared his view but hadn't dared put it in writing. "Sean was fairly new to the industry and this was early in his career. He obviously went on to become the top-rated retail analyst in South Africa, but it took huge courage for a young analyst early in his career to write a report like that."[3] Holmes's report was unusual in other ways, too. Often, the sort of investment research that is published by South Africa's stockbrokers is polite and deferential. Egregious governance scandals are described as "unfortunate incidents"; atrocious acquisitions that end up costing shareholders billions are characterised as "questionable" or "ill-timed". But Holmes's report – a searing critique that advised investors to "sell" and run as far away from Steinhoff as they could – was anything but ambiguous.

"We are concerned about the quality of Steinhoff's earnings, especially given its poor financial disclosure and lack of transparency," he begins. Holmes spoke of a "pattern of aggressive accounting treatment", flagging worries about the company's "relatively weak balance sheet" and "unnervingly" bad disclosure. "We find the rate of business acquisitions disturbing, especially where it is unclear how they fit the business strategy of a furniture manufacturer and retailer ... [This] distorts comparisons and poor financial disclosure further clouds the issue."

Like Butters, Holmes pointed out that Steinhoff's levels of murky "intangible assets" had begun to spike, and now made up nearly three-quarters of the company's entire net asset value. In 2006, for example, Steinhoff had bought trademarks to the value of R2.5bn – yet it refused to say who they'd bought them from or what these trademarks even were. "Very little evidence exists that these trademarks have created any value thus far."

And Holmes said that if you examined Jooste's recent acquisitions, it seemed pretty clear that he was lavishing large amounts of money on buying duds. "Despite the R13.5bn spent on investments over the past six years, the company has failed to improve profitability. Return on average total assets (a key ratio used to illustrate profitability) decreased from 11% in 2001 to 7% in 2006." It was an uncompromising diagnosis.

Almost immediately after the report went out, JP Morgan received an ominous phone call. Jooste, evidently seething, summoned Cuffe and JP Morgan's most senior banker in South Africa, Jon Zehner, to his Wynberg office in Johannesburg for "a chat". "He sat us down in his boardroom, and two other Steinhoff directors – Jan van der Merwe and Piet Ferreira – were there too," says Cuffe today.[4] "Markus began pacing around, telling us how we just didn't understand the business. He went on about how it all began, how Bruno had started it in Europe. It was all such a hard sell that I'm surprised there weren't small violins playing in the background." It was characteristic Markus: a mix of charm, arrogance and haughty self-importance. He'd casually patronise JP Morgan by suggesting it almost wasn't their fault: they just didn't have the smarts to understand the brilliance of Steinhoff's structuring.

Cuffe was unmoved. Please point out where we've made a mistake, he asked Jooste. It wasn't any one issue, Jooste said, but rather the fact you don't understand Steinhoff.

"I said to him: if, as you say, we've made some huge mistake, then you'll have the last laugh. If we've got it wrong, our reputation will be ruined, and Steinhoff's share price will keep going up. We'll look like fools," Cuffe recalls.

That's not good enough, said Jooste: we demand you withdraw the report.

"He went from being silky smooth to being quite aggressive," says Cuffe. "It was quite a transformation. In the end, he was so furious when he didn't get his way that he began swearing, and eventually he stormed out of his own office. It was farcical – Piet Ferreira looked around awkwardly, not quite sure if Markus was coming back or whether he should show us out." (Someone else who was in the boardman for the meeting says Markus didn't storm out.)

Jooste seemed particularly hurt that Holmes hadn't shown him a copy of the report before publishing it. But in the months leading up to its publication, Steinhoff had flatly refused to provide any of the financial documents that JP Morgan asked for.

This was Steinhoff's playbook for when it ran into trouble: obfuscate, ignore or bully. (It's important to remember that, while many of Steinhoff's executives are now eager to pin everything on Jooste after his fall in December 2017, the truth is that numerous executives must have been complicit in hiding information – and complicit in strong-arming anyone who questioned this.)

Unable to wrestle JP Morgan into submission, Steinhoff's instinct for a street fight meant it wasn't going to let this go.

At that stage, Sean Holmes had been emailing Jan van der Merwe, Jooste's lieutenant, with questions about Steinhoff's financial structuring. Holmes was eager to stress-test his assumptions.

But Van der Merwe was clearly no stranger to Jooste's strongman tactics. He promptly forwarded Holmes's email to a number of JP Morgan's clients – the investment houses that bought their research, such as Old Mutual and RMB Asset Management – with a snide message that Holmes was clearly looking for inside information. "It was a direct attempt to damage our reputation and block Sean," says Cuffe. "This bullying, interfering with our clients, presumably to get them to drop us, was intimidation like I'd never experienced from any other company we'd covered."

Of course, a central reason why Jooste was so outraged by JP Morgan's behaviour is that Steinhoff had injected a lot of energy into soft-soaping the analysts and fund managers. Many of them had drunk Jooste's Kool-Aid. Steinhoff's presentations, which it would host for investors, were legendary parties that often extended into the early hours of the morning. In Cape Town, those presentations usually took place at the One & Only at the Waterfront or the stately Vineyard Hotel in Newlands.

One analyst who attended a fair number of those Steinhoff presentations, but who didn't want to identify himself, said: "It was really just a giant party for the 'who's who' of Stellenbosch, more than a results presentation." "Afterwards, the single malt whisky and brandy would flow, often past 1 am. The few analysts there, among the friends and family, loved it too, because Markus would have a few drinks and chat openly about all kinds of inside information," says another. It helped reinforce the cult, the sense that you were part of the select inner circle who had boarded Steinhoff's rocket to the moon. And for those analysts who stayed till the wee hours, giddy from their proximity to Markus, they'd be hard-pressed to be too critical.

Greg Davies, the head of equities at Cratos Capital, said those investment presentations were all about puffing the cult of Markus. Any line of questioning that even hinted at scepticism would elicit disapproving titters from Steinhoff's keepers – specifically, its banker, Standard Bank, or its sponsor, Jannie Mouton's PSG Capital.[5]

Analysts who asked about Steinhoff's poor cash flows, its low-quality assets and its aggressive accounting were frozen out by those who *got it*. "It was like a tribe. Markus was seen as a superstar whom the investment community just didn't appreciate enough. The story was always that those who didn't see his vision would soon be sorry," says Davies.

Terence Craig, chief investment officer for Element Investment Managers, says that about 70% of the people at these Steinhoff results presentations in Cape Town were either Jooste's staff or friends of the top brass. "It was incredibly difficult for anyone to ask any real questions. It reminded me of the bravado of the IT boom: whenever Markus spoke, people would clap and cheer. If there was ever the hint of a tricky question, Markus would smile and slap you down – bully you out of asking anything else." For Craig, this was another sign to walk away. "If you look at all the companies shortly before a big crash – Enron, or even Nedbank in 1999 when it was run by Richard Laubscher, they'd get really aggressive with you if you asked a tough question. That's always a sign to be extra cautious."

Craig Butters says that one thing that allowed him to take a more objective view from the outside was that he didn't attend many of the Steinhoff presentations or spend much time in one-on-one meetings with Jooste. "I kept a low profile at the presentations I did attend, and never stayed for drinks afterwards. Perhaps this distance is what allowed me to focus on the numbers, without getting too sucked into how magnetic a personality he might have been."

Many analysts, not to mention some journalists who routinely covered Steinhoff, prized their access to Jooste and his team, and were loath to jeopardise it. So, as you can imagine, those investment houses who'd become part of Jooste's cheerleading squad were furious with JP Morgan. In one case, Cuffe and Holmes went to see a Sandton-based pension fund manager, who was also one of JP Morgan's largest clients. "The fund manager stood up and began shouting at Sean about Steinhoff. He was banging his fists on the table, repeating the words: you're talking *shit*, you're talking *shit*," says Cuffe. It was that sort of reaction, as well as the warning that Holmes better be careful or he'd find himself "pinned to the wrong side of a mattress", that led to JP Morgan cutting off all coverage of Steinhoff. Later, after Holmes left to join Deutsche Bank, and Cuffe went to work as a consultant, JP Morgan did a 180-degree turn. But then, this Damascene conversion was entirely in JP Morgan's interests. The bank was well aware from whose table the scraps would be falling. From Steinhoff's various prospectuses and reports, it is clear that JP Morgan ended up earning a packet as an "adviser" to the listing of Steinhoff Africa Retail

(STAR) in 2017. As one of two "joint bookrunners" for the STAR listing alongside Standard Bank, JP Morgan earned a chunk of the R226m in fees paid to nine advisers – probably around R30m.[6]

But the bank's renewed faith in Steinhoff came back to bite it – just as it bit every one of the titans of global banking. After Steinhoff's collapse in December 2017, JP Morgan stunned investors in New York when it revealed a few weeks later that it would have to take a $273m hit in its own financial results as a result. This was partly from a $143m loss on loans it had made to Christo Wiese to buy shares in Steinhoff, and another $130m it had to set aside for bad debt. Marianne Lake, JP Morgan's chief financial officer, described this loss as "far and away the largest loss in that business we've seen since the [2008 financial] crisis".[7] "It will happen from time to time, though maybe not this significantly or this suddenly," she said. "While we're obviously disappointed with the outcome here, this is a large and diversified business that even after this loss is very profitable."[8]

But JP Morgan wasn't alone. What had happened was that JP Morgan was part of a consortium of banks – including Goldman Sachs, Citigroup, HSBC and Nomura – that had lent €1.6bn to Wiese in September 2016 so he could buy more shares in Steinhoff. Their collateral for these loans was €3.2bn worth of Steinhoff shares. It meant that when Steinhoff's share plunged 61% in a single day, the banks took a thrashing along with all Steinhoff's investors. So, by January 2018, the South African accounting scandal that began in the winelands of Stellenbosch ended up giving the biggest names on Wall Street an $800m bloody nose.

Besides JP Morgan's loss, Bank of America also revealed that it had taken a $292m hit from a "single client", whom it didn't name – but who was obviously Wiese. It clearly irked Bank of America's CEO Brian Moynihan, who said: "We weren't happy with it from the top of the house through to the actual people who are involved in it."[9] Citigroup was equally embarrassed, and it also steered clear of naming Wiese or Steinhoff as it talked vaguely about a "single client event" that was the cause of a $130m loss in its equities division, and a $267m credit loss in another part of its business.[10] Mercifully, Goldman Sachs was at least direct. Speaking to analysts, Goldman's finance director, Marty Chavez, was blunt: "I wanted to come right out and mention that we took a $130 million loss on a single structured loan, and that was Steinhoff."[11]

There's no small irony that, in the end, Markus Jooste duped even the world's largest investment bank, a bank so notorious for its ruthlessness that it was once famously described by *Rolling Stone* magazine as the "great vampire squid wrapped around the face of humanity, relentlessly jamming its blood funnel into anything that smells like money".[12]

*   *   *

Talk of how Jooste's muscle tried to lean on JP Morgan spread rapidly through the market. Darren Cohn, who used to work as an analyst at brokerage UBS, the South African arm of the largest Swiss bank in the world, says it made him sceptical of the furniture company. "I knew Jooste's reputation, that Steinhoff aggressively attacked anyone who was negative about them. We knew what had happened to Sean Holmes. But I wanted to be objective, and have a look at the numbers for myself."

Cohn reckoned that Steinhoff's shares were cheap, being sold for less than three times its annual profit. This was far cheaper than most shares on the JSE, which typically sell for far more than ten times their profit. "However, given the company's high debt levels, as well as its reputation, I decided to go through each and every note in the financial statements with a fine toothcomb."

It didn't take long to find red flags. In particular, Steinhoff referred to three "joint ventures" in its financials, and it provided abridged financials for two of them. But for the third, it said the financials were "available on request" – which was a curious anomaly. Now, what Steinhoff had said is that those joint ventures were "family owned" companies that lacked the cash to build more stores and expand. Steinhoff said its plan was to provide the capital, and then buy the whole company later. "I was concerned that what was actually happening was that Steinhoff had off-balance sheet debt, and that the capital was actually [being used] to repay that," Cohn said.

Cohn's interaction with Steinhoff's head of investor relations, Mariza Nel, didn't reassure him at all. (Nel was viewed, by analysts at least, as being part of Markus's inner circle. This may be why Jooste went to such pains in his "resignation letter" to say that Mariza knew nothing.) Nel told Cohn not to worry, as the joint ventures would soon be "out of the system", as Steinhoff only planned to invest a further R100m in those businesses. This was hardly a reassuring response. And Cohn never got the financials for that third joint venture company.

"At that point I had a choice: either refuse to [cover Steinhoff at all] until I had sight of the full financials, or be strategic and patient. Given how aggressive Steinhoff became with anyone questioning them, I thought that it would serve investors more if I were patient." So he initiated coverage with a "buy" call on Steinhoff. A few years later, in 2012, having got nowhere in understanding the joint venture companies, he dropped coverage of Steinhoff entirely. "Steinhoff had continued to invest heavily in those companies. I chased after Mariza Nel for the full financials, but she never responded to my emails or calls. We simply could not continue to cover the company without being able to fully assess the risks."

Other analysts talk of being bullied, too, telling how, when Jooste was tackled about something he wasn't keen to discuss, his Jekyll and Hide switch would trigger. One pension fund manager (who did not want to be named) recalls how, in 2009, he went to speak to Jooste at his office in the old Steinhoff building in Wynberg, Johannesburg. He raised three issues: the disturbing number of "off-balance sheet companies", the fuzzy accounting, and a number of questionable deals that didn't seem to make sense. Jooste started off with his usual charming *shtick*: me, I'm just a dumb retailer, what do I know about accounts? All we do is make sales and record this in our books. We're just couch salesmen, really; don't ask us about fancy accounting words.

This wasn't unusual. Those who knew him say that Jooste would often seek to beguile people through a calculated humblebrag act, which he usually pulled off with deft precision. "He liked to pretend he was this unsophisticated Afrikaner who simply bought companies for R100, and sold them for R115, but it was just an act," the fund manager says. "The reality is, Markus knew the intricacies of accounting better than anyone, and when you called him on it, he would just flip entirely. It was the scariest thing I've seen. It was Jekyll and Hyde."

In theory, furniture retailing is meant to be a simple business: you either make furniture and sell it, or act as a wholesaler by buying furniture from someone, and selling it on at a margin. But Steinhoff was far past that. It was an entirely more convoluted beast. For one thing, Steinhoff was making a whole lot of its money in "interest income" on loans it had made to other companies that nobody knew anything about. But Steinhoff wasn't a bank: what good reason did it have for clocking up mountains in interest from murky companies you knew nothing about?

And then there was that curious deal in which Steinhoff sold a bunch of its properties to Hemisphere in 2008 – a deal which Butters had also red-flagged. But when the fund manager wanted to discuss Hemisphere, the switch tripped in Jooste's mind. Evidently furious, Jooste stood up and walked over to the fridge in his office, took out a bottle of water, and stared out of the window as he drank it – ignoring his guests as if they were wallpaper.

Element Investment Managers was one company that also hit a wall when it tried to get answers from Steinhoff. In 2010, Element's chief investment officer, Terence Craig, met Danie van der Merwe (Steinhoff Africa's CEO at the time) and Piet Ferreira (who was putting together many of Steinhoff's deals at the time). Says Craig: "At that stage, we didn't trust their numbers. About 90% of their value was in these murky intangible assets, and they'd been paying an incredibly low tax rate. So we kept peppering them with questions about how it looked like they were round-tripping sales."[13]

After about forty minutes of Steinhoff's executives ducking questions, they said to Craig: "Look, we just don't have answers to your questions. We'll have to go ask Markus and get back to you."

To Terence Craig, it was ridiculous that an executive director and senior manager couldn't answer questions about Steinhoff's finances. "The impression I got was not that they didn't know the answers; the impression I got was that they knew, but didn't want to tell us." Craig and his team said goodbye and never contacted Steinhoff again. "After the meeting, I told our team: this is the reason why we should never own shares in Steinhoff," he says. It was evidently a mutual decision. Soon, Element's invitations to Steinhoff's results presentations began to dry up. As far as Jooste was concerned, they were dead to him.

Evan Walker, who works at 36ONE Asset Management today, was one of those who initially bought the Steinhoff story, even though he didn't particularly like Jooste. "I never trusted him," he says. "I did think he was potentially creating a good business but we were always sceptical of the amount of deals and the amount of clean deals. But as a South African investor you only have a few offshore companies to invest in."[14]

Others might not have trusted him either. But they still were willing to hitch themselves to Jooste's chariot, secure in their religious faith in him as a deal-spinning messiah. Before Steinhoff's collapse, Simon Brown, a sassy market pundit who runs a company called Just One Lap, summed the position up with precision. "Generally speaking, there are two views when it comes to Steinhoff. This first is 'I don't understand its balance sheet but I trust Markus Jooste', and the second is 'I don't understand its balance sheet so I'm not investing'."[15] Brown's point was that *nobody* understood the balance sheet, but if you were part of the cult of believers, you were willing to leap into the darkness anyway.

* * *

While there were genuine sceptics in the years before Steinhoff's collapse, there were an equal number of "experts" who would rattle on about the company's "exciting prospects". Rather like finding white South Africans today who will admit to supporting apartheid, locating those cheerleading analysts today isn't especially easy. There are also others who, shamelessly, will boast how they "spotted Steinhoff" years ago. Everyone is an expert about what happened yesterday.

The fact is that on 4 December, the day before Jooste resigned and the share price collapsed off a cliff, there were 17 analysts who covered Steinhoff, 11 of whom recommended that investors "buy" the share, 6 who recommended they "hold", and exactly zero who called it as a "sell". On the face of it, this appears to be an epic failure on the part of the "experts" who are paid to tell you which companies to avoid.

Butters says he believes this is partly structural: stockbrokers are typically housed in large banks or finance firms, which, on the other side of the Chinese wall, make a living from either advising companies on deals or providing them with the finance. "There is an implicit pressure on analysts to be positive because then those investment banks will be looked on favourably. At a company like Steinhoff, all the investment banks were falling over themselves to win a slice of its business for all the acquisitions it was doing."[16]

And the fees that the investment bank charged Steinhoff for structuring deals in Europe were gargantuan. Page through the prospectus that Steinhoff issued before doing its 2011 deal to buy Conforama, and you'll see it paid R150m in "expenses" – R40.3m of which went to Citigroup, R40.4m to HSBC, and R42m to the Royal Bank of Scotland. In 2014, when Steinhoff bought Pepkor, it paid R40m to various advisers, including R30m collectively to various banks, including Investec, Deutsche Bank, Citigroup and Barclays.

Two things you'll notice. Firstly, all these banks that buzzed around Jooste and scooped up the honey also have a stockbroking arm, which is meant to provide "independent advice" on companies. Secondly, the brokers who were critical of Steinhoff *do* seem to have cost their banks valuable investment banking business. Take JP Morgan again: despite being rated as the top global investment bank, it didn't get a share of Steinhoff's dealmaking fees for many years after the Sean Holmes fiasco.

If loyalty was the one characteristic that Jooste prized above all else, then any display of disloyalty would elicit the sort of grudge you'd expect to find more commonly in a Sicilian crime family. That ill will, he'd struggle to forgive.

Barry Norris is the founder of the London-based Argonaut Capital, which began doubting the Steinhoff story in about March 2017. At the time, Argonaut began "shorting" the share – essentially, betting the price would fall. Norris says he believes most analysts (bar a few) "missed" the Steinhoff issues because of the sort of structural tensions that others hint at. "The analysts at these brokers, attached to the big investment banks, aren't *really* there to provide advice to fund managers. Rather, they're there to help the banks make money on these big transactions. It's rare for them to make a sceptical call because, firstly, they could get sued, and, secondly, they risk losing business," he says. And there was plenty of money in that, since Steinhoff was raising a lot of capital to plug the holes in its balance sheet, not to mention the almost weekly takeover offers. "All the investment banks wanted to make fees on doing that business."

Fraser Perring, who heads a research outfit named Viceroy which published a devastating report on Steinhoff two days after the retailer collapsed, agrees.

Perring, a former social worker from the UK, says the analysts who work for the big banks are often put under pressure to keep good relationships with the companies they cover.

"There were plenty of analysts who covered Steinhoff yet it took us – me, a social worker and two exceptionally talented kids from Australia (Gabriel Bernarde and Aidan Lau, both 24-years old) – to pull together what had happened at Steinhoff," he says.

With precious little sceptical research out in the market, large investors poured far too much money into Steinhoff. In particular, Perring reckons the government-owned Public Investment Corporation (PIC), which invests the pensions of civil servants, had no business investing in Steinhoff. "What was the PIC doing investing pension money in this piece of shit? Did it just take 42 brandies and three meals for them to agree to invest money in Steinhoff?"

By the time Steinhoff exploded in December 2017, the PIC owned 8.5% of Steinhoff. This wiped more than R16bn from government employees' pensions.

Other analysts speak of an "unspoken pressure" to be positive about Steinhoff. One told of how, when he was preparing to discuss Steinhoff's takeover of JD Group, and just how bad this was for shareholders, during a roadshow, he was told "not to put out a negative recommendation on a Steinhoff deal during a presentation".

What remains a remarkable feature of the Steinhoff story is that despite all this scepticism on the part of some of the largest investment houses in the world, the Steinhoff ship continued to steam along as if these icebergs didn't exist. "At one stage, about half the institutions in the country wouldn't touch Steinhoff," says Andrew Cuffe. "About half the analysts covering the retail companies also thought it was dodgy. This changed. By the time it all went south, I think just about every institution was exposed to Steinhoff to some extent."[17]

The fact is, banks continued to lend to Steinhoff, and switched-on investors like Christo Wiese put money into the company, despite the red flags. The question is: why?

There is one potential answer, best summed up by a notion that first gained traction thanks to Adam Sweidan, chief investment officer of the London-based alternative investment firm Aurum Fund Management. Speaking in Australia in 2014, Sweidan referred to "a herd of black elephants gathering" to describe events such as fresh water pollution and global warming.[18] "When they hit, we'll claim they were black swans which no one could have predicted, but, in fact, they are black elephants, very visible right now." This "black elephant", in other words, is a combination of the elephant in the room that everyone knows about but doesn't want to discuss and the "black swan" event that is supposedly unforeseen but has the potential to cause untold devastation. Andrew Cuffe believes this aptly describes the unspoken knowns about Steinhoff, dating back more than a decade. "In the investment community, Steinhoff really was the elephant in the room that everyone knew about but few wanted to talk about. And in the end, when Steinhoff collapsed, we all know what sort of black swan impact *that* had on our market."

The truth is, the view that Steinhoff was a patchwork quilt of suspect profit and fanciful trademark values wasn't exactly a fringe opinion floated tongue-in-cheek in flat-earth chatrooms. But only a few people – including Craig Butters, Andrew Cuffe and Sean Holmes – were willing to risk becoming pariahs by saying so out loud.

6

Jockeying for position

"It's said that all those who go racing are rogues and vagabonds. That may not be true – but it is true that all rogues and vagabonds go racing." These are the words of Sir Abe Bailey, one of South Africa's first Randlords who made such a fortune on the country's mines that, by the time he died in 1940, he was believed to be one of the wealthiest people on the globe. Bailey was also one of the early patrons of South Africa's horseracing industry. He became the largest racehorse owner and breeder not only in South Africa, but also in England. Famously, Bailey staked an immense sum on his horse Lovematch to win the Johannesburg Summer Handicap one year, netting the largest-ever winnings at that stage: £64,000.[1] "All my life, I have been a gambler," he once said. "I have not in mind the meaningless habit of putting a pound or two on a horse and waiting for a jockey to pull it first past the post – that's just feeble fumbling with fate. I mean, going all out on something which may yield big returns in life – love, politics, everything that touches human activities." The gambler, he said, is drawn to instances where the odds of success are terrifyingly slim – the slimmer they are, "the more fascinating they become".

It is an instinct you could believe was shared by Markus Jooste, who, for roughly a decade, became the shining street lamp of South Africa's racing industry, around which all the moths flitted, seeking to share some of the reflected light. By the time of his downfall, he was considered by some pundits to be the second-biggest racehorse owner in the world, after Sheikh Mohammed bin Rashid Al Maktoum, the ruler of Dubai.[2]

The story began in the early 1990s, when Jooste said he was approached by two other owners – Albert Rapp and Colin Fram – to take a share in a horse called National Emblem. The liver chestnut horse had been bought for R100,000 in 1993, but ended up taking home R1.9m in prize money, crossing the line first in fifteen races. Jooste said that "the success of National Emblem then, and now, is probably the cornerstone of my involvement in racing . . . he was the first horse I owned".[3]

It was only a few years later, around 2002, when Jooste began to seriously parlay his newfound Steinhoff wealth into horses. He was immediately, and profoundly, successful. It helped that he was heralded as a messiah in an industry that, were it a barfly, would be perpetually losing its wallet, theatrically patting down its pockets for stray notes, before hitting up the next guy for a drink. Some racehorse owners have been famously skint, but Jooste arrived with a reputation for having plenty of cash, and no great reluctance to lay it out. As Jooste himself put it when he was interviewed early on in his racing career: "No one should ever go into racing to make a profit."[4]

He first made headlines when he splashed out millions at Australia's Magic Millions sale in January 2002; then, over Easter that year, he did the same at the Inglis sale in Sydney, before, in May, buying the rest of National Emblem that he didn't already own.[5] At that point, National Emblem had retired, and was standing at South Africa's largest stud farm, Klawervlei, on the banks of the Breede River near Bonnievale in the rural hinterland of the Western Cape. At stud, National Emblem was a fantastic success: by 2005, he'd sired 206 winners – including horses like Nhlavini, Rebel King and National Spirit. In 2004, Jooste also took a share in Klawervlei. Others who also bought into Klawervlei included Danie van der Merwe, Frikkie Nel, Jan van der Merwe, Bernard Kantor and Chris van Niekerk.

Klawervlei is run by John Koster, whose grandfather Ralph first began breeding racehorses in the 1930s – a tradition continued by his father Peter. Koster says Jooste first got involved when Danie van der Merwe persuaded him to have lunch with Markus. "It changed my life forever . . .

it took no less than twenty minutes with Markus to realise this partnership was an opportunity of a lifetime – his vision and leadership is beyond comprehension. Markus is very strong on family and tradition," Koster said a few years back.[6]

Jooste's appetite grows exponentially after that. At his peak, Jooste would have about 350 horses training in South Africa – and many more abroad. He also wasn't shy to spend millions importing horses from overseas. Jooste's trainer, Charles Laird, once gushed that "Markus is bringing in horses, while we are losing many of our top ones to Dubai and elsewhere". There was, for example, a colt he imported from Aidan O'Brien's stable in Ireland called Albert Hall, who raced in a partnership between Jooste, Jim Lewis and a shadowy Englishman named Malcolm King. At the time, Laird described King as "a big player in the UK, and this will be his first horse in South Africa".[7] (King, who fancied himself as a debonair James Bond-style character, would later be outed as a central character in some of Steinhoff's dubious early deals.)

Initially, Markus raced under his own "silks" – the personalised colours worn by the jockey – of maroon, white and yellow. This was no great surprise, given that Steinhoff's insignia are maroon. He then raced in partnership with his wife Ingrid and registered the now well-known "Springbok" colours of emerald green jacket with yellow stars and black sleeves.

After that, he "restructured" his racing interests, and the horses were all shifted into the name of Mayfair Speculators – the company owned by his trust – which took over the green, yellow and black colours. Soon enough, Mayfair's distinctive colours dominated racetracks around the country from Turffontein, Greyville and Kenilworth to the Vaal.

* * *

But Jooste's desire for control extended beyond the track itself. During an interview with the *Sporting Post*, he said as much: "I make the chain of activity a complete cycle. At Steinhoff we grow the trees, cut the wood, make the furniture and sell the furniture. My racing business is modelled on the same lines."[8] He was true to his word. He manoeuvred to get himself appointed to the board of Phumelela, a company which had been set up with the express goal of "corporatising" the racing industry, but which had to inject part of its profits back into it. Jooste was also appointed to the board of the Racing Association, a broad body of racehorse owners set up to "protect and support the interests of the sport of horseracing". Then, he was appointed a trustee of the Horseracing Trust, which owned 35.2% of Phumelela and which was meant to channel dividends back into the industry. All this meant his tentacles were everywhere. Jooste could hold sway over how money flowed in the industry, and how it was reinvested (or not) into racing.

Such creeping control wasn't appreciated by everyone, as you can imagine in a sport that tended to attract sceptical personalities, averse to conformity. Soon, talk began to filter out about how Jooste had "captured" South Africa's horseracing industry.

Until 2005, there had actually been a clause in the Racing Association trust deed that specified that you couldn't be a director of the association, the trust and Phumelela all at once. But at that year's Racing Association AGM, Jooste's board proposed a "special resolution" to abolish that rule, allowing him and Chris van Niekerk to serve on all three bodies. So, a group of "concerned owners" wrote to Jooste and Van Niekerk, arguing that they shouldn't be "wearing more than one hat" and should consequently resign. In any event, they said, there hadn't been the required 25% quorum of members at the 2005 AGM to pass the resolution.

One of these owners, Brett Maselle, an advocate, approached Markus Jooste at a cocktail party in Germiston and told him "to do the right thing" and quit. An aggressive Jooste jammed his finger in Maselle's face and told him to "get your facts straight". Jooste said he'd obtained a legal opinion which indicated that they hadn't broken any rules. Maselle tried for months to get hold of the legal opinion. Eventually, he received a sniffy letter from the Racing Association declaring that "the legal opinions . . . are internal" to the association. Today, Maselle still doubts whether the legal opinion ever existed.[9]

As to whether Jooste "captured" horseracing, Maselle says there's no question about it. "Markus Jooste was in control of horseracing, it's as simple as that. People were scared to do anything without him. Markus controlled many of the people in all the organisations, and even installed Steinhoff people on the Racing Trust."[10] Eventually, in 2014, Jooste and Van Niekerk resigned from the trust – but on their own terms. Nobody would push them around.

Jooste's craving for control went a step further. For ninety years, the yearling sales hosted by BloodStock South Africa in Johannesburg were *the* big event for breeders to sell their horses. But Jooste had little influence on the way BloodStock ran its sales. So, in 2011, he and a group of Cape owners set up the Cape Thoroughbred Sales (CTS) as a rival sales company. CTS effectively went to war, even hosting its 2014 "Ready to Run" sale over the same weekend as their older, more staid competitor. This unsettled everyone.

Mike de Kock – a trainer whose horses have won every major race in South Africa including four Durban July Handicaps, two J&B Mets and nine Summer Cups – said in 2014 that if "salesgate" continued, it would polarise buyers and dilute the quality of the horses on offer.[11] "Sort out your nonsense," he told both CTS and BloodStock.

CTS was having none of it. In 2016, it doubled down, offering the richest payday yet in racing – $1m in prize money, which comfortably exceeded the Durban July's R3.5m prize. But there was a catch: it was only open to horses bought at the CTS sales. This seemed to be a gimmick designed to hurt their rivals – strong-arm them out of the business. What it meant was that Jooste had become South Africa's biggest racehorse owner, a director of all the most influential organisations directing the sport, a driving force behind the Cape sales, and part owner of the country's largest stud farm. As one insider told journalist Angelique Serrao: "If you essentially own the horse through the stud farm selling it, and you also buy the horse through a separate company you own, you are going to get the best price for that horse. So, the horse prices are marketed to be bigger and stronger than they might in reality be."[12]

Take the Cape Premier Yearling Sales, hosted by Jooste's company CTS, in 2016. Not only did Jooste's Mayfair Speculators buy the most number of horses – 22 yearlings for a total of R24.5m – but his Klawervlei Stud also clocked up the highest aggregate of sales, R38m. For good measure, Mayfair broke the record for the highest price paid for a thoroughbred yearling, spending R6m to buy Silver Coin, in partnership with Australia's Coolmore Stud.[13] This underscored what everyone knew: Markus was the fundamental, defining personality in South African horseracing. As the *Sporting Post* put it: "We have never experienced dominance of the magnitude displayed by Markus Jooste."[14]

Robyn Louw, a columnist for the *Sporting Post* and vocal commentator on the local racing industry, says that in the history of the sport in South Africa, no one has sought to wrangle total domination in the way that Jooste did. "It was really quite astonishing to watch – the way he got appointed to all those racing bodies," she says.

But if you strip out the politics, Jooste seemed to have a shrewd eye for the horses. On victories alone, his top horse was probably Legal Eagle, which was bought for R425,000 in 2013 but which, by the time he was named Horse of the Year in 2017, had won more than half his starts and earned winnings of more than R10.6m. The others were also from the top shelf, including The Conglomerate (which won the Durban July in 2016), 2017 Cape Derby winner Edict of Nantes, J&B Met winner Hill Fifty-Four, and Variety Club, which won races for Jooste in Dubai and Hong Kong.

Not only was Jooste intent on "owning" the South African racing industry, but he'd soon take a healthy stab at doing the same outside the African continent too. Here, again, he was enormously successful. Within a few short years, all the owners you'd meet on the track at Paris's Longchamp Racecourse, Melbourne's Flemington Racecourse, or Dubai's Meydan Racecourse knew Jooste or knew of him. His flash was legendary. In 2014, in France, he caused tittering at the Arqana August yearling sale when Mayfair first snapped up a filly for €1m, then bid €1.1m for a colt.[15] And in 2016, Jooste partnered with Michael Vincent Magnier (part of the famous Irish racing family) to bid £1.3m for a colt sired by Frankel, said by some to be the greatest racehorse of all time, at the Tattersalls Yearling Sale in the UK.[16]

By buying quality equine flesh, victories were assured. In September 2016, his horse Juliet Rose won the Gr2 Qatar Prix de Royallieu in Chantilly in France, at one of the most prestigious race days in the world.[17] Derek Brugman, Jooste's racing manager, gushed that Jooste was "really very happy" about the Juliet Rose's victory because "the investments in France are beginning to come to fruition".[18]

At his peak, Jooste had about 350 horses in training – a sizeable investment which would have cost him about R125m per year for stabling and training. It surprised no one that Markus and Ingrid Jooste were voted "owners of the year" for more than a decade. Their horses dominated the winner's enclosure. It seemed nothing could shake this all-encompassing dominance.

Then the Steinhoff explosion happened in December 2017, and everything changed.

*   *   *

When the Steinhoff debacle broke, the National Horseracing Association (NHA) stuttered, unsure how to deal with the scandal involving one of their own. Jooste relinquished his personal burgundy silks and resigned from Phumelela. Mayfair Speculators, under pressure from the banks, then sold all of its prized equine flesh in South Africa. Legal Eagle was sold to Braam van Huyssteen, the founder of Tekkie Town (which was bought by Steinhoff in 2015) for R3.2m; Edict of Nantes was sold to a buyer in Hong Kong for $750,000 (R9.9m) and promptly shipped overseas; and Talk of the Town (bought by Mayfair for R3m in 2016) was reportedly bought by NHA chairman Ken Truter.

The unseemly frenzy to snap up Jooste's horses was distasteful for some. Brett Maselle wrote an open letter shaming the other owners for rushing to do deals to buy Jooste's horses. "One would think that after hearing about these frauds any person would run a hundred miles away from doing any business with Jooste and Mayfair."[19] To Maselle, this illustrated how many in the industry – especially those in positions of influence – were willing to airbrush the cloud over Jooste out of the picture. It's not surprising, he says, given how so many of them were Jooste apparatchiks, owing their position to him.

But, unlike in the business arena, Jooste still has plenty of friends in racing. Hassen Adams, the chairman of Grand Parade Investments, says the accusation that Jooste "captured" the racing industry is "the greatest untruth I've ever heard.[20] It's just so scurrilous, really. Markus spent hundreds of millions in the racing industry. He has been an incredible asset to racing, no question. So what he might have done on the other side of his life is really no concern of mine." Adams, who is one of the biggest racehorse owners in the country himself, and a member of the group that set up Cape Thoroughbred Sales with Jooste, is one of Markus's most loyal defenders to this day. He still meets up with him, and speaks to him often. "Why shouldn't I? He's done nothing to me," he challenges. "He's a friend, and one of the most generous and genuine people I know. These rumours that this guy took all his money and planted it overseas, that's just not true. He used it to build the biggest stud farm in no time, to become the biggest racehorse owner in the country in no time, and to build the biggest sales company in no time. Whether or not it's his money, I don't know. But he put money into the sport."

Adams's view – that Jooste put South African horseracing on the map, in a way that nobody else has done before or since – is not uncommon. Michael Leaf, the former head of a black empowerment investment company and a fellow racehorse owner, agrees with Adams.[21] "Look, Markus was elected to all these roles in the industry because of his corporate career – everyone felt he'd do a good job of making racing a proper business, and he did. The Steinhoff issues are unfortunate, but was he good for racing? Unequivocally, yes."

Adams adds that Jooste splashed out huge amounts of money overseas, in turn attracting foreign investors back into our racing industry, from the UK, Australia and the Middle East. No other South Africans have thrown this amount of money into racing before. He also scoffs at any suggestion that Jooste enriched himself, through ensuring Phumelela paid out to its shareholders money that should have been reinvested in racing. Adams says any racehorse owner knows, right from the start, that they're only going to lose money when they start in the game. "Money isn't the *point* of racing. If you haven't owned a racehorse, you'll never know the adrenaline rush it gives you when your horse wins. It's a sport, and that's what you pay for."

Bernard Kantor, the co-founder of the global banking group Investec, who was also Jooste's partner for years in racing, agrees. "It's a passion, it's what people who can afford it do with their spare disposable income. Some do it for the ego, others as a hobby, but few will do it for the money. For me, if I never saw another racetrack in my life, it wouldn't worry me – but I love the breeding part of it."[22] What he doesn't like – what infuriates him, in fact – is constantly being hauled into the Steinhoff story. "I've never owned a share in Steinhoff, I wasn't on the board. I'm so sick of this," he fumes. "Yes, I was Markus's friend – but just because you're some-one's friend doesn't make you guilty of anything." For this reason, he is still loyal to a man with whom he'd been a business partner for more than a decade: they co-owned horses, they co-owned the Klawervlei stud farm, they co-owned the Cape Thoroughbred Sales, and they were both directors of Phumelela. He describes Jooste as "one of the kindest, most generous men I've ever met. The work he did in communities, and for people, is often forgotten." Kantor says that Jooste was indisputably good for the industry. "Markus was never happy to be an under-bidder at an auction. If he liked a horse, he'd pay whatever he had to, to get it. He had courage that way, and he was passionate about the industry." But, he adds, whatever Markus Jooste did, he'll have to account for it.

Still, Kantor, like Adams, believes the horseracing industry will recover. "The industry felt it, but, after about six to eight months, it began to recover. Buyers have begun to reappear, and there is a recognition that you can now get a decent horse at a decent price." Having said that, Kantor believes that the vacuum left by someone like Jooste will inevitably mean there is less money in an industry already under severe strain. "Look, some of the trainers, smaller owners and breeders may not make it. And this could have a knock-on impact: if owners can't pay trainers, they can't pay grooms. But the truth is, we've been flooded by too many people in the industry who don't understand the costs involved and should not be there." What happens, he says, is that owners are conned into buying horses by struggling trainers. But these "new owners" often have little feel for the costs and, over time, can't afford the bills. So money dries up, which has a knock-on effect on the trainers and the grooms. "Of course, the blame will be angled towards Phumelela, who will now sit with the problem. But Phumelela does not train horses. So why does it become their problem?" asks Kantor. Markus Jooste's ejection from the industry simply brought these issues to a head.

In the racing fraternity, many people close to Markus portray him as some sort of fallen hero, undone by his own human frailty. Take Chris van Niekerk, for example. Van Niekerk, whose impeccably coiffed silver hair, intense eyebrows and deep voice give him the demeanour of a 1970s crooner, has been a loyal ally to Jooste, both in business and on the racetrack, for more than a decade. He first met Jooste on the racetrack at the Steinhoff race day at Turffontein. At the time, he was CEO of timber company PG Bison when Markus and Danie van der Merwe, another racing enthusiast and the current CEO of Steinhoff, came to chat to him. Until that point, Van Niekerk said, the Steinhoff executives he'd met only wanted to talk price – which he found exhausting. "Danie said: 'Let's stop talking price. Let's talk strategy.' And that changed the whole environment, that changed the whole relationship – not only personally, but also between the two companies."[23] Soon after, in May 2002, Steinhoff bought PG Bison. From then on, Van Niekerk and Jooste were inseparable at the track. Other owners considered them a package deal. So it was no huge surprise that he and Markus were a tandem package on the board of Phumelela, the Racing Association and the Racing Trust.

The Steinhoff collapse, and Jooste's departure, hit Van Niekerk hard. In January 2018, a few weeks after Jooste's sudden resignation, Van Niekerk stood up to give the opening speech at the Cape Premier Yearling Sale, held at the Zeitz Museum of Contemporary Art at the Waterfront in Cape Town. In what was described as an "emotional speech" by those who heard it, Van Niekerk, rather grandiosely, invoked the words of Napoleon Bonaparte in characterising Jooste's fall: "I wanted too much. I strung the bow too tightly. I believed too much in my own good fortune."[24] Van Niekerk told the audience: "I'm not here to sing anybody's praises or to cast any judgement. I'm in the sad corner. I'd rather remember the value added over the years to the industry and to people's lives."

Of course, Van Niekerk's sentimental portrayal of Jooste wasn't altogether surprising, considering their long partnership. Van Niekerk added: "There will be another, a new champion owner of the year. And let me remind you, even though Elvis left the building, the music never stops." Some, apparently, applauded Van Niekerk's comments. Others scoffed at it. As one said: "Napoleon left a trail of tears and misery behind him, and Jooste has done the same. Napoleon had an ego the size of a battleship and Jooste was the same." The problem is that the racing industry now appears to be so heavily populated by "Markus's people" that the taint of Steinhoff can be detected everywhere.

Brett Maselle says it's no surprise that so many people are still fiercely loyal to Jooste. "Most of these people made their living out of Jooste. So obviously they'll not want to believe he did anything wrong. They want the good days to return."[25] This uncritical reverence for anyone willing to slap down a cheque is understandable, given how expensive it is to keep a racehorse, but it doesn't reflect particularly well on those involved.

There's another remarkable tale, which reveals much about Jooste's ambition and desperation to be recognised by the industry. The Epsom Derby, first run in 1780, is the most prestigious race in the world. It is the original "Derby", attended by the Queen every year, where horses owned by royals from all over the world compete. It's also the richest horse race, with prize money of £3.1m, watched by no less than 1.8m people on TV. If you can make it to Epsom, Frank Sinatra might have said, you can make it anywhere.

Famously, the best vantage point to watch the race is considered Epsom Hill, at the centre of the track. It is called the "People's Hill" because, unlike the track itself, there's no starched dress code of top hats and tails and, for two centuries, no entrance fee. William Powell Frith's famous Victorian painting *Derby Day* captures the Hill's carnival atmosphere. Families arrive, spread out picnics, pitch their kids onto fairground rides and listen to live music.

Then in mid-2017 Jooste boasted that he'd "stolen" the famous Hill. "Just call me the Robin Hood of Epsom," he famously told *Business Day*'s racing reporter, David Mollett.[26] Evidently, Jooste had wangled a ten-year deal to rename the Hill "Poundland Hill", a marketing gimmick alluding to the chain of discount stores that Steinhoff bought in 2016. As it happened, the Epsom Derby is sponsored by banking group Investec, whose co-founder is Jooste's racing partner, Bernard Kantor. Investec, which first got its banking licence in Johannesburg in 1980, had taken over the sponsorship of the Epsom Derby in 2009 when the previous sponsor, Vodafone, pulled out. The UK *Daily Telegraph* reckoned the sponsorship deal was worth £30m.

Kantor said it was a "no-brainer" for Markus to rebrand the Hill. "The Hill is the real history of this incredible day and this incredible race. In the old days you used to get five hundred thousand people at the Derby and most of them were on the Hill." Strangely, while it was meant to be public land, Steinhoff announced that anyone who wanted access to the Hill for the Derby would have to spend one pound at a Poundland store. The British press, true to form, tore into Steinhoff. *The Guardian* said it was a curious partnership, since the idea of an "elegant, glamorous image of Derby Day appears to be a sharp contrast to Poundland's pile-it-high, bargain-basement profile".[27] The tabloid newspaper *The Sun* dubbed it "an outrage". Race-goers "will not just be reminded of the fact that they have taken the budget option to Derby Day, they will know that it was those in top hats and tails sipping champagne in plush boxes across the racecourse who thought this was an appropriate rebranding exercise".[28]

Britain's yellow press will, no doubt, have been overjoyed that in April 2018 Epsom torpedoed the Poundland deal. "Due to the widely reported issues concerning Steinhoff, we have mutually agreed that Poundland, one of its brands, will not be involved with The Hill at the Investec Derby Festival in June," said the Derby's GM, Simon Durrant. Jooste's bid to etch his company's brand onto the face of the world's most famous horserace had flopped.

* * *

Ian Jayes, a former racehorse owner and trainer, is another who claims Markus Jooste is responsible for the decay of what were already pretty elastic morals in the industry. Now 78 years old, the combative Jayes was one of the few people who took on Jooste – and believes he was drummed out of the industry for his trouble. "Horseracing is one of those sports where money is almost like a god," he says. "I've been in this game a long time, and in the early years people like the Oppenheimers never boasted about how much their horses cost. When Markus came in, it was all about how much the horses cost, how much he was putting in, how he was this saviour . . ." He says that within a short time, Jooste and his partner, Chris van Niekerk, had their tentacles everywhere. What Jayes queried, particularly, was how more than R30m of public money found its way into Phumelela's coffers.

There's a backstory to this that dates back to the grim days of Grand Apartheid in South Africa. During that time, horseracing was the only game in town for people intent on gambling. In the dusty homelands, there were casinos like Sun City, but these were hours away from Joburg or Pretoria. Instead, gamblers like Jooste's father would hit the betting shops – like TAB or Tattersalls. As a result, government taxed the racing industry heavily. Some of this tax money was placed in the Horse Racing Development Fund, which was set up by government to dish out grants for "the development of the horseracing industry". So, for example, if a racing club wanted to build accommodation for grooms, it could apply for a grant.

But after Phumelela was listed on Johannesburg's stock exchange in 2002, ostensibly to "corporatise horse racing", Jayes says the company took over the financial responsibility. According to him, R3.6m of the R17.5m set aside for stabling and building grooms' accommodation was used to upgrade the Vaal racecourse, while the other R13.9m found its way into Phumelela's profits. "It is just astounding," he says. "How can this money, meant to be used to improve the industry, end up being distributed as profits for the shareholders of Phumelela? It is nothing less than an asset grab."

Jayes wasn't alone in thinking this. In 2013, at a hearing at the Competition Tribunal, Chopela Simoto, chair of the Grooms' Association, said that Phumelela had promised to spend R17.5m on stabling and building housing for grooms – and hadn't done a thing.[29] So Jayes went to the Racing Association AGM and Phumelela's AGM, and asked how this had happened. He says he was treated like a pariah. "The attitude was that Markus and Chris van Niekerk are strategic thinkers who've saved our industry. How dare you question their vision."

Phumelela, however, disputes Jayes's version of events. In 2011, former Phumelela CEO Rian du Plessis said that Gauteng government officials had agreed in 1996 that "there were no terms and conditions attached to the proceeds on dissolution of the fund". And he said his lawyers, Sonnenberg Hoffmann and Galombik, had investigated and found "no irregularities" in how this money was transferred to Phumelela.[30]

Jayes still doesn't buy this story. That is why he, along with another owner, Phindi Kema, has lobbied South Africa's erratic Public Protector, Busisiwe Mkhwebane, to investigate the horseracing industry and, in particular, how the development fund money was pilfered. It is worth noting that Jayes and Kema had designs of their own on the industry, having set up Africa Race Group, which sought to become an operator in its own right. In April 2018, Mkhwebane said she'd investigate the industry, including Phumelela's "questionable" formation in 1998, and what had happened since. (Phumelela, however, isn't worried. It said Kema "has a history of instituting meritless complaints", calling some of her allegations "hilarious".)

But Jayes's story doesn't end there. During the height of his fracas with Phumelela, he was still training about fourteen horses at the Vaal, where he'd rented stabling on the track from Phumelela. Then one morning, he opened a letter from Phumelela: you have three months' notice to vacate the stables, it said. "It was vindictive," says Jayes. "Shortly before, I'd told the Competition Commission about my concerns over the industry and the trust money. I believe this was their payback. It shows the vindictiveness and power of the Markus Jooste clique and their willingness to abuse it." Jayes says Phumelela had never done this before – not even to those trainers who still owed a lot of money in arrears rent.

So, out of options, tired and frozen out of the industry, Jayes retired. "I hear that Jooste is now out of the industry, that Mayfair has sold all its horses. But that doesn't get to the heart of it. His cronies are still there, running all the major organisations. His tentacles remain."

*　　*　　*

Rian du Plessis, the eloquent and smooth former CEO of Phumelela, says any talk of Jooste having "captured racing" is "just nonsense". Du Plessis was never likely to have agreed with this sentiment, though. He remains one of Jooste's closest and most loyal confidantes, even to this day. Their friendship dates back to 1979, when they were both members of the Wilgenhof residence at Stellenbosch University, as first-year accounting students. Jooste trusted Du Plessis so implicitly, in fact, that he appointed him as a trustee of his family trust. "Ask yourself," says Du Plessis, "to what end would Markus want to capture the industry? So that his horses could win races that they shouldn't have won? Of course not. The reality is, the man put a lot of money into racing and he has lost a lot of money."

Du Plessis says the racing industry will survive Jooste's impromptu departure from the fraternity, just as it has survived other whirlwind departures of charismatic, big-spending owners who vanished almost overnight. "You need to bear in mind that Markus's 350 horses in South Africa represent only about 5% of the 6,500 horses in training now. Sure, they were high value, but all of those horses have now been sold and are with new owners." He says that if those horses had all been put on auction at the same time, it could have been a "disaster" for the financial position of South African racing. "Unsold horses might have then had to be re-homed or even put down, but we managed an orderly sale. We avoided a catastrophe."

Bernard Kantor also flashes with anger when talk arises of "racing capture". "Really, it's absurd. It's small, petty-minded people talking absolute shit. Phumelela has an independent board, has its own governance structures. There are people there who've never met Markus. Do people really think that he's sitting down in the Cape somewhere pulling all the strings at Phumelela? It's just ridiculous."

Kantor's view is representative of many in the existing power structures in the industry. They hadn't seen the fraud, hadn't lost through the bloodletting in Steinhoff shares, and their perspective of Jooste was a universe away from the cartoon villain they'd read about in the newspapers. Phumelela, and the racing industry, have nothing to do with Steinhoff, they say.

John Koster, the MD of Klawervlei, says Markus Jooste's presence "took us to the next level".[31] "We were able to participate internationally. We went from a family business to a corporate business. We travelled overseas quite a bit, getting to see how they breed horses in other parts of the world." However, it is understood that Jooste is negotiating to sell his stake in Klawervlei. Koster won't say as much, except that "there are negotiations going on". But he does say that the appearance, and then disappearance, of a big personality in the industry has happened plenty of times before.

Perhaps. But Joey Ramsden, who trained many of Jooste's horses, believes Jooste's rapid departure will leave an immense gap in the racing economy that will be hard to fill. "It will also be felt in employment, not just among the trainers but also the grooms. In my case, I've gone from training 120 horses to half that."[32] Ramsden and Jooste had a famously strong relationship. Today, Ramsden describes that December morning, when he heard about the Steinhoff implosion, as an immense shock. "I only had positive experiences with Markus. He was a huge benefactor to the industry, and a model owner. He was very generous to many people – not me specifically, but people in need. So, the whole Steinhoff thing, I was as surprised as anybody."

7

Ikea 2.0

———

As the decade ticked over to 2010, Markus Jooste began entertaining a fanciful notion that he hadn't seriously thought possible until then: toppling Ikea as Europe's top furniture retailer. It was a fantastically ambitious plan. Ikea, after all, had become *the* gold standard of retail in the seven or so decades since it was formed in 1943 in Sweden. Its minimalist Scandinavian-designed furniture, based on the principle of 'high design' at 'low prices' and sold in ready-to-assemble flat packs, had captured the consumer zeitgeist. With its 300 warehouse-style stores in 47 countries, the Ikea catalogue is said to be "twice as widely distributed as the Bible". Nearly a billion people visit Ikea stores every year, and legend has it that one in ten Europeans is conceived in an Ikea bed.

By 2010, Steinhoff – having already swallowed Unitrans and Homestyle, and then making a play for JD Group – was already being dubbed "the Ikea of Africa". But that wasn't good enough; Jooste wanted Steinhoff to *be* Ikea.

In the early days, this sounded like the sort of pie-in-the-sky fantasy that entrepreneurs tell themselves before they go to sleep at night. Few seriously reckoned Steinhoff could ever seriously pull off a challenge to Ikea. But this changed after 2010. One Steinhoff executive, discussing the company's trajectory in 2013, seemed almost to surprise himself when he admitted: "Yes, I think we have a chance to tackle Ikea – which was impossible ten years ago."

For years, Jooste had something of a crush on Ikea's business concept. The fact that Ikea had its own factories, its own raw materials, and supplied its own furniture into its own stores, from tree to table, was catnip. It's what Steinhoff wanted to do too. As Jooste remarked: "We learnt that from [Ikea's founder] Ingvar Kamprad. He's the guy who showed it to us. He produces his own stuff, sells his own stuff and owns his own property. We purely follow what he did. Our only problem was we couldn't build a brand – so our strategy was to buy the number one or two around Ikea in every country."[1]

Jooste had a whiteboard in his office in Germany, on which he plotted every European country and every retailer in that country: who was who, who owned what, who was doing what. Always, ahead of them on the chart, there was Ikea.

So, how to surpass them? On every iteration of the plan, Jooste kept coming back to Conforama – the French discount retailer that began life in Lyon in 1967 and became known by its blunt slogan "Where life is cheaper". Page through a Conforama catalogue, and you'll see the usual fare of discount home stores: sofas for €250, large 230-litre refrigerators for €299, chaises longues for €400. In the European Union, where economic growth has struggled to breach 2% for more than a decade, it's the sort of model that works. It is why, today, Conforama's market share in France is now 16% – just behind Ikea's 19%.[2]

In 2007, Conforama was controlled by PPR, a company 41%-owned by the Pinault family. The Pinault family also owned Gucci, and Jooste figured that with such different brands, the family weren't aiming to stick around the discount market forever. So in 2007, Jooste went for tea with Jean-François Palus, PPR's chief financial officer, to feel him out about a possible deal. Palus told him: in life, everything is for sale, so when we want to sell, we'll contact you.

Later that year, Palus called Jooste back. We're serious about selling, he said. Come have a look. But Palus had a caveat: our price is €2.5bn – it's non-negotiable. So, Steinhoff had a look, even signing a "confidentiality agreement" in May 2008. But the price was just out of Steinhoff's reach.

Then, in August 2008, Lehman Brothers went into bankruptcy, and a global financial freeze swept the globe. Alan Greenspan, the former chair of the US central bank, the Federal Reserve, described it as a "once-in-a-century type of event". All the metrics suddenly shifted. Europe's retailers took a battering over the next two years, and in late 2010 Jooste got his chance. "I'll never forget, I was at a function in December in South Africa for lunch – a work function," Jooste recalled. "And I suddenly got this call on my mobile phone from [Palus] and he said: 'This is your chance.' I flew over the next day, and the team went with me."[3]

Within days – on 12 December – Steinhoff had signed the deal to buy Conforama for €1.2bn. It was less than half what the Pinault family had wanted just two years before. And, as luck would have it, this was the exact moment in economic history when interest rates in Europe were at their lowest since the Second World War. There have been few more felicitous times to buy a colossal retail chain. It changed everything, Jooste reckoned. "Suddenly, we were something in the furniture game. Suddenly, we were known in every country in the world . . . From that day on, every retailer in Europe contacted me, every door opened, every discussion was open," he said.[4]

Conforama's network included 186 stores in France, 15 in Italy, 13 in Switzerland, 18 in Spain and Portugal, 3 in Croatia, and 1 in Luxembourg. While the size was dazzling, Conforama today is hardly the most prized asset. Prudential's Craig Butters describes how, during Paris' 2013 "sales week" in June, Conforama was the only one sitting in the cheap seats, waiting for a dance. "In every store in Paris, one could hardly move – Conforama was completely empty," says Butters.[5]

One thing the Conforama deal did do, however, was suddenly inject a €1bn property portfolio into Steinhoff. In every town in France and Switzerland, Steinhoff suddenly owned some property or other – from sprawling, warehouse-style properties on the outskirts of cities to small boutique-style stores.

The way Jooste described it, Conforama was the catalyst for the split of the Steinhoff empire into three arms. The monster had got too big. Firstly, he decided to create an "African industrial company", which would hold PG Bison and Unitrans, called KAP; secondly, there would be the "African retail company" called JD Group, which would hold stores like Joshua Doore, Incredible Connection, Timber City and Unitrans Motors; and, thirdly, there would be the remaining Steinhoff business, which was already starting to look discernibly more European. Doing this, said Jooste, would be the first step to creating "a retail organisation that can compete with Ikea on a worldwide basis".

*   *   *

To make its three-leaf clover model work, Steinhoff would first have to take control of JD Group, to act as the foundation for its African retail empire. It did this through an ingenious takeover, which was another breathtakingly exquisite Markus Jooste classic.

But to understand just how risky it was for Steinhoff to buy the JD Group in the first place, one needs to understand how the furniture industry works. And one also needs to understand how, since the 1990s, the industry broke itself by beginning to sell furniture on credit. This wasn't just the JD Group – it was Profurn, Ellerines and Lewis Stores.

For years, furniture was a simple business. You walked into a store, picked a lampshade, paid for it and walked out. But in the 1990s furniture stores figured out that if they could offer goods "on credit", which could be repaid over as long as three years, more people could afford to buy from them. Before long, however, credit wasn't just a mechanism to unlock people's buying power and help them purchase beds and sofas; it was *the* fundamental way in which these stores made money. So, they morphed into microlending businesses, with a handy sideline in furniture. The tail began wagging the dog.

Take the story of Martin Mkhabela, an insurance salesman for Old Mutual in Limpopo, one of South Africa's poorest provinces. In 2015, when Mkhabela's bed broke, he walked into a Lewis store in the small town of Burgersfort, and told the salesman he was looking to buy a bed. They showed him a Restonic Ambassador Dream Top, on sale at R4,699. The salesman convinced him to take a Masterguard mattress protector as well, so, in all, Mkhabela agreed to spend R5,078.[6] But – and here's the thing – he agreed to buy it "on credit" and pay it back over three years. Suddenly, a R785 "initiation fee" was slapped on, plus an R800 "delivery charge", a R513 "maintenance agreement", a R57 monthly "service fee" and R109 every month for "customer protection insurance". Mkhabela ended up getting a replacement bed (marked at R4,699) for more than three times that sum: R16,156. He seemed surprised when he was told how much he was paying: "How can it cost R16,000? It's abnormal. I'm surprised because they just told me I must pay R448 a month," he said.[7]

There were many like Mkhabela who hadn't calculated the monthly impact of such a deal. In 2007, the government realised that debt levels were ballooning, and that many people found themselves trapped in debt, taking out one loan to repay another. So, it passed a new National Credit Act to remedy this. But companies like JD Group, Lewis and Ellerines weren't employing high-priced financial whizzes in their businesses for no reason – they found a way around it. If you looked hard enough, there was always another "initiation fee", an "insurance charge" or some fee you could sucker people into paying. For example, Lewis had a clause in its contracts saying that if you missed a payment, they could charge you R12 for a phone call, to ask you why. By 2014 the credit regulator's numbers said there were 4.2m people in arrears. So, extrapolating this, the simple act of making a phone call was costing these customers who already couldn't pay, an extra R2.4bn per year.[8]

With admirable introspection, JD Group's Peter Griffiths told me in 2015 that easy credit perverted the industry. "That's where it all went wrong," he said. "The model became so intertwined that it became difficult for customers to work out the cost of the product versus the cost of the financial services."[9] The business model, Griffiths said, wasn't sustainable. Sure, it all looked fine when more and more people were borrowing. But when the economy stuttered, there was a tsunami of bad debts just over the horizon, about to roll in.

By early 2018, 25 million South Africans had taken credit somewhere, though nearly half – 9.7m people – were considered "not in good standing". More than 5.5 million South Africans are more than three months behind in repaying loans.[10] These overwhelming levels of debt remain one of the most serious blights of the post-apartheid economic era. As *The Economist* put it: "With interest rates high and financial literacy low, many loans lead to financial ruin. They may even widen the gap between rich and poor, since people who besmirch their credit records by missing payments on small loans will then struggle to get mortgages."[11]

JD Group was one of the pillars of this creaking system. For years, it had navigated the tightrope adeptly. It helped that it owned some of South Africa's most recognisable and strongest brands. Many South African homes, you'll find, have one of its pieces of furniture – whether it's a 23-inch TV set bought from appliance store HiFi Corporation or a four-piece lounge suite from Bradlows.

At the centre of the group was Joshua Doore, most famous for a jingle dating back to the 1970s which assured shoppers that "You've got an uncle in the furniture business". Its promise was to give them "brand name furniture at factory prices". There was also Morkels ("Your two-year guarantee store") for furniture and appliances; mass market furniture discounter Price 'n Pride; and southern Africa's largest technology retailer, Incredible Connection, which sells fancy iPads, MacBooks and computer paraphernalia.

All these brands, mostly focused on poorer shoppers, had been assembled under one umbrella by David Sussman, an unsubtle, brawny bear of a man. Sussman had got his first break when he'd started two Price 'n Pride stores in 1983. He was, like Markus Jooste, a dealmaker at heart. So whenever a rival hit the wall, he'd buy their chain. It worked so well that by 2000 he ran a chain of 678 stores. It was, as the Competition Tribunal chairman David Lewis would point out, a "meteoric rise".

Almost from the start, Sussman had been great friends with Jooste, ever since his stores began stocking Gomma Gomma furniture in the 1990s. Initially, he didn't give Jooste much hope when he pitched up at JD Group. "We knew [Gomma Gomma] was in trouble, so when Markus and Michael Delport came to see me . . . the thought did strike me: here are two guys, they've come out of the canning business – do they really understand what they're letting themselves in for?"[12] But Sussman says that with Markus "chemistry existed from day one". The two cemented their relationship travelling together to meet Bruno Steinhoff in Germany. On that trip they'd stay up late at night, drinking whisky and plotting their vision of merging their two companies to create a united furniture empire.

That didn't happen for years, however. It was only in 2012 that Steinhoff finally wrested control of the JD Group. Remarkably, even though JD Group was worth R11.3bn at the time, Steinhoff managed to get it without paying a cent. Equally astounding was that Jooste did this without issuing a single new Steinhoff share.

This is how he did it. In May 2011, Steinhoff "sold" Unitrans Auto (which includes Hertz car rental and other dealers) and Steinbuild (which included Timbercity and Penny Pinchers) to JD Group for R3.1bn. Sussman's company paid this price by issuing 49m shares to Steinhoff, which gave it 22.4% of JD Group. Step two: Steinhoff "sold" its industrial assets – Unitrans and PG Bison – to KAP International, which gave it shares in payment. This took Steinhoff's holding in KAP to 88%. Step three: Steinhoff then did a barter deal: it swapped a chunk of its shares in KAP for more shares in JD Group. The upshot was, while its shareholding in KAP was now reduced to just 62%, it got 50.1% of JD Group.

Voila! Steinhoff had gained control of SA's largest furniture retailers, JD Group and KAP, simply by shunting shares around the table.

Not everyone liked the tactics. More than 16% of JD Group's shareholders voted against the offer, for example. But it didn't matter – Markus had sold the vision of a unified retail empire adeptly. Sussman, speaking at the time, marvelled at the fact that anyone could not like the plan. "Quite frankly, I don't understand why anyone would vote against it," he said.[13] Mark Hodgson, an analyst at Avior, said that Steinhoff's offer was "a bit cheeky" and "not particularly attractive": Steinhoff had paid too little to get control of JD Group. It smacked of a disregard for shareholders. Piet Viljoen, a highly rated analyst who began his career lecturing at the University of Pretoria before moving through various investment companies and starting Regarding Capital Management in 2003, didn't like Steinhoff's modus operandi. "It's not something we're comfortable with," he said in 2012. "It's not clear to us whether those acquisitions have created value or not, which is why we don't own any shares in Steinhoff."

JD Group proved to be a bomb, relying as it did on its "interest" earned on loans to paper over the fact that the core business really was sick. Already, JD Group's target market – the "value conscious mass-middle market" – was in big trouble. By the time Steinhoff took control, the amount of bad debt inside JD Group was crippling. "So much of the book was rotten, it completely took us by surprise," says one former Steinhoff executive. Speaking a few years later, JD Group's CEO, Peter Griffiths, said that "to wean yourself off credit isn't easy – we're a lot more careful and stringent on our credit scorecards [and] people who would have been given credit a few years ago are being turned away today". But by 2013, JD Group's customers had borrowed R8.2bn from the company to buy furniture and appliances. And more than a quarter of those customers had stopped paying for at least five months – a sign of a seriously rotten lending business.

In December 2013, shareholder activist Theo Botha pitched up at the JD Group AGM and asked why Sussman's company had set aside far too little money to cover these bad debts. Sussman and the other directors rubbished Botha's argument. "The company [is] comfortable with the level," he said. He was hopelessly wrong. Within weeks, JD Group had to hike its provisions by R602m (a 66% rise), and wrote off R495m in bad debts. It meant that JD Group had made a R138m loss for the six months to December 2013.

It was a sorry tale. Overall, JD Group's loan book had growth to R10bn, but it was riddled with cancer: more than R5.2bn was "non-performing". Its customers had simply stopped paying back the loans.

The results raised eyebrows, given the fact that eight people on JD Group's fourteen-member board had accounting qualifications (like Len Konar, Jooste himself and Peter Griffiths). Yet, JD Group had messed up its accounting provisions horrendously. Little wonder that at that half-year results presentation, JD Group locked out photographers. Perhaps it didn't want pictures of its executives with tears rolling down their cheeks in the next day's newspaper.

* * *

Jooste must have been furious. He'd bought a lemon, and now its rocketing levels of bad debt meant that more money had to be set aside as "provisions". The creeping JD Group cancer threatened to cripple Steinhoff's balance sheet. He needed to get JD Group's horror show off Steinhoff's books, fast. So, not for the first time, Jooste found a hat with a rabbit in it. Steinhoff told investors that it had sold JD Group's "consumer finance book" to an unnamed "international consumer finance provider" for an "unnamed sum". It soon emerged that Steinhoff had been negotiating to sell JD Group's loan book to the French banking group BNP Paribas for R4.6bn.

On the last possible day of Steinhoff's financial year, 30 June 2014, JD Group said it had "received an offer, subject to due diligence and conditions precedent, to dispose of its consumer finance division (excluding the insurance business JDFS), which provides instalment sale financing on furniture products and unsecured products". This clearly wasn't a done deal: BNP Paribas was still trawling through its "due diligence". But no matter: in its accounts for the year to June 2014, Steinhoff said it would exclude the ruinous impact of JD Group's loan book. "The announced sale of the consumer finance division . . . resulted in this division being reflected as a discontinued operation in the income statements for both 2014 and 2013," Steinhoff said in financials signed by Jooste and Deloitte.

This was important. In accounting parlance, if you can convince your auditors something is a "discontinued operation", you don't have to include its losses (or profits) in your financials. And deliciously, all the liabilities and assets of such a business (like its bad debts) are classified as "held for sale" in a single line on the accounts and also aren't included in your balance sheet.

It's difficult to give due emphasis to just how critical this card trick was to Jooste's Steinhoff narrative. The JD Group consumer finance division had made a R1.97bn loss for the year, from R4.7bn in revenues – yet this was now being stripped out of Steinhoff's books, as if it had all been a bad dream. So, had that BNP Paribas "offer" not arrived hours before sunset on the last day of its financial year and had JD Consumer Finance's numbers been included, JD Group would have made an immense R1.4bn loss, rather than a R537m profit. For Steinhoff, it would have dramatically lowered its operating profit to R10.6bn, from the R12.6bn that it reported to shareholders.

And this would have tipped over a number of other dominoes. For a start, Steinhoff's operating profit margin would have actually dropped to 8.6%, down from 10% the year before. But thanks to stripping out the consumer finance division, Steinhoff could report a margin increase to 10.8%. (In its 2014 report, Jooste triumphantly spoke of how the goal had been to "increase margin".) Steinhoff's earnings per share and its net asset value would also have looked worse; its liabilities would have been higher; and its ratings agencies would have been asking a lot of questions.

Quite how serious this was to Jooste is clear from the "Steinhoff leaks" (of which more later), which show the extent of his desperation to cover the JD Group hole. In one of the leaked emails, Jooste wrote to Dirk Schreiber, the German head of Steinhoff's European operation, that he had to impair JD Group's loan by R3.6bn, which would "put [our] results out of balance". So, he proposed that out of the purchase price, a company called Genesis (not controlled by Steinhoff) would get a "commission" of €130m (R1.9bn) for negotiating the sale of the JD Consumer Finance book to BNP Paribas.

This seems ludicrous: why should Steinhoff pay 27% of the BNP Paribas price as a commission? Well, one possible answer is that Genesis could then recycle €100m back into Steinhoff, boosting Steinhoff's profits by that amount.

Schreiber wrote back, suggesting various alternatives. In the end, they settled on doing the deal through Talgarth – the company that would later set auditor Deloitte's antennae ringing in 2017. "Let's use Talgarth, who has been involved all the years, to receive the €130m, and he is also the one with the debit balances to pay the interest," Jooste wrote. Jooste and Schmidt also discussed various options to fiddle the ratios – keeping margins above a certain level, and cost of sales lower. It was all about reverse-engineering the financials to arrive at a number they liked.

It would seem that Jooste's efforts to dress up Steinhoff's financial accounts to hide JD Group's bad debt in the bluntest, most obvious way possible was at the core of his undoing. The gerrymandering, at least in 2014, helped Jooste dodge a missile. Well, sort of. The problem was that in the event BNP Paribas *didn't* buy the finance division.

In September 2015, Steinhoff tried to blame this failure on the Competition Tribunal, which had imposed conditions on BNP buying the company. "This process, which is ongoing, has resulted in the transaction completion date being extended beyond one year from initial recognition of the business as a disposal group," it said. For the year to June 2015, JD Group's finance division was still classed as a "discontinued operation" in the financials.[14] That was in fact lucky. For Steinhoff took a red pen to the loan book, writing off R1.5bn of the value. By June, the loan book's net assets were calculated at R3.3bn – a far cry from the R10bn when it was bought a few years previously, or the R8bn of the previous year.

Two months later, on 16 November, Steinhoff's chief financial officer, Ben la Grange, and its finance director, Frikkie Nel, revealed that actually the BNP Paribas deal wasn't happening at all. They said in Steinhoff's annual report that at the end of October 2015, "JD Group has, after much consideration and extensive discussions with [BNP Paribas], decided not to proceed with the transaction".[15] The reasons, apparently, included the "change in the economic environment" and the "financial and commercial aspects of the transaction". Investors weren't told what actually happened. Still, it seemed that BNP Paribas had finished looking at the quality of the loan book they were getting, and weren't going to pay anything near the R4.6bn initially announced. But have no fear, said La Grange; we have made "substantial progress with the disposal of the business to an international investor with worldwide interests in providing credit to the lower [(income] customers".[16] Steinhoff said it expected that "definitive agreements" with this buyer would be signed before the end of 2015.

At this point, Jooste must have realised he couldn't risk bringing JD

Group's atrocious loan book back onto Steinhoff's balance sheet. He had to make another plan. Thereafter Steinhoff said nothing further about who was buying the JD Group loan book. The only reference is a one-liner in its 2016 annual report, which read "Steinhoff disposed of JD Group's financial services division, including insurance operations, to a European private equity consortium."[17] However, filings with the Competition Commission in March 2016 showed that JD Financial Services was actually being bought by a company called Wands Investments. Tracing this through the usual web of shelf companies, it turned out that Wands was owned by Fulcrum, which in turn, was owned by a murky Swiss company called Campion Capital. Campion Capital, it would later emerge, is pivotal to Steinhoff's smoke and mirrors. At the time, virtually nothing was known about this nebulous Swiss company. The competition authorities certainly didn't have much of a clue, describing it only as a company that also happened to own an "unsecured lending business operating under the name Capfin".

Had they dug deeper, they'd have uncovered a company with all the authenticity of a plastic edelweiss. In a nutshell, Campion was, for all intents and purposes, a thinly disguised off-balance sheet version of Steinhoff, run by Steinhoff's former top executive in Europe. Officially, Steinhoff didn't own Campion, but, unofficially, it would seem that Jooste still called the shots.

So, what role did Campion play when it came to the JD Consumer Finance transaction? Well, the most likely scenario is that Steinhoff "lent" money to Campion, to allow it to "buy" JD Consumer Finance. This would enable Jooste to keep its atrocious losses far away from Steinhoff's accounts, even though, as the funder, Steinhoff was entirely exposed to the swings and arrows of JD Group's bad debts. Given how atrocious that business actually was, with a deeply rotten loan portfolio, you'd probably have had to pay someone to haul away the carcass if it was a real arm's-length deal. But it wasn't: it was an in-house deal, designed to dress up Steinhoff's balance sheet. Jooste, it seems, had created an "off-balance sheet vehicle" to ensure JD Group's rotten loans didn't pollute Steinhoff's balance sheet.

One Steinhoff director says the board did ask plenty of questions about the JD Consumer Finance deal. "I can tell you that we spent many hours debating it," he says. "There were many of us who were sceptical – who hadn't even believed that Steinhoff should have bought JD Group in the first place. But Markus constantly told us that Fulcrum was an independent private equity company in its own right".

A former Steinhoff executive says Jooste told him that the point of selling JD Consumer Finance to Fulcrum was to clean up Steinhoff's accounts before the listing in Germany, in December 2015.

At the time, stockbroking firm Imara SP Reid warned that Steinhoff "has, for a long time, been as much of a private equity fund acting in the furniture space as a composite business [and] has been perceived, not unfairly, by fund managers as opaque".[18] Worse than simply opaque, actually. It appeared to be flogging businesses to front companies it had set up itself, in an attempt to make its financials look much better.

As it happens, the JD Group three-card trick wasn't Campion Capital's first rodeo, designed to flatter Steinhoff's accounts. So who was Campion Capital, really? Deciphering Campion's real identity, it turns out, holds the key to understanding the events that crippled Steinhoff.

8

Three-Card Trick

———

In the middle of the Valaisan Alps, at the crossroads from where you can branch off either south-east to Italy or north to France, there's a small Swiss town called Martigny. It's only ninety minutes from Geneva, but in winter, when it's carpeted in snow and you can't even see the foothills of the Rhône Valley mountains, which spear up around the town, Martigny feels as if it is the most remote place in the world. In summer, enveloped by mountains, there is something Stellenbosch about it. In fact, with just fifteen thousand residents, it's even smaller than the Cape winelands town. Martigny is better known for its vineyards, the castle Bâtiaz that overlooks the town, and its restored Roman amphitheatre than as a hub for global entrepreneurs. Yet, it is in Martigny, at 14 rue du Léman, that Campion Capital has its headquarters, in an anonymous office opposite the Hotel Forclaz-Touring.

Apparently, Campion Capital was set up here as a global private equity fund in June 2014. Campion's registration documents list three people as its officials: Siegmar Schmidt, Alan Evans and Jean-Noël Pasquier. All three supposedly contributed 50,000 Swiss francs to Campion Capital's founding equity. All three have deep links to Steinhoff.

Schmidt, a bloated and balding German accountant, was in charge of Steinhoff's European finance from 1999 to 2013. It seems he lives in Bad Zwischenahn, a ten-minute drive from Bruno Steinhoff's home in Wester-stede. In theory, Schmidt left Steinhoff in 2013, after which he referred to himself as a "consultant". Schmidt would argue he is now "independent" from Steinhoff. But the emails leaked from the Oldenburg investigation show that Schmidt was right in the thick of it, conspiring with Jooste to dress up Steinhoff's accounts in 2014. For example, in an email, Jooste asked Schmidt to "raise an additional 100-million Euros . . . from a subsidiary company" so that the financials comply with "our plans/forecasts". Schmidt replied, reminding him of "the balance sheets we pushed up in recent years" – providing useful cash that could be deployed to inflate some or other business. The implication is that the Campion structure was dreamt up within Steinhoff as a way to do "off-balance sheet deals" that wouldn't register in its accounts – and Schmidt was deployed to make this happen.

The first sign that the relationship between Schmidt and Markus Jooste was less than salubrious emerged in 2013. In June that year, Steinhoff said it has reached a deal to "acquire the entire issued share capital" of Kika-Leiner – one of Europe's largest retail companies, with 7,500 staff, shops in 73 locations (mostly in Austria) and sales of €1.2bn. Then, mysteriously, and without telling anyone why, this deal vanished. Instead, in November 2013, it turned out that a company called Genesis, controlled by Siegmar Schmidt, would actually be buying Kika-Leiner for €375m (R5.5bn), "facilitated" by Steinhoff. In other words, Steinhoff would "lend" the money to Genesis to buy Kika-Leiner, by giving Genesis 120m Steinhoff shares.

There are distinct echoes in the Kika-Leiner transaction of the early forestry deal of 2001 which we have already discussed. In that case, Steinhoff had said it was acquiring the forests in Knysna from Barloworld, only for it suddenly to decide that it needed a "third party", Fihag, to buy the forests. And, exactly as with the forestry deal, a few months later Steinhoff said it actually did want to buy at least part of the Kika-Leiner group. In June 2014, Steinhoff announced it would be buying part of Kika-Leiner from Genesis, its property portfolio, for €452m (R6.6bn).

This seemed an irredeemably rotten deal from the outset. After all, why would Steinhoff not just buy the whole business outright for €375m instead of paying more than that for just half? Why would Steinhoff do a deal that effectively gave a former manager more than R1bn, essentially for nothing? Actually, the situation was even worse. Portsea Asset Management said in a June 2017 report on Steinhoff that after scrutinising Austrian and German commercial records it had found that "in fact, Steinhoff Europe was the initial owner of Kika-Leiner in November 2013 [and] in June 2014 ownership moved to Siegmar Schmidt".[1]

How is it that a multi-billion-rand asset can simply disappear off a company's books, and end up being owned by someone else? Especially a company like Genesis, which had only been spirited into existence five minutes before and had exactly zero track record.

In December 2017, Viceroy Research would also identify the Kika-Leiner case as the first of many baffling deals, saying it "believes this scheme was enacted purely to enrich management". If only that were the whole story.[2]

* * *

The second Campion "official" is Alan Evans, whose history with Markus Jooste goes back more than a decade. An Englishman, born in 1950, Evans represented Bruno Steinhoff's company Fihag, which helped insert Kluh Investments into the middle of the forestry deal with Steinhoff. This deal ultimately ended up earning Jooste millions. He was also a shareholder in the Australian company Freedom Group when Steinhoff bought out shareholders in 2003.

"Alan was one of Markus's guys, everyone knew that," says one Steinhoff insider. "For each rugby World Cup, every four years from 1999, Alan would come along as Markus's guest. I got to know him then. He seemed harmless."[3]

Others who knew Evans described him as "quiet, painfully shy", who always seemed to be around Markus Jooste, but more as wallpaper than as any defining presence. In Swiss documents, Evans gave his registered address as St Helier on Jersey, one of the Channel Islands. He was listed as Campion's president until July 2018.

But despite his apparently grey persona, Evans's history is far more colourful. His name arises too in the Panama Papers, the leaked list of clients of the Panamanian law firm Mossack Fonseca, as a shareholder of Global Financial Investment Holdings, which owns shares in a range of companies, such as Warren Trustees. People who know Evans say he's the guy you'd hire to set up opaque offshore companies where nobody can be traced.

In 2003, an eighteenth-month investigation by *Poland Monthly* placed Evans at the centre of an offshore account scam involving Poland's largest insurance company, PZU, as well as Russia's partly state-owned energy company, Gazprom. "Managed by British national Alan Evans, the Warren Trustees Group, a loosely structured outfit of lawyers and accountants specializing in offshore deals, aided and facilitated what appear to be illegal offshore trust funds, accounts and transfers," the magazine said.[4] It was dicey precisely because, at the time, Poles were not allowed to set up individual bank accounts in other countries unless they lived there.

"Evans managed the accounts of at least 700 different trust funds, with many funds changing names or having double or triple accounts at different addresses in Dublin, Trenton NJ, the Bahamas and other locations around the world," the magazine said. The companies he created were often layered into a series of trust funds, which was "a technique both effective and traditional in money laundering circles". And the companies registered were supposedly "simultaneous experts in real estate acquisition, insurance, reinsurance, government permit acquisition, construction, Internet technology and project development – not to mention in trust fund law and financial advisory services". There are disturbing echoes of exactly these tactics in Steinhoff's off-balance sheet vehicles: a confusing array of new trusts, with money and assets shifting in and out in a dizzying spiral, and a series of faceless shelf companies.

The third face of Campion is the French-born accountant Jean-Noël Pasquier. He's the least known of the three. He appears to have worked as a tax consultant, and in this way he may have met Evans back in March 2011. That was when he joined a consulting company called Applegate FS in Geneva. When it was set up in 2011, Applegate described its purpose as "all activities in the fiduciary field, such as accounting, taxation and auditing; all advice relating to the management and administration of companies". Though Evans wasn't a director of Applegate, he had an email address linked to that business.

Pasquier, like Evans, pops up in many of the Steinhoff off-balance sheet companies since 2015. He is, for example, still listed as a director of Fulcrum, which bought JD Financial Services, GT Global Trademarks and Campion.

Campion does have a website. There, it describes itself as having "strong Swiss roots with an international exposure". Those roots, it turns out, are about as Swiss as croissants and boerewors: its assets are entirely South African, and it's run by a Frenchman, an Englishman and a German.

Campion's website boasts that it "advises private investors and shareholders of medium and large-sized companies on issues relating to private equity and investment management". The website doesn't reveal who runs Campion, what exactly it does, or what its investments are. The online description consists of less than 150 words. It might as well have had a Hotmail address. In every respect, Campion appears to be a thinly veneered disguise for a Steinhoff "off-balance sheet company".

It's unclear why Siegmar Schmidt chose the name of Campion Capital. Perhaps it was to soak up any reflected glory from other, legitimate companies – like the specialist capital-raising firm Campion Capital, which is based in London and which takes its name from its British founder, Will Campion. "We were actually quite pissed off when we read about it," says Will Maydon of the legitimate Campion, who works with plenty of South African wealth managers and institutions like Standard Bank, Nedbank, Coronation and Allan Gray.[5] "We'd read about the issues around Steinhoff, and they've never had any links to us." Maydon says that after the scandal broke, he spoke to a number of asset managers in the US and UK who knew Steinhoff. 'The consensus was that they would never have invested in the equity of Steinhoff as they couldn't understand [why] Steinhoff was paying to purchase a number of low-grade businesses."

Truth be told, Campion Capital, Siegmar Schmidt's supposed "private equity fund", was a classic "off-balance sheet vehicle". Even though it claimed it was entirely "independent" from Steinhoff, and run by "outsiders", the reality was it had only ever done three deals in its life. It bought JD Consumer Finance (as we've seen), the financial services arm of Pepkor, called Capfin, and Steinhoff's trademarks through a company called GT Branding. All of them were linked to Steinhoff. This only reinforces the conclusion that this was no arm's-length company doing deals overseas. Rather, it would seem to be a company run by insiders meant to help Jooste shift nasty liabilities off Steinhoff's balance sheet, hide losses and create fictitious revenue.

Despite this, despite Siegmar Schmidt's links to Steinhoff, and despite the fact that it appears wholly reliant on Steinhoff loans, you won't find any mention of it as a "related party" in any of Steinhoff's documents. Nor, in fact, was Campion declared as a related party to the Competition Commission. If you're looking for a serious non-disclosure, this would be a good place to start.

*   *   *

Campion's purchase of Steinhoff's brands in 2015 was perhaps the most obvious of its three murky deals. Even the most mediocre tax avoider knows how to put together a prosaic "trademark and brand" fudge. Many of the top global companies have done it, like Apple and Google: set up a company in a low-tax jurisdiction (say, Switzerland) and let it buy your trademarks or brands. Then, let that Swiss company charge an immense "royalty fee" to your holding company, which allows it to squirrel the bulk of the profits away to a place where they won't be heavily taxed.

In 2015 Steinhoff sold a portfolio of about 200 of its brands and trademarks, which it held in a company called GT Global Trademarks, to a Swiss company called GT Branding for €488m. In Steinhoff's 2014 annual report, it said the deal "makes provision for the continued use by the group of the trademarks, as well as potential future benefits resulting from the wider marketing of the trademarks by the management company". In other words, people who read this announcement would have believed that Steinhoff was selling its brands to a company meant to focus on promoting them. It would get a large upfront payment of €488m, and would pay an annual royalty fee to use them. What no one would have guessed, though – what Jooste's company hid from investors – was that, actually, the only way GT Branding could afford to pay that €488m was thanks to a loan of $810m which it got from Steinhoff. Nor did anyone know that Steinhoff immediately bought 45% of that Swiss company, while the other 55% was held by – no prizes for guessing – Campion Capital. In other words, it was a big circular deal – all done with Steinhoff's money, but benefiting the other shareholders of Campion Capital.

Needless to say, Steinhoff didn't declare this as a "related party" to anyone. Had it done so, investors could have checked for any shady dealings – such as whether Steinhoff had lent far too much money, and how it was being repaid. Yet, anomalously, GT Branding's own financials (accessible in Switzerland) do disclose the $810m as a "related party debt". But most people wouldn't have seen those Swiss accounts. They'd have been none the wiser that, in fact, Steinhoff was on the line for what went down at GT Branding.

What was worse is that when Steinhoff was asked about this, it lied. In April 2017, the London-based Portsea Asset Management spent a fair amount of time picking through Steinhoff's accounts. In particular, it flagged the fact that Steinhoff said it had lent €994m to certain companies it hadn't named. So Portsea contacted Steinhoff, and asked who had borrowed this money. They were told the money had been lent to "Chinese suppliers". It was a patent lie, and it took Portsea all of five minutes to see through it. "We can state with a high degree of certainty that Steinhoff's loans and investments are *not* to Chinese suppliers, but at least CHF 809-million (Swiss francs) are loans to GT Branding," said Portsea. "And, we believe, the remainder are likely loans to the Campion entity that purchased JD Consumer Finance." Portsea's report exposing this sham was published in June 2017 – months before Steinhoff crashed. Its conclusions were pretty similar to that of Viceroy, which reported a few months later.

But this was only half the con. Not only had Steinhoff lent the money to Campion to buy GT Branding (which it hid), it also included "interest" repayments on these loans in its revenue, as it reported to shareholders.

If you look at Steinhoff's audited accounts for the year to June 2016, it claimed it made profit of €1.4bn. But this included "income from investments" of €248m. Most of this, €219m, came from a category which Steinhoff only described as "loans" and "other". Now, this was a pretty hefty number, accounting for more than 15% of Steinhoff's final profit that year. Yet nowhere in its financials did the company bother revealing how it had made that money, other than to describe it as just "loans" and "other income".

But don't fret, Steinhoff said, if you want to know where this came from, "details of loans and investments are available at the registered office of the company for inspection". So, in mid-2017, before the Steinhoff bubble popped, Portsea Asset Management contacted Steinhoff and asked exactly what this "loan and investment" profit consisted of. "We were told this would not be possible," Portsea reported.

By this stage, there were red lights blinking all over the place for Portsea. It went and checked the accounts, and found out that Steinhoff was only paying its suppliers after a seven-month wait – when the average in the industry was just more than two months. "It does not make sense that Steinhoff is not paying its suppliers on the one hand, and lending to them on the other," Portsea said. In essence, it was all a mirage. Steinhoff had "lent" money to GT Branding, which was used to buy Steinhoff's own assets, and the left-over cash was used to repay "interest" to Steinhoff.

Later, Karl Leinberger, the chief investment officer of Coronation Fund Managers, said Steinhoff's ownership of GT Branding "should have been disclosed". Leinberger says that when Fulcrum bought JD Financial Services, "we had questioned the sale with management, and the risk of an undisclosed related-party transaction, only to be given the plausible explanation that no related parties were involved". Instead, Leinberger was told it had been sold to a "European private equity firm with other sub-Saharan lending businesses". Of course, the only lending businesses it ever owned came about thanks to Markus Jooste.

In November 2017, a few weeks before Steinhoff crashed, Reuters published an article revealing details of the GT Branding deal for the first time.[6] Professor Emilios Avgouleas, who holds the chair in International

Banking Law and Finance at the University of Edinburgh, was quoted as criticising Steinhoff for keeping the deal secret. "It's a material transaction and arguably it can lend itself to all kinds of distortions of the share price," he said.

Rather remarkably, once his dirty little secret was revealed, Jooste doubled down. He put out a statement saying, "All reporting requirements have been met – this has been confirmed by our internal legal team and external experts."[7]

Had anyone bothered to ask why it was that a shelf company in Martigny, in the middle of the Alps, had suddenly become a hub for emerging market microlending companies, it could all have been so different. Had the auditors picked up the fact that it was all just one in-house related party picnic, they would have insisted that Campion, GT Branding and the others should all have been put back into the Steinhoff pot (or "consolidated", in accounting lingo). This would have led to JD Consumer Finance's bad debts being included among Steinhoff's liabilities, and the "interest" that Steinhoff reported as profit would have had to be excluded. In other words, Steinhoff would have looked a whole heap less shiny than the glimmering picture presented to investors and ratings agencies.

*   *   *

Michael Jacks, a methodical, soft-spoken accountant, had spent plenty of hours picking apart the Campion Capital three-card trick in 2017, in the weeks before Steinhoff collapsed. As an analyst for various hedge funds – he now works for the Dubai-based Arqaam Capital – Jacks had seen some pretty convoluted structures before then. But Campion was on another level entirely. "I'd been asked to begin covering Steinhoff in about August 2017, and one of the first things I noticed was the extent to which Steinhoff took a keen interest in controlling both the narrative of research reports and analyst earnings estimates," he says. For example, Jacks had contacted Steinhoff to ask them about the low tax rate, and was given "semi-plausible" answers around using inter-group loans to reduce the tax rate. But, significantly, Steinhoff asked him "not to include" those details in his report.

Then, after the Reuters article questioning the GT Branding deal, Jacks contacted Steinhoff to ask them to explain the relationship. They blustered, and couldn't answer him. Which only made him more suspicious. So, Jacks began digging in the Swiss business registry. "I discovered an immense off-balance sheet structure with Campion positioned at the top. All the entities had at least one of three common directors – George Alan Evans, Jean-Noël Pasquier and Davide Romano – and one of two addresses – rue de Léman 12 or 14," he says. It soon became very clear that Campion wasn't independently owned or managed, as Steinhoff had been saying. "It seemed rather more plausible that Alan Evans and the others were intermediaries acting on behalf of Steinhoff, or its directors, and Campion was being used to hide liabilities and pump up its profits."

Take Campion's third deal, with Capfin (which was done through Fulcrum). Rather like JD Group's "financial services" arm, Capfin was the quintessential predatory lender. It boasted how it made "fast, easy cash loans" of up to R10,000. Its main customers were people who walked into Pep or Ackermans stores, and wanted to buy clothing or appliances on credit. As with JD Group, Capfin customers would end up paying backbreaking interest rates. For example, if you'd taken out a R5,000 loan from Capfin in 2012, you'd have to pay back R6,925 barely six months later, with fees. That's an annual rate of 78% interest plus fees – at a time when the prime interest rate charged by banks was just 8.5%.

The story is that back in January 2013 a company called Southern View Finance (SVF) was created and listed in the tax haven of Bermuda, with the sole aim of buying Capfin. SVF is owned by a company called Mayo, but being registered in the shady and opaque British Virgin Islands, it doesn't have to say who owns it.[8] However, it turns out that Southern View Finance's shareholders included Christo Wiese and Brait. Wiese says other Pep managers, including Pieter Erasmus, were also investors. Discussing the matter today, Wiese says there was nothing nefarious in the Capfin deal.

"Back in Pepkor, Southern View was our micro-finance business. We took it out of Pepkor and listed it separately for a number of reasons. For one thing, it bedevils your balance sheet to have a finance company in a trading company, and we also wanted to do financing deals with other entities."[9] This included providing financing for similar retailers in Poland and Eastern Europe, presumably also in the Pep chain. What it meant was that a number of Pep shareholders owned Southern View, including Wiese, Brait, Pepkor's MD Pieter Erasmus and other Pep managers. Essentially, Pepkor would sign up clients and earn a fee for doing so, and Southern View would provide the finance, collect the interest and manage the debtors' book.

But soon after, in August 2014, Capfin hit a road bump. The National Credit Regulator (NCR) ruled that Capfin's advertisements had "misled or deceived customers", as it did not "require customers to provide support-ing information or documentation to verify their income".[10] The regulator found no less than 25 cases of reckless lending at Capfin. So in February 2015, it cancelled Capfin's licence. Standard Bank and FirstRand, which had lent to Capfin, sensibly pulled their funding lines. But no matter for Steinhoff: its finance arm became the "lender of last resort", providing a loan facility to Capfin of R500m. Quite why Steinhoff should be funding a company it didn't own, who can say.

Then, the final leg: in July 2015, Southern View sold Capfin to Cam-pion's company Fulcrum for R4.6bn – 35% of which went to Brait. It remains unclear how Fulcrum, part of a shady off-balance entity in Swit-zerland, could have found this sort of money. Wiese says the deal with Fulcrum happened after the Pepkor deal, when there was a discussion about what to do with Capfin. "Jooste then said, No, this company called Fulcrum would buy the business. It was reported to the Steinhoff board, and we understood that Fulcrum was owned by Campion, which was an independent private equity firm that Markus had done deals with before." The price Fulcrum paid for Southern View Finance was apparently based on a formula using Steinhoff's profit, with a discount applied because Capfin wasn't listed. We now know, of course, that Campion was inde-pendent in the same way the Zimbabwe Electoral Commission is independent: arguably, and probably not at all.

Wiese said he was in a difficult position on this negotiation. "Remember, I was the largest shareholder in Steinhoff and the largest shareholder in Southern View, so I recused myself. They negotiated and came to a deal, which I thought was fair. It was perfectly correctly handled by Pieter Erasmus. They signed the deal, and it was the end of it," he says.

In June 2016, now under Campion's control, SVF published financials which showed how ludicrously profitable giving loans to the country's poorest consumers can be. Though Capfin had lent out R1.46bn in loans, of which R504.7m was "bad debt", it still made a profit of R186m. It's a ridiculously convoluted helix, probably purposely so. The bottom line is that the loan repayments, being made by many poor black South Africans under threat of blacklisting, are being recycled across the world and then hidden – through London, Bermuda, and then into Switzerland.

Why create so many hoops? Initially, Michael Jacks thought it might just be a tax structure, designed to take the profits from Capfin out of the country, into a "low-tax" country like Switzerland. After looking at it for a while, he reckoned the motive could have been far more sinister. "At best, it looked like a very aggressive tax structure; at worst, it looked like an outright fraud in which Steinhoff was trying to hide assets and liabilities off its balance sheet using a vehicle established and controlled by its own people." His thesis is that Steinhoff always really controlled Capfin in substance, even though it was supposedly sold from Pepkor and found its way to Campion. The fact that Steinhoff stepped in to lend to Capfin when the banks pulled out implied that control existed. "Ben la Grange was Steinhoff's chief financial officer," says Jacks. "I can't imagine a circumstance under which he would not have had to sign off on or at least know about the R500m loan facility granted to Capfin."

Once Jacks thought he'd figured out that Campion Capital was really just an inside job, he went to meet some of Arqaam's clients, urging them to avoid investing in Steinhoff shares or else risk getting caught up in something more serious than just a scrap over a few numbers. Some listened, and sold their shares. It was already the end of November, days before Steinhoff would come tumbling down. "I had begun writing my report detailing what I'd found about Steinhoff and Campion, but we believed that we didn't have enough facts to publish. So instead I went out and met and spoke with every client that would take my calls, laying out what I had found and why I thought it was serious."

Steinhoff had promised to answer his questions about those off-balance sheet companies when they published their 2017 financials in the first week of December. Infamously, that never happened, as Deloitte refused to sign those accounts. The day after Jooste's resignation, Jacks published his report. It was entitled "Steinhoff: Off Balance-Sheet Offsides", with the subheading: "Evidence of Swiss off balance-sheet structure, with multiple layers, highlights potential accounting and tax irregularities".[11] In the report, Jacks said: "Campion Capital and related companies appear to be entities that are, in substance, controlled by Steinhoff and should potentially have been consolidated." The implications were devastating: if Campion had been consolidated into Steinhoff's accounts, dating back to 2014, then this would have radically altered its profits, liabilities and assets. Steinhoff was far, far less profitable than anyone knew.

There is another part to the story. Later, Campion would sell Capfin's "loan administration" and "call centre business" back to Steinhoff. This was a vital part of the con, as it meant Steinhoff could then "repay" the money to Campion that it had spent setting it up. After all, for any proper laundering operation, you need to have money going right around. Steinhoff lends money to Campion to "buy" assets like JD Consumer Finance, which allows it then to claim "repayments" on this loan in its profits. It also then "buys back" companies from Campion later, probably for an inflated amount, which allows it to make all these shady loan balances disappear. "None of this was real money," says one person who has scrutinised these transactions. "There were loans made to these off-balance sheet companies that were never going to be repaid, all to make Steinhoff's accounts look better."

Beneath the lid, the Steinhoff you thought you knew wasn't the real Steinhoff.

* * *

STEINHOFF
INTERNATIONAL HOLDINGS N.V.

Before the December 2017 crash it was a global business empire with about **130 000** employees and **11 000** retail outlets in more than **30** countries

USA
- Mattress Firm

AFRICA
- Pep
- Ackermans
- Tekkie Town
- Shoe City
- Dunns
- John Craig
- Refinery
- Flash
- Powersales
- HiFi Corporation
- Russells
- BUCO
- Bradlows
- Incredible Connection
- Timbercity
- Sleepmasters
- Rochester
- Steinbuild
- Hertz
- Unitrans

UNITED KINGDOM
- Poundland
- PEP&CO
- Harveys
- Bensons for Beds

EUROPE
- Pepco
- Abra
- Emmezeta
- Lipo
- POCO
- Conforama
- Kika-Leiner

AUSTRALIA & NEW ZEALAND
- Best&Less
- Harris Scarfe
- Postie
- OMF
- Plush
- Mozi
- Freedom
- Snooze
- Fantastic Furniture

KEY
- General Merchandise
- Household Goods
- Automotive

Above left: Markus Jooste, second from right, with university friends, circa 1980.

Above right: Jooste, only two years into the job of Steinhoff CEO, in 2002 on the shop floor of one of the firm's furniture stores. *Picture: Gallo Images/Sunday Times/ Raymond Preston.*

Above: Markus Jooste (front row, centre, with beard) with fellow students outside the Wilgenhof residence at Stellenbosch University, circa 1980. Rian du Plessis, later to become Phumelela CEO, is behind Jooste, left with moustache.

Above left: Steinhoff's listing on the Frankfurt Stock Exchange in Germany in 2015. From left: Bruno Steinhoff, Ben la Grange, Danie van der Merwe, Christo Wiese and Poco founder Peter Pohlmann. *Picture: Steinhoff website.*

Above right: The stuffed polar bear, shot 45 years ago in Alaska, in Bruno Steinhoff's office in Westerstede, Germany. *Picture: Rob Rose.*

Sessel "*Gabi*"

Left: The Gabi chair from East Germany that put the early Steinhoff on the map. *Picture courtesy of Bruno Steinhoff.*

Above: Bruno Steinhoff at the company's Frankfurt listing. *Picture: Steinhoff website.*

Above: Markus Jooste leads in Variety Club and jockey Anton Marcus after winning the 2013 Grade 1 L'Ormarins Queen's Plate at Kenilworth Racecourse in Cape Town. *Picture: @hamishNIVENphotography.*

Above: The listing of Steinhoff Retail Africa (STAR) on the JSE in September 2017. From left: Riaan Hanekom, Vusi Khanyile, Ben la Grange, Jayendra Naidoo, Allen Swiegers, Heather Sonn and Markus Jooste. Star changed its name to Pepkor Holdings in 2018. *Picture: Pepkor.*

Top: Celebrating Edict of Nantes' win in the Grade 1 Cape Derby at Kenilworth in 2017. Back, from the left: Brett Crawford, Gwendelynne Macgregor, Bernard Kantor, Derek Brugman, John Koster and Markus Jooste. Front, from left: Michael Jooste, Markus's son, Frankie Dettori and Barry Donnelly. *Picture: @hamishNIVENphotography.*

Bottom left and right: On 13 December 2018, Huffington Post broke a story about Berdine Odendaal, allegedly Jooste's mistress, accompanied by a number of pictures of her from social media. The site reported that she had a number of properties registered in her name at the exclusive Val de Vie estate near Paarl, which is also where Jooste had a palatial home until he sold it in May 2018 for a reported R13m. *Pictures: Facebook.*

Right: Steinhoff ad banners dumped after they were removed from Stellenbosch University's rugby field in January 2018. *Picture: Gallo Images/Bloomberg/ Waldo Swiegers.*

Middle: Steinhoff's AGM in April 2018 in Amsterdam. Supervisory board chairman Heather Sonn talks to Steve Booysen, head of the audit committee. In between is company secretary Ewoud van Gellicum. *Picture: Gallo Images/ Bloomberg/Jasper Juinen.*

The homestead of Markus Jooste in Voëlklip, that previously belonged to the Rupert family. Photo: Edrea du Toit/Rapport

The writing's on the wall...

Although painted over with white paint the very next day, on the night of 27 December 2017 the perimeter wall of a house in Voëlklip belonging to Markus Jooste was spray-painted with 'unflattering' graffiti.

Jooste had earlier resigned as CEO of Steinhoff, after financial irregularities at the multinational furniture retailer surfaced and made headline news.

This luxury homestead where the perimeter wall was defaced, in 10th street, Voëlklip, runs almost an entire street block and used to belong to the Rupert family. According to the Hermanus Police no complaints were reported about the graffiti.

The spray-painted words 'thief' and 'con artist' were painted over the next morning. Photo courtesy of HuffPost SA.

Above left: Former banker GT Ferreira in 2006. Ferreira and the farm workers' trust of his Tokara wine estate lost more than R1bn in the Steinhoff collapse. *Picture: Gallo Image/Business Day/Moshe Sekete.*

Above right: Christo Wiese and Danie van der Merwe (directly behind Wiese) at a parliamentary hearing into Steinhoff in January 2018. Wiese announced in April 2018 that his Titan Group was suing Steinhoff for R59bn related to cash investments made in the company in 2015 and 2016. *Picture: Gallo Images/Netwerk24/Adriaan de Kock.*

Right: From left, Renier van Rooyen – a legendary retailer and long-standing business partner with Christo Wiese in Pep – Wiese and Whitey Basson, the former Shoprite CEO who thwarted plans to move Shoprite into the Steinhoff empire. *Picture courtesy of Johann van Rooyen.*

Opposite bottom: The *Hermanus Times* covers the defacing of the wall surrounding Jooste's home in the seaside town on 11 January 2018. The word "thief" was spray-painted on the wall of the villa Jooste had bought from the Rupert family. The paper also reported that a vacant piece of cliff-top land owned by Jooste had become a tourist attraction. Two onlookers were heard saying "appalling, just appalling" while shaking their heads the day a reporter visited the scene.

Above: Ben la Grange answering questions with his advocate, John Dickerson, by his side in Parliament in August 2018. *Picture: Gallo Images/Foto24.*

Above: Markus Jooste and his team of lawyers in Parliament in September 2018 in what was his first official appearance in public since the company's collapse nine months earlier. *Picture: Gallo Images/Brenton Geach.*

The emergence of Campion, and its influential role as a "cleaner" to disguise the pockmarks in Steinhoff's accounts, formed a critical moment in the Steinhoff story. It suggests that Markus Jooste, who'd been feted as *the* brilliant dealmaker, who'd famously got a half-price deal on Conforama, couldn't let the reality of the numbers speak for themselves.

Part of the Jooste legend was that unlike other entrepreneurs, he avoided the lemons. The truth was, like everyone else, he had a patchy record. On the credit side, there was, of course, Cornick and Conforama – but he'd bought just as many rotten apples, besides JD Group.

Take Homestyle in the UK, which had 440 outlets, partly supplying beds and mattresses, and partly furniture under the Harveys brand. In May 2005, Steinhoff paid £105m (about R1.2bn at the time) to buy 61% of the company, which was listed on the London Stock Exchange. Two years later, it offered to buy the rest, at a price 23.5% above Homestyle's share price at the time. Brokerage JP Morgan described the price paid in 2005 for Homestyle as "demanding, considering that the company appeared to be technically insolvent at the time of the acquisition, if trademarks (R1.5bn) are excluded". It meant that Steinhoff immediately shoved Homestyle trademarks worth R2.5bn onto its balance sheet. What piqued JP Morgan's interest was that Steinhoff "failed to disclose any detail on the nature of the trademarks or from whom they were acquired". When JP Morgan asked about the matter, Jooste's team met them with silence.

But this was the way it was: Steinhoff had been frantically buying companies for more than they were worth, to boost their profits. "It is not clear these investments have added any additional economic value," said JP Morgan at the time. This frenzy cloaked the fact that in some cases, the existing businesses weren't doing that well. Strip out all the purchases, and for the seven years after 2000, Steinhoff's profit growth would have been a pedestrian 8% per year, barely higher than inflation.

Speaking in 2018, Bruno Steinhoff says there was a marked difference from the earlier incarnations of Steinhoff that he created and the company under Jooste. "In my time, there was organic growth. I liked to build things. But in Markus's time, we started to buy lots of things," he says. The acquisition spree hid two central facts: firstly, that the operational business was, in many cases, quite weak, and secondly, that Steinhoff had a pathetically frail balance sheet. The truth was, Steinhoff's assets were hopelessly inflated, and its liabilities understated. On its balance sheet, for example, Steinhoff had €9.1bn in "goodwill" and €7.3bn in "intangible assets" – two airy-fairy categories of assets meant to somehow pin a value to your brands. But putting such an immense value on these intangible assets is like shooting an arrow into the audience at the opening night of a Broadway musical while blindfolded: somebody is always going to get hurt.

* * *

While we shouldn't diminish the role that Siegmar Schmidt, Alan Evans and Jean-Noël Pasquier played, there were a number of other people who were just as instrumental in helping Markus Jooste do what he did. Dirk Schreiber, the de facto head of Steinhoff's European business, obviously deserves an honourable mention. The leaked emails show that Schreiber was instrumental in helping create the deals and documents needed to cook the accounts. Quite why Schreiber helped Jooste is harder to gauge. In a video recording made in 2013 to commemorate Steinhoff's fifteen years as a JSE-listed company, Schreiber speaks of his desire to belong. He describes how, in 2006, when he was consolidating accounts for Siegmar Schmidt, there was "quite a difficult" project they were working on. "Markus Jooste invited us into the team, and allowed me to sit around the table, like 'one of us'. I think that was my key moment. It was where I realised that I [was] becoming part of this team, I was becoming part of the family, and I was getting all this trust and all this freedom to work on the project and to make [it] successful," he said.[12]

But the most mercurial of all Markus Jooste's mysterious confidants was a crusty British businessman named Malcolm King. King, dough-faced, with not much of a discernible chin and famously curt, fancied himself as something of a swashbuckling James Bond.

Though several sources say that King lives in the Cotswolds, in England, in South African company records, he lists his address as being in the tax haven of Jersey – a 45-square metre island off the French coast that has famously loose tax rules. (Alan Evans, the director of Campion, also lists his address as being in Jersey, and there is certainly circumstantial evidence that he and King knew each other well.)

Evidence obtained during a joint project by investigative journalists Ama-Bhungane and the *Financial Mail* suggests that King met Markus Jooste through a mutual friend – someone who has been pulling the levers of corporate South Africa for three decades: Gary Harlow.

Like Jooste, Harlow qualified as a chartered accountant in the early 1980s, and has since been on the boards of 14 public companies. Mostly, he has focused on running a company called Unihold, but many people still know Harlow from his days as a special consultant to the African National Congress (ANC), which became the ruling party, in the early 1990s.

During the mid-1980s, however, Harlow was one of the initial shareholders at Gomma Gomma, alongside Elizabeth Bradley, Markus Jooste and Michael Delport.

King liked to come across as something of a debonair racehorse owner. He, Jooste and someone called Jim Maxwell co-owned two horses – Breedsbreeze, which ran four times, and Rivaliste, which ran twice in the UK in 2010 and 2011.[13]

Rian du Plessis, the former CEO of Phumelela and a family friend of Jooste, says that he first met King in 1999. "We became personal friends in the seventeen years that my family and I lived overseas."[14] King, say those who know him, is a piece of work. He is an avid, furiously keen hunter, and he boasts, according to a Steinhoff insider, that there are only six animals in the world that he hasn't shot. Hunting websites picture him crouching lasciviously over some corpse or other, with captions like "Congratulations to our hunter from the UK Malcolm King with successful completion of the rare hunt for Chartreuse chamois, it was difficult to obtain a licence and a reliable outfitter, a real job was done, which resulted in a fine trophy filled collection".

There are pictures of him standing proudly over the body of a forest hog he killed in Ethiopia in March 2014 (apparently the second-largest ever shot); over the body of an endangered Konya sheep in Turkey's Bozdag mountains; and over an endangered goat-antelope, the Bukharan markhor, in Tajikistan. It tells you most of what you need to know about him.

In South Africa, several news articles have fingered Malcolm King as a convenient popular front for Markus Jooste, though he furiously denies this. King evidently finds the questions over his murky relationship hard to stomach. When I tracked down his cellphone number and called him in the UK, he was startled. "Who's that . . . no, no," he said, before killing the call.

After I emailed him, King then got a lawyer from Leeds in the UK, Matthew Howarth, to send a message threatening legal action should any reference to him be defamatory or misleading.

King ignored most of the questions sent to him, saying, "We have no further comment to make regarding his relationship with Mr Jooste." King said he was "not prepared to discuss relationships which are private and confidential".

This is unfortunate for him, since he ended up being the public face of the consortium that bought the wine farm Lanzerac from Christo Wiese in 2011, in a sale first proposed and apparently put together by Markus Jooste himself. Even though Wiese says it was Jooste who approached him to buy the farm, you won't find Markus's fingerprints anywhere near Lanzerac. Instead, the only two directors of Lanzerac Estate Investments since 2012 are Malcolm King and Paula King. One of the former directors of Lanzerac says he understood that "Malcolm King owns it" – but wasn't sure if Jooste was involved. According to King, speaking through his lawyer, the wine farm "was purchased by Pavilion Capital Investments" and Jooste "does not have an interest in Lanzerac Estates". But he won't say anything more: "the details of the purchase of Lanzerac are subject to contractual confidentiality". If this is so, it doesn't explain why Jooste would have approached Wiese about the deal, and implied he was part of it.

Interestingly, court papers show that Jooste's company Mayfair Speculators had lent money to Lanzerac. Equally curious is the fact that it was King's company Coy's Properties that owned the luxury pad at the Bantry in Cape Town, where Jooste's alleged mistress, Berdine Odendaal, lived. It seems that in that case, too, King helped ensure Markus's fingerprints were nowhere near the scene of the crime. Asked why he owned that property, whether he charged Berdine Odendaal a market-related rental, and why he chose to sell the apartment after Odendaal's relationship with Jooste was first outed, King denied this had anything to do with Jooste. "Coy's Properties is owned by Pavilion Capital Investments. The property was sold and achieved its market value at a time of political uncertainty in South Africa." Perhaps. Yet, it is odd that he thinks South Africa suddenly became so much more "politically uncertain" months *after* the kleptocratic administration of Jacob Zuma was expelled and replaced with the far more benign Cyril Ramaphosa.

King appears to have not only a personal relationship with Jooste (which he is clearly skittish about discussing), but also a commercial relationship with Steinhoff. This is because documents show that the company he chairs in the UK, Formal Investments, is implicated in other odd deals involving Steinhoff. Formal Investments is registered at Palm Grove House in Tortola in the British Virgin Islands, though it operates from a building called Freedom House in Cheltenham in the UK. Interestingly, Steinhoff's UK business is located in Freedom House too. Formal Investments has three directors: Malcolm King, his son Nicholas King, and a South African named Robert Boschoff. Its purpose is "property investment", apparently. So whose properties does Formal manage? Yes: Steinhoff's. Since 2014, Steinhoff has owned a company called Alvaglen Estates, which is registered in the Bahamas – a Caribbean island renowned as a tax haven. However, two of Alvaglen's warehouses are managed by King's Formal Investments, according to Bloomberg.[15] It's unclear how many other properties Formal manages. After Bloomberg reporters asked questions of Formal, it snatched the portfolio off its website. But its accounts show it made just £1,043,099 in revenue for the year to June 2017, and just £26,794 in profit. Asked about Formal's relationship to Steinhoff, King said it was "covered by contractual confidentiality agreements" and so he would make no comment.

Alvaglen, as it happens, is critical to understanding the links between Markus Jooste, Alan Evans and Malcolm King. It is this property company, set up in 1999, that provides perhaps the only nexus that ties them all together.

Unluckily for Evans and King, the Panamanian law firm called Mossack Fonseca managed their tax affairs for years. But in 2016, 11.5 million files from Mossack Fonseca leaked out, laying bare the minutiae of tax dealings at more than 214,000 companies, including those belonging to Evans and King. Thanks to the Panama Papers, we now have a paper trail that shows how Alvaglen was flipped between Evans, Steinhoff and King in a breathtaking whirl of transactions – most likely involving an increase in its value every time. The trail of transactions suggests that the confusing flipping of assets was designed to avoid tracing the beneficial owners, through an almost impossible-to-follow chain. Nonetheless, let's take a bash. Between 2001 and 2004, Alvaglen's shares were owned by Evans's Warren Trustees (yes, the same body that got into such trouble in Poland). Then, on 28 June 2004, Warren sold Alvaglen to Steinhoff. Steinhoff then held the stake in Alvaglen for five years, until 11 November 2009, when it sold it to a company called MB Nominees, registered at Alan Evans's address in Geneva, Switzerland, which held it for five years. (Significantly, Evans still appears as a director until 2007 – during Steinhoff's time as an owner.)

In 2014, the washing machine was switched to spin. On 17 January, MB Nominees sold Alvaglen to a company called Wanchai Property, which was registered at King's Formal Investments. Just four days later, on 21 January, Wanchai flipped Alvaglen to two other companies, Pavilion (King's company) and M&D Holdings (also registered at King's Formal Investments). Then, just four days later, on 25 January 2014, Steinhoff bought Alvaglen back from King's companies.

In other words, Alvaglen swapped owners three times in just eight days. It's a dizzying whirlwind. What could be the point of it?

Asked about the reasoning for the Alvaglen transactions, King's only response was: "It is denied . . . that ownership of Alvaglen was swapped three times in eight days." He doesn't explain why the Panama Papers say otherwise. Nor does he say what his company paid Evans's MB Nominees for Alvaglen, or what Steinhoff paid him for Alvaglen just days later.

Conspicuously, he does not comment on the view of one expert I spoke to who said the point of this whirlwind of property transfers was to "avoid detection, and so that in all likelihood the properties can be revalued upwards at each turn, which will ultimately boosts Steinhoff's assets". That expert, who is close to Steinhoff, points out that when Steinhoff bought back properties, it most likely did so at "vastly inflated values, which means those in the middle make plenty of money". It's an interesting view, since the middlemen in the Alvaglen transaction were Evans and King. Just after Steinhoff bought Alvaglen, its property assets (held through its property arm Hemisphere) went through the roof. Hemisphere's accounts, which have been obtained from the Dutch company's office, show that in 2014 Hemisphere's value soars from €599m to €2.058bn. This suggests Steinhoff may have paid more than €1.4bn to King's company to buy Alvaglen back.

The Dutch newspaper *Het Financieele Dagblad* reported on how Alvaglen was shifted between various companies all within eight days in 2014. Jan van Koningsveld, director of the Offshore Knowledge Centre, described those machinations as "striking". "Because of these disguised structures, nobody can find out who the actual shareholders are."[16]

It's now clear that Hemisphere's (and, probably, Alvaglen's) portfolios had been vastly overvalued. Whereas before its collapse, Steinhoff claimed it had €2.2bn in properties, this was slashed by half, to just €1.1bn. It was final crushing evidence that the values of Steinhoff's properties had been artificially inflated way beyond what was reasonable. One interpretation is that this could have been done to allegedly give the sellers an immense kickback, which could then be later shared.

King, of course, won't discuss how instrumental Alvaglen was in Hemisphere's obscene overvaluation. Instead, at every turn, he claims all details are "confidential" and his relationships "private". Of course, many people know all about Malcolm King's relationship with Jooste. One Steinhoff insider describes visiting his sprawling estate in the Cotswolds, after Steinhoff's 2015 World Cup junket to London. So, it was no immense surprise when King's company Pavilion Capital lodged a R420m claim against

Jooste's company Mayfair Speculators. This is unequivocal evidence of a mysterious flow of money between Jooste and King – which King won't explain. Quite remarkably, King "subordinated" his claim to Mayfair, which meant that he agreed that all other creditors would be paid first. Consequently, King would only get around 39c for every R1 he was owed – losing 60%. "It made absolutely no economic sense for him to do that," says one of the creditors. "I don't understand it – perhaps he just didn't want his claim to be looked at too carefully – who knows?"

What's clear is that King's dealings with Jooste go far deeper than anyone suspected. This might explain King's insistence that all his dealings with Jooste are "private and confidential". Of course, they're unlikely to remain that way forever. After all, a cynic might suggest, in a conspiratorial whisper, that King's companies could have been "repaying" Jooste part of the profits made from deals involving Steinhoff. If so, it wouldn't be the first time that Jooste made a mountain of cash through a secret side-deal involving Steinhoff.

The Rise and Fall of Christo Wiese

―――――

"In some ways, I'm quite lucky to have lost only R59bn. If this thing had happened just one year later, I would have lost *everything*." These are the words of Christo Wiese – the man who describes himself as a "failed lawyer", but who has been described by others as South Africa's answer to Walmart founder Sam Walton or celebrity investor Warren Buffett, or even as the real-life counterpart of JR Ewing, the scheming oil baron in the soapie *Dallas*.

Since the early 1980s, Wiese has been *the* ace dealmaker of corporate South Africa, wresting control of some of the finest brands in South Africa. By 2015, his portfolio included cash retailer Pep, Africa's largest supermarket chain, Shoprite, and gym chain Virgin Active as well as a trolley of London high street retailers.

That brain-numbing R59bn he lost in Steinhoff was about half his fortune. It's more money than all but a handful of people on the globe stand any prospect of ever amassing, let alone seeing vanish. And yet, it could have been worse.

Steinhoff's dénouement happened at the eleventh hour of an endgame that Wiese had been planning for four years. The way it was meant to end was that Steinhoff would have controlled the STAR African retail business, which would have been made up of Pep, the JD Group and, the biggest prize of all, Shoprite. These are the cream of African retailing, clocking up more than R200bn in sales every year. Combined, they would have formed the most powerful conglomerate ever to operate on the continent. And the man destined to pull the strings at the apex of this vast retail empire would have been Christo Wiese.

By December 2017, this plan was about 90% complete. "It was almost done – all of it," says Wiese, speaking in his office in the industrial grey of Parow, in Cape Town.[1]

The Christo Wiese of today is still sprightly, sharp enough to anticipate the end point of any line of questioning, and relaxed enough to lapse into an amusing anecdote about a friend on a whim. He's 77 years old, but about ten of those years have been added since December 2017.

"Steinhoff controlled Pep, it controlled the other retail businesses and Shoprite was already halfway into the structure too. The Public Investment Corporation and I had agreed to put all our shares in Shoprite into STAR, and in return I would have got shares in Steinhoff." Had that actually happened, Wiese's fortune, which had stacked up into a considerable heap after his five decades in business, would have all but vanished. Had he got shares in Steinhoff for his stake in Shoprite, he would have lost the jewel in his crown. Had Jooste not been exposed when he was, but rather a few months later, Wiese would, effectively, have been *done*. It's a poignant illustration of how the fate of such immense fortunes can hang by an exquisitely delicate thread, the finest margin separating safety and utter devastation.

To understand how this happened, and what Christo Wiese nearly lost, it helps to start right at the beginning – to start in the desert.

*   *   *

Christo Wiese's ascendancy begins in the small town of Upington on 10 September 1941. Upington, even then, was in the middle of nowhere – about 800 kilometres from either Johannesburg or Cape Town. Though you might not notice, because of the Orange River, which flows through the town to create a mirage of fertility, Upington is the gateway to the vast Kalahari Desert. This is the desert memorably described by Laurens van der Post, the great dreamer-philosopher and embellisher, as "the great wasteland". And Upington is the green oasis on the fringe of that desert.

While Wiese remembers his early years in Upington as privileged, living as he did in a good home with a good car, the town never lost its flavour as a semi-desert frontier settlement. He grew up with the rhythm of nature in his ears. You can see echoes of that sensibility in Wiese's character today. For example, he still owns a private game reserve in the Kalahari, still goes hunting as he did when he was young, and his choice of business ventures – like diamond mining – evokes that rustic start.

When he was young, his father Stoffel ran a Kalahari sheep and cattle farm and a garage; his mother managed a florist and a bridal shop. Their example bred an early instinct for retail. Christo was the family's only son and so, as he'll admit, a little spoilt.

Initially, Christo went to school in Upington, but for the final two years he went to boarding school at Paarl Boys' High, about an hour away from Cape Town. There's a revealing anecdote about his early entrepreneurial instinct. During his school days, a travelling carnival came to town. There was a game where you'd roll a ball – either a blue, white or red ball – and if it landed on the colour you picked, you'd win. Christo studied the game, collected his friends' pocket money, then bet on it. He lost badly. "I was taught a valuable lesson – you can't beat the house. You can imagine how popular I was. All our pocket money was gone for the term," he says.

After school, he went on to study law, attracted by the theatrics of it, by the romantic notion that a logical argument could carry the day. Surprisingly, his first few years at university were not at Stellenbosch, the de facto choice for promising Afrikaner students in those days. Wiese says this was because his father was a *Bloedsap*, an Afrikaner loyal to the United Party of Jan Smuts, and despised the prevailing ethos of the National Party, which had beaten the more centrist United Party in 1948 and immediately introduced apartheid. "My dad held a very strong view that good United Party kids who went to Stellenbosch became Nats, and he wouldn't have that. So for my first year, I went to Cape Town University."[2]

However, Wiese says his "less than illustrious academic record" led to his return to Upington with "the firm conviction that I was not cut out for academics – I wanted to be a businessman". So Stoffel Wiese tried to help him. He bought a radiator repair business, which he let Wiese have a bash at running. But it proved too hot a prospect. "Radiators were repaired with carbide, which is a very hot thing. And my dad bought this little building in Upington which, I swear to you, was the only building in Upington where the sun was shining 24 hours per day. That made me think that studying was not such a bad idea," he told business journalist Bruce Whitfield.

So he had another crack at law – this time at Stellenbosch, where he did finally get his degree. But it seems Stoffel's initial insistence that his son study at UCT paid ideological dividends, for Wiese was one of only a few students who campaigned against apartheid on the Stellenbosch campus in the mid-1960s.

And, then, a moment of serendipity. But for a chance discussion on one of his student vacations back home from Stellenbosch, his life might have gone in another direction entirely. Across the road from his father's garage in Upington was another garage, owned by a friend. One morning, Wiese walked over to chat to him, and they soon got talking about someone who'd been married to Wiese's cousin Alice for a few years by then – a man named Renier van Rooyen. Renier is going places, Wiese's friend said. He's got five clothing stores right now, but he's looking for investors. He wants to go national.

That night, Wiese brought the subject up with his father. Perhaps we should consider putting some money into Renier's venture, he said. The old man took the bait. He sold his other businesses, and put all of his money into this new clothing company. Renier also struck a deal with Stoffel: that once Christo finished university with a law degree, he must come join the new company. If it was still around, that was.

*   *   *

Renier van Rooyen is the forgotten colossus of South African business. His isn't a name that springs to mind when you consider the outstanding characters in the development of the country's modern economy. He's not, for example, a household name in the same way that you'd consider Anglo American's Ernest Oppenheimer, Liberty's Donald Gordon or, more recently,

Discovery's Adrian Gore or African Rainbow Minerals' Patrice Motsepe. Yet without Van Rooyen, you could argue that the complexion of modern South African retail would be entirely different. For one thing, we wouldn't have had Shoprite as we know it today, and we certainly wouldn't have had Steinhoff.

Van Rooyen was born in 1931 in Kenhardt, about an hour away from Upington. He was the child of a poor livestock speculator who died when he was young. He grew up as the archetypal scrappy frontier kid, trying his hand at various jobs, including a part-time gig as a messenger for the court in Upington.[3] A compelling account of his early years, written by Renier's son Johann, would record that this job of tallying the possessions of people defaulting on debt gave him critical insight into the dangers of buying on credit.

"Not only were people being enticed by easy credit to buy things that they could probably not afford, but in most cases, companies that were forced to issue debt summonses lost most of the money owed to them," wrote Johann.[4]

So, in 1955 Van Rooyen opened "The Bargain Shop". It was nothing more than an unpretentious house with whitewashed walls, jimmied into a shopfront. There was no fancy signage. What there was, however, was plenty of demand for the clothes he was selling, at prices far lower than in the more conventional shops in town. Soon, Van Rooyen opened BG Bazaars (legend has it the initials BG probably stood for *bakgat* – a shorthand description of something excellent) and that soared too.

In 1965, Van Rooyen got together a small group of investors to take his stores countrywide. Mostly, the people who backed him were family and friends, including his sister Baba, his brother Gert and Stoffel Wiese. The name chosen for the new venture was picked from a shortlist of ten – including Van's, Up's, Ric's, Ren's, NW and Pep. Renier van Rooyen settled on the last option. The name Pep, his son would record, instantly captivated him: "although it did not really have an intrinsic meaning it corresponded with his own boundless energy and enthusiasm".

The first Pep store was converted from a BG Bazaars Store, and opened in De Aar – another remote town in the Northern Cape about 400 kilometres south of Upington, at the junction of the railway line between Kimberley and Cape Town. In December 1965, two new Pep branches opened, in Postmasburg and Kimberley.

Pep became an unlikely sensation. Newspapers of the day printed pictures of long queues outside the Kimberley branch for the opening – with women standing under umbrellas and sun hats to shield themselves from the heat. Word of Pep's opening specials began to spread to other towns: men's trousers and ladies' shoes going for 99c apiece, baby shoes for 5c each, and handkerchiefs for 1c. Pep's Bloemfontein debut, for example, would appear to have been the rural South African equivalent of a modern-day Black Friday sale in a Florida mall: when a throng of four thousand overenthusiastic shoppers broke the glass doors, fifteen policemen were called in to deal with the stampede.

In 1966, Pep realised it couldn't choreograph this new venture from Upington. So Renier, Alice, their three kids and the family German shepherd climbed into the family car, and hit the long dirt road to Cape Town. They settled in Bellville, one of Cape Town's northern suburbs. Pep soon opened up a warehouse in Woodstock, before shifting to Kuilsrivier soon afterwards.

Pictures from those years show Van Rooyen, earnest eyes sparkling with intent, standing alongside a slim and dark-haired Wiese, often impeccably dressed in a shiny suit.

Wiese slotted easily into Pep's motley crew from Upington, which included a deep-sea diver, a train driver, a teacher and a carpenter. As second-in-charge to Van Rooyen during the early years, the young Wiese was tasked with identifying new properties for Pep's expansion. This was no small responsibility. By February 1968, Pep had 18 stores, and was making R1.6m in sales; by 1969, it had 58 stores and was clocking up sales of R2.9m. Not even a fire, which destroyed more than R1m (about R100m in today's terms) in stock at the Kuilsrivier warehouse in 1971, could hold the firm back.

As luck would have it, that fire happened just three days after a promising accountant had started at Pep as its financial director – a fresh-off-the-boat 25-year-old Whitey Basson.

Recalling that event today, Basson says: "It was about 6 pm, and I was sitting in the office with Tom Ball when we noticed smoke coming through the roof."[5] They rushed down to the warehouse, where they saw flames burning their way through the stock. "I didn't sleep that night at all. My wife was coming over, bringing sandwiches to all of us at the warehouse who were battling to save whatever we could." The next morning, not having slept a wink, Basson got in his car and travelled to nearby Bellville, scouting out alternative premises. By midday, he'd signed a lease on a new warehouse, and by 3 pm deliveries for Pep were already streaming into the new warehouse.

This story encapsulates why Renier van Rooyen rated Basson so highly. During the mid-1970s, Basson effectively ran Pep. He had Renier van Rooyen's power of attorney, and nothing happened at the company without Basson's say-so. "Renier had worked himself into the ground by that stage," says Basson.

Basson, who would become an essential player in the Pepkor story, had been close to Wiese at Stellenbosch University. Their political inclinations were similar, in part because Basson was also part of a *Bloedsap* family, his father Jack Basson having been a United Party politician.

Whitey Basson had studied accounting, did his articles at Ernst & Young, and then began working at PwC. At PwC, he ended up auditing Pep's accounts, where Renier first spotted him. Today, Whitey Basson describes Renier van Rooyen as the "finest retailer I've ever worked with". "He and Len Shawzin from Truworths were the only retailers I know who could open a box of trousers and say, this one you can sell for R5.99, this one you can sell for R7.99, and these are awful, give these ones away. They could put a price on something without even looking at the cost price. They knew their products – and you don't get that often."[6]

Van Rooyen was a stickler for methodical planning. He'd make extensive notes for his staff all the time. For example, there are notes to staff in the early 1970s which record instructions like "Customers are always right. Never make use of derogatory [racial] comments". Untypically for the era, he insisted that black and white customers use the same dressing rooms, despite what his son describes as "considerable opposition".

Then, in 1972, Pep listed on the Johannesburg Stock Exchange at R2.75 a share. In those days, brokers traded on the floor of the JSE, and the demand for Pep shares led to chaotic scenes, according to *Die Transvaler* newspaper. Pep's shares ended the day at R3.30.[7]

The brochure that accompanied the listing spelt out Pep's philosophy in a line: "We do not sell cheap goods – we sell goods cheaply." As Van Rooyen put it: "We don't sell rubbish: at a given price our wares are of a good quality, a fact realized by our customers. Poor people are not stupid – they cannot afford to be."

Things worked out pretty well for those traders who'd scrambled to get Pep's shares on that first day. In its first year as a public listed company, its before-tax profit doubled to R1.6m, on sales of R34m. The number of stores grew from 163 to 222.

Then Wiese decided he wanted to give the law profession a bash. So, a year after the listing, he left Pep. For one thing, it was because he figured Pep had "lost part of its magic as a family business" after it became a public company. For another, it was because he'd just got married to Caro Basson, and wanted the more predictable hours he'd get by practising at the Cape Bar – arriving home before sundown every day, rather than just a few days a month.

There was another reason, though. "Renier was the number one guy," he says. "I would not have had it any other way – he was a better number one than I would have been. But I also knew that I wasn't really cut out to be a number two man."[8]

Before Caro agreed to marry Christo, however, she laid down some conditions: there are two things you must never do, she said – never go into politics, and never make movies. There was a reason for this: her father Japie Basson had been a renowned maverick politician, who'd been booted out of the National Party, and drifted through the various incarnations of white opposition politics, before helping form the Progressive Federal Party (PFP). But in 1977 Wiese stood, unsuccessfully, as a PFP candidate in the country's national elections. He explains that the PFP's leader, Frederik van Zyl Slabbert, called him one day with the proposal when he was in London. "He asked, 'Would you consider being a candidate in Stellenbosch?' I said I'd think about it, so I called my wife, and she said, 'No, that's fine.' Because she knew that as a PFP candidate in Stellenbosch, I stood no chance."

In the end, Wiese contested the seat in Simonstown, but lost. Later, however, Wiese broke with the PFP, when he served on the State President's economic advisory council, the president being the much-despised *Groot Krokodil*, PW Botha.

During his sabbatical from Pep, Wiese bought a diamond mining company called Octha Diamonds, which mined for alluvial gems on the banks of the Orange River in the Richtersveld, for several million rand. It was, in many ways, a return to the Kalahari. It was at Octha that he first encountered Markus Jooste as an articled clerk working for accounting firm Greenwoods in the early 1980s.

Though he remained a non-executive director of Pep, working part-time while running the diamond company, the years between 1973 and 1981 represented a break from the expanding clothing company.

In the years Wiese was away, Pep changed its spots. The metamorphosis happened thanks to a phone call that Whitey Basson received, sometime in 1979, from a man called Martin Shane. Shane had heard on the grapevine that Basson was thinking of leaving the clothing industry and was looking to get into the food business. At the time, Shane was acting as an intermediary for a small, eight-store grocery chain in the Western Cape called Shoprite, whose existing family owners were squabbling with each other. He reckoned Whitey, in his personal capacity, might fancy taking it over.

"I'd wanted to leave Pep at the time and try something different," says Basson. "So I'd travelled to Germany, I'd travelled to Austria to see what they were doing with food, because that's what I was keen to try. Then Martin called me about Shoprite."

Basson went to speak to Van Rooyen about the proposal. He loved the idea – let's start a proper food division, he said. So Van Rooyen struck a deal with Shoprite's owners: Pep would buy it for R1.9m (though the grocery chain had R1m in the bank, so the price was effectively only R900,000).

Renier van Rooyen told Whitey to take himself and five guys to Shoprite's factory office in Lansdowne, in the southern suburbs of Cape Town, and do what had to be done to fix it. "It was an old family business at the time," says Basson. "So we arrived and had to rebuild it virtually from scratch. We had to redo the shelves, we had to buy typewriters, everything."

Analysts thought it a terrible idea. There was no way the tiny Shoprite chain could compete with the grocery giants like Pick n Pay and OK Bazaars, they said. "If Renier had listened to the analysts, he would never have bought Shoprite," said Wiese later, in an interview with *Succeed* magazine in 1999. But Shoprite was to prove perhaps Van Rooyen's savviest move. In its first year under Whitey Basson's brawny arm, the scrappy but inconsequential Shoprite made just R13m in sales and profit of R400,000. But by 2018, it was the Muhammad Ali of local retail, with sales of more than R140bn, and profit of R5.4bn.

Soon, the minnow was eyeing the whales. First, in 1992, it swallowed the larger food chain, Checkers. Then, in 1997, it bought its larger rival, OK Bazaars, for the grand sum of R1 – a chain of 319 stores which, under the stewardship of SA Breweries, had managed to burn R185m in three years. Within nine months, Basson had found R200m in savings – partly by integrating advertising departments and getting things done faster with fewer people. It was the making of Whitey's formidable reputation.

* * *

Then in 1982, for no evident reason, Renier van Rooyen walked away from it all. At the age of 51, the premier retailer of his era told his friends he was simply tired, and was worried that he'd lose interest in the business. "I have a garden, and I never get into it; I have a yacht, and never get on to it," he told the *Financial Mail* at the time. It meant that Christo Wiese returned as chairman, the top position at Pep. Van Rooyen sold two-thirds of his shares to Wiese for R7m – at R12 apiece.

At his leaving party at Cape Town's Mount Nelson, Van Rooyen gushed that he was "handing over to Christo, who is not only my close friend, but a man who will make a wonderful chairman". Wiese, for his part, said Pep would be run the same way as it had been for decades. "Although there are certain differences in style between us, there is no difference at all when it comes to our business philosophy," he told the *Sunday Times*. Wiese pledged to run the companies along the lines of Renier's five principles of building a business – faith, hard work, enthusiasm, compassion and positive thinking. "We all know the world has problems and challenges, but if you don't get up in the morning focusing on the positives, then life must be hell," he said. The Christmas edition of the in-house *Pep News* of 1981 introduced the new top dog, Wiese, fresh-faced in a blue suit with an unruly mop of brown hair laying siege to his ears.

But while it all went well for some years, things took a nasty turn in 1985 on the day that PW Botha scowled through his "Rubicon" speech. The rand went into freefall when it became clear the country's tunnel-vision leaders were resistant to change and reform. Interest rates vaulted overnight, which meant that Pep's debt of R142m, which had been raised to give the retailer a deep enough wallet to build new stores, became cripplingly expensive. "We lost an awful lot of money because we had converted our rand loans to dollar loans, and of course when the rand collapsed, a lot of people were wiped out," said Wiese years later. "We lost R90m. In 1986 that was a lot of money. I went to London and I managed to buy a currency option, which in those days was completely unheard of. That helped us to stem the worst of potential losses."

Wiese had no choice: he had to overhaul Pep. So, first, he listed Shoprite on the JSE, selling 15% of it in the process. Then, he set about selling all Pep's peripheral businesses, including some of the factories. These moves staunched the bleeding. One year later, the debt had gone entirely, and Pep had R100m in cash in the bank. It was, Wiese said, his most challenging time in business – before Steinhoff, that is.

Over the next decade, Wiese reshaped Pep into a multinational conglomerate. Shoprite was obviously doing fantastically well, gobbling Pick n Pay's market share with all the abandon of a sugar glutton at a cruise ship buffet, but Pepkor had also bought retailers overseas – Brown & Jackson in the UK and the 84-store chain Best & Less in Australia, for which it paid R360m. All this meant that by the turn of the century, the business started by Renier van Rooyen in a small, rambling shop in De Aar, which had made sales of just R102,000 in its first year in 1965, earned R27.7bn in sales and R480m in operating profit in 2000. It had more than 2,700 stores. Wiese, standing triumphantly at the podium that year, declared it "the best results in Pepkor's history".

It was so big, in fact, that Wiese decided to break up the conglomerate. So, Pepkor handed its shares in Shoprite to its individual shareholders (cutting the maternal strings to Pepkor), and created another separate company to hold the UK Brown & Jackson business, called Tradehold. Pep had gone back to its roots as a company focused on "cash value clothing" for low-income customers, with three arms: Pep, Ackermans and Best & Less. It was simple, uncluttered, and it was a recipe that worked.

It worked so well, in fact, that in October 2003 private equity company Brait swooped in with an offer to buy Pep entirely for R2.1bn, in conjunction with Christo Wiese. This would mean that after 31 years as a publicly listed company, Pep would be taken off the stock exchange. Shareholders quibbled, arguing that the offer was far too little for a quality asset. But their cries were like whispers in a concert hall. Wiese called all the shots – though he owned just 21.3% of Pepkor, he held nearly half the voting rights.

After Wiese was prevented from voting on the deal (the takeover panel ruled, fairly, that he wasn't independent), Brait raised their offer by 20% to R2.6bn. It was just enough in the end: 70.8% of shareholders voted to accept it, and Pep went private. There Pepkor stayed, almost anonymous, for a decade. Wiese, meanwhile, became even more powerful.

* * *

During those early years of the new century, everything Wiese touched turned to gold. He became the most powerful businessman in the country. The day before Steinhoff cratered, Wiese's personal fortune stood at around R100bn – if you believe the various rich lists published every year. He had shares in Steinhoff, STAR, Invicta, Brait and Pallinghurst. Wiese would later joke that he had no idea whether those "rich lists" were correct about him, recalling the words of Nelson Bunker Hunt, who, for a spell, was the richest person on the globe thanks to his investment in silver. "People who know how much they're worth aren't usually worth that much," said Hunt.

To outsiders, it appeared that money, gathering lots of it, had become Wiese's *raison d'être*. The accumulation of money, they believed, was everything to him. Asked what his barometer of success was by *Business Times* journalist Adele Shevel, Wiese said it was about more than building a thriving business. "I know people who achieved in business, but are desperately unhappy people," he said.

But, Shevel asked, would you truly consider yourself successful if you hadn't made a lot of money and built companies?

"I would have to say no to that question, because of the prevailing culture in the world in which we live," he says. "Often you see someone who has achieved very little materially but is often happier. I sometimes look at people who lead very simple lives but have come to terms with certain things."

It didn't help that Christo Wiese put in place a confusing jumble of tax structures, shifting money around between various trusts in a dizzying asset shuffle. Then in April 2009, Wiese was stopped at London's Heathrow Airport with £674,920 in cash in his bags, on a flight from London to Luxembourg.

Did you declare this money? the customs official asked.

No, because I don't *have* to declare it, Wiese replied. If you're travelling within the EU, you don't have to declare any of it, and last time I checked, Luxembourg was in the EU.

The British customs officials confiscated the money. But Wiese went to court and got every penny back. In court, his lawyer said: "The amount of money was consistent with Dr Wiese's stated wealth, representing less than two weeks' income and a minute fraction of his assets." He explained that the cash came from diamond deals in the 1980s that he'd kept in a safe deposit box at a bank in London because of the restrictions on foreign exchange at the time in South Africa.

Many felt that Wiese's sole motivation, especially in the last few years before Steinhoff's collapse, was just to get money out of South Africa. One Steinhoff insider says that Jooste had sensed Wiese's desire to externalise money outside South Africa, and ruthlessly exploited this. "Everything was about getting his money out," he said. "If Markus could dress up a deal in these terms, that it would allow him to externalise funds, he knew the odds of Christo asking too many critical questions was low."

If there's one criticism that infuriates Wiese, it is this. "By the time I did the Pepkor deal, I already had probably about 30% of my assets abroad. That was more than enough, so it certainly was not a driving force for the deals," he says. Doing deals overseas happened because his South African retail businesses had become too large, so if he'd tried to buy anything else, the competition authorities would probably have vetoed it. "There's this thing people often say, that Markus Jooste 'caught me' because of my desire to move assets overseas. That's nonsense. All I wanted to do was house all my assets under one umbrella. I had more than enough overseas."

Over the years, Wiese watched the bottom line ruthlessly. He was not, unlike many of his peers, someone who'd cling onto an investment for sentimental reasons. "Anyone who says something is never for sale is a fool or a liar or both. You can't make a categorical statement about selling businesses," he said in 2014. "I certainly won't sell a rand for 100c, but will be happy to sit down with someone who offers me 300c for a rand." It was a philosophy that made him fantastically wealthy, and the envy of many.

Wiese tells this great story – he communicates frequently in anecdotes – about Whitey Basson's son Cornell. The way it goes is that Cornell Basson was working in another company, and his boss called him in, and asked him: Does your dad ever talk to you about business? What does he say?

So, Whitey's son replies: "He told me you must just watch Oom Christo – he's never worked a day in his life, and he hasn't done too badly."

* * *

Someone else who'd had a hawk's eye trained on everything Christo Wiese did was Markus Jooste. From today's vantage point, it seems as if Jooste groomed Wiese, realising what sort of gravitas the country's largest investor could bring to his business. It was a slow dance.

In 2006 Wiese was invited to Steinhoff's financial results presentation at the Mount Nelson Hotel. "I was curious, so I went," says Wiese. "I got on very well with them, as it turns out, so over the next few years, they invited me to go hunting with them in England and Spain. I got to know them all on a personal level." The personalities chimed: Bruno, Weise and Jooste loved to hunt; they loved to lego together businesses; and they all had retail in their blood.

Not many people know this, but it was during these years that Jooste first made a play for Shoprite. This was in 2009 – more than two years before Wiese owned a single share in Steinhoff. At that time, Markus met Christo and suggested they combine Shoprite and Steinhoff. But not only had Craig Butters just warned him off Jooste, but Wiese wasn't sold on the idea. "I backed off from that deal," says Weise today. "This wasn't because of anything Craig Butters had told me, but because I thought the debt levels in Steinhoff were too high. I said to Jooste: at this stage of my life, I don't want this. Shoprite has hardly any debt, so this just doesn't suit me." Jooste would have to wait.

The story illustrates, again, just how valuable an asset Shoprite really was. At one stage, Rob Walton, son of Sam Walton, who'd built the world's largest retailer, Walmart, even subtly hinted to Wiese that he might fancy buying Shoprite. Wiese politely declined. Asked why he wouldn't sell, Wiese's answer was: "Why would I?"

Jooste's next opportunity came in 2011. At that time, Wiese was look-ing to sell Lanzerac, the wine estate that he'd bought in 1991 (from the South African Reserve Bank) for just R9m. Lanzerac was a mess when Wiese took it over. The hotel on the property had lost its star grading, and it was struggling for tourists. So Wiese overhauled it, rebuilt the hotel, replanted the vines, and built a modern cellar. But Lanzerac wasn't Wiese's only wine farm. In 1999 he paid R100m for the Lourensford wine estate, which he bought from canning family scion David Gant. (Gant, as you'll remember, had bought Markus Jooste's first company.)

Explaining his decision to shed Lanzerac, Wiese says: "I'd been building up Lourensford, and my children aren't really interested in wine estates. I mentioned this to Jooste, and he came to me and said, 'Look, I'm putting together a consortium, and we'll buy Lanzerac from you.'"

It's an interesting revelation since the only public announcement at the time was that Lanzerac had been sold to a "foreign consortium". There was no mention made that Markus Jooste was pulling the strings from off stage.

Publicly, at least, the shadowy, Jersey-based businessman and racehorse owner Malcolm King was the face of this consortium. Jooste's fingerprints are nowhere. Instead, the only two directors of Lanzerac Estate Investments, since 2012, were King and his daughter Paula.

However, there was a catch to the Lanzerac deal: Jooste's consortium wanted to pay using Steinhoff shares. Wiese asked them why. "They had some fancy explanation for it – but I looked at it and did some research on the Steinhoff share. It was a highly liquid share, so I could have sold it if things turned bad. It suited me fine," he says.

Then Jooste came to him with another scheme. Look, he told Wiese, I know you have a lot of shares in PSG. Steinhoff is already a large shareholder in PSG, but we want to be the biggest shareholder – so will you swap your PSG shares too for shares in Steinhoff?

"Markus told me that he would be swapping his own 20m shares in PSG into Steinhoff. So I figured, shit, if *he's* doing that with his own shares, he must be *really* confident in Steinhoff's future. Why wouldn't I do the same?"

Jooste's decision to swap his own PSG shares into Steinhoff reassured Wiese. "Markus invested his own money, in front of me, into Steinhoff. If he hadn't done that, I probably would have kept my PSG shares, and not have got involved in Steinhoff at all," he says.

So, Wiese took possession of 42.7m shares in Steinhoff, worth R1.06bn at that stage. While it still put him far behind Bruno Steinhoff (with his 171.9m shares, or nearly 10% of the company), it gave Wiese 2.4% of Steinhoff. It's what's known as a nice start. To cement the relationship, Wiese became a non-executive director of Steinhoff in March 2013.

Arguably, this was Jooste's pretext all along: if he could convince the country's wealthiest entrepreneur to hop on board the Steinhoff steam engine, the company would gain the esteem it had craved for years. Wiese says he remained quietly on the Steinhoff board for two years, watching how Jooste ran the company. What wowed Christo in particular was that everything Jooste said he'd do, he did. "He did things I thought were impossible. He had to get permission to list in Frankfurt, and he had to raise R18bn offshore. Markus *did* that – almost as easily as if he was making a phone call."

Wiese discussed his plans with his son Jacob. "I said, we must put all our interests under the Steinhoff umbrella. We have to make sure there's a control structure in place, but we must do this. We can build something really fantastic here."

Once satisfied, Wiese and Jooste prepared for the next step in the plan: merging Pepkor into Steinhoff. But before doing this, Wiese spent days with Jooste looking through Steinhoff's books. He also asked his bankers, RMB, to scrutinise the books. "I asked them to do *one* main thing: check the cash flow. I wanted to be sure that there would be proper cash flow to pay my dividends. They gave me a report saying, don't worry, there's plenty of cash there," he says. Wiese then had a heart-to-heart discussion with Jooste, in which he laid down his final conditions for selling Pep to Steinhoff. "I told him: look, Markus, you go through two stages of life: getting rich, and staying rich. I'm now in the second phase, and there are some assurances I need from you. First, I want to have some sort of voting pool so that it'll be difficult for a predatory raider to take over the company; and, second, we must never take so much debt onto our balance sheet that we lose our investment grade rating, and beyond what the non-core assets could be sold for." In other words, Steinhoff must agree to keep its debt to a manageable level. And if anything went wrong, they could sell enough of their assets at the stroke of a pen to get back an investment grade rating. "It was an immutable and firm agreement. Markus agreed," says Wiese.

This was a critical point. To keep that investment grade rating he'd promised Wiese, Markus Jooste was almost obliged to shift debts like

JD Consumer Finance off his books. He may have been so desperate to keep Steinhoff's credit rating intact that he took a shortcut, shunting JD Consumer Finance into Campion. Could this have been his motivation for what he did? "It's possible," says Wiese today. "Look, he knew that was our one unbreakable agreement, so perhaps he made sure that this wasn't broken – whatever he had to do. It's possible."

* * *

Then, in November 2014, Christo Wiese took his most fateful decision over his five-decade business career: he (and Brait) would sell Pepkor to Steinhoff. At a price tag of R62.8bn, Steinhoff's takeover of Pepkor was *the* biggest corporate deal in South Africa until that point. (It was subsequently trumped by Anheuser-Busch's $102bn takeover of SABMiller.) But R62.8bn was still real money. Even for Christo Wiese.

More fatefully, Wiese and Brait agreed to take Steinhoff shares as payment. This meant that Wiese controlled 23.9% of Steinhoff, thanks to his 654.8m shares. And he owned 34.9% of Brait – so there was no mistaking who was calling the shots.

At the time of the deal, Pepkor, which had begun life as a single store in the Karoo, was now a vast global chain with 3,742 stores in 16 countries, annual sales of R38bn and profit of R4bn. But the new combined 'Steinkor' would be an even larger beast: it would have 6,000 stores across the globe, churning out sales of more than R156bn.

Wiese celebrated the deal with a braai. And Jooste gushed that he'd be able to work with Wiese to "leave a company behind that will always be there". It's a sentiment that hasn't aged well.

A year later, Jooste would describe Pepkor as "*the* deal of Steinhoff of the century".[9] "It's our biggest acquisition ever, and it's the one that went down the most seamless in terms of integration. Our influence at Pepkor with Pieter Erasmus and his team again was purely on corporate matters and financing, on treasury, on currency management. The day-to-day business they run as effectively as before."

Around that time, Johann van Rooyen, the son of Pep's founder, who had studied at Stellenbosch in the same year as Jooste, bumped into him at the Durbanville racetrack. Van Rooyen had been invited by his brother-in-law, Peter Gibson, who was CEO of Horseracing South Africa – one of the many parties on the racing scene with whom Jooste did not see eye to eye. "They'd just done the Pepkor deal, so I said to Markus: 'Congratulations. I believe you're joining our Pep family.' He replied: 'No, Pep is joining the Steinhoff family.'" The anecdote illustrates exactly how much of a merger this really was. Markus would be in charge, absolutely.

At the time, there was a sort of obvious logic to the deal: Pep operated in Eastern Europe and Australia, while Steinhoff's Conforama, Kika-Leiner, Bensons and HomeChoice dominated Western Europe. "Steinhoff's footprint in Western Europe is totally new for the whole Pepkor group," said Jooste. "We can give them an introduction into countries like Spain, Italy, France, Germany and Switzerland, where they've never been before."[10] But this wasn't the only rationale. The truth was that the Pepkor deal was *vital* for Markus Jooste. Years of shoddy purchases – like JD Group and Homestyle – were catching up with Steinhoff. Its cash flow was beginning to look anaemic. Pepkor could thus be the remedy. As a blue-chip cash retailer, it finally brought some real cash to the rinky-dink Steinhoff. It wasn't just fragile paper profits.

Even the cynics believed this could prove the turning point for Steinhoff. Finally, it could become a real company, with real cash flows and real prospects, not just a shimmer of tongue-in-cheek journal entries. Andrew Cuffe, the former head of research at JP Morgan, was one who believed that Pepkor could allow Steinhoff to swap the dark arts of accounting profits for actual cash flow. "If some considered them the Mafia until that point, perhaps that deal was Steinhoff's way of going straight – like buying some legit dry-cleaners," he says.[11]

But there were many inside Pepkor who didn't like the deal one bit. A number of Pepkor executives didn't trust Markus Jooste for a second. Pieter Erasmus, who was running Pepkor as its MD, was one of those who apparently didn't get on with Jooste at all, insiders say. "Pieter used to refer to Markus and his crew as the Bentley brigade, as they'd always pitch up in their fancy convertible Bentleys. They weren't retailers," one insider says.

However, another cloud soon descended over the largest South African deal, thanks to Jooste's fast-and-loose style of negotiating. When executives are haggling over such a deal, a company is meant to put out a "cautionary announcement", which lets investors know something is on the boil. It also means that the company's top brass aren't allowed to buy or sell shares while they have "inside information". To breach this rule would be to breach rules on insider trading.

Brait evidently felt it needed to put out such a "cautionary announcement" about the negotiations to sell Pepkor to Steinhoff. So, on 19 September, Brait warned shareholders it was "in negotiations which, if successfully concluded, may have a material effect on the [share] price".[12] The troubling part was, however, that just days before Brait's warning, five Steinhoff directors splashed out R146m to buy shares in Steinhoff. They included Bruno Steinhoff (R66.6m), Wiese (R53.1m), Markus Jooste (R25.8m), Theunie Lategan (R549,500) and Frikkie Nel (just R80,500). Was there any chance that they didn't know of the looming Pepkor deal when they bought those shares? If they had known, it would have constituted "inside information", and they'd have benefited once the shares rose after the deal was announced.

It seems unlikely that they didn't know – especially since Brait had told the world it was already in negotiation. And it was clear that any knowledge of the deal would have involved "price-sensitive information", as Steinhoff's shares rose from R51 to nearly R60 after the deal was announced. This meant that, in total, the value of the shares bought by the five Steinhoff directors had risen R16.3m after the deal.

Keith McLachlan, an analyst for Alpha Wealth, was one person who reckoned it was pretty suspect: "Shouldn't Steinhoff have been under cautionary? . . . Christo surely knew of the deal, yet bought Steinhoff futures," he asked. At Steinhoff's AGM, a week after the Pepkor deal was announced, veteran shareholder activist Theo Botha pointedly asked the company about what, on the face of it, appeared to be insider trading. "Minority shareholders sold shares, and they [didn't have] the same information as the board of directors. So I feel that was actually unfair, because the directors were in a position to know about this [deal]," he said.

Len Konar, Steinhoff chairman, rejected Botha's argument. "I'm going to disagree . . . we acted appropriately, professionally, properly." Konar added: "There is speculation out there, there is professional jealousy."

Stehan Grobler, Jooste's *consigliere*, chimed in too, saying that when the five directors bought the shares, "the hard bargaining that culminated in the final conclusion of the transaction was then not under way as yet". It sounded like a thin excuse and overly lawyered..

One Steinhoff insider told me at the time that, contrary to what Grobler said, it was not a recent deal. "The Brait cautionary speaks for itself. Steinhoff and its board have been working on the deal for at least four months," he said.[13] To outsiders, it seemed suspicious. Still, it took the regulator in charge of monitoring insider trading – the Financial Services Board (FSB) – more than six months to even open an insider trading investigation. Solly Keetse, the head of the FSB's market abuse directorate, said the probe was into "individuals who were privy to price-sensitive information and who traded ahead of the announcements". Wiese was unperturbed: "I've no idea [why the FSB did this], but I'm totally relaxed about it," he said at the time.[14] "There never was any insider trading. No deal was done by the time that announcement was made."

A few months later, the FSB quietly shelved its insider trading investigation. It wasn't the first time, either. The FSB had done the same thing in 2003, when Craig Butters lodged a complaint with it about Markus Jooste's trading in a company called Arch Equity. "The FSB responded by attacking me and even complaining to my boss," says Butters. Which tells you pretty much everything you need to know about the regulator.

* * *

After the Pepkor deal Christo Wiese's ultimate plan was halfway there. The final step would be to merge Shoprite into Steinhoff to create an African retail conglomerate. As a precursor, Steinhoff had to split into two: a European company and an African company. So, in 2015, Steinhoff said it would list on the Frankfurt Stock Exchange in Germany. This would be followed by the splitting out of the African-focused assets into a new company called STAR (Steinhoff African Retail).

Many thought this was an awful idea. Not least was Whitey Basson, the CEO of Shoprite, who'd been with Christo from university, right throughout the Pepkor years. Basson distrusted Markus Jooste. He didn't like the way Jooste flashed his cash around, he didn't like that he knew little about retail, and he didn't like Steinhoff's businesses. Whitey despised the idea of a merger. Asked about this, Wiese says only that "Whitey and Markus had a difference in styles – they just didn't gel".

Ask Basson the same question today, and he sighs. "Ag, man, I'm so *tired* of talking about Steinhoff. My office is in Dorp Street in Stellenbosch now, and it's all anyone in the restaurants wants to speak about. Let's talk about something else."

Basson retired in November 2016. But before he did so, he made his feelings known, in a characteristically blunt way. "No, I don't know if it's a good idea," he said when asked about a merger. "What would you benefit by putting Anglo American and Toyota together?" he added.

The discrepancy between his view and Wiese's was patently evident because, at the exact same time, Wiese was also standing up on podiums and talking of how Shoprite would be "a natural fit" for Steinhoff.

Those close to Whitey Basson say there were plenty of things about Steinhoff that rubbed him up the wrong way. "He spent a lot of time looking at Steinhoff," says someone who knew him well. "In the end, he had a pretty good idea of how it worked. There were businesses in Steinhoff that he didn't like, which he thought were poor quality. And his view of Markus Jooste himself wasn't overly complimentary either." Basson apparently didn't believe that a retail conglomerate of this sort, in different arms of retail – clothing, food, furniture, mattresses, cars, hardware and a thousand other lines – could possibly have the sort of focus you need to do well. Throw in the fact that you're now trying to do this across different countries on opposite sides of the world, and he wasn't sure anyone could pull it off.

Nor was Basson alone in his scepticism. The London-based Portsea Asset Management eviscerated Steinhoff's business model in a research report, months before it collapsed. "We can count on one hand the number of retailers that have been successful retailing multinationally in a single retail segment – Zara, H&M, Ikea and Nike come to mind. But we know of no retailer, bar Steinhoff, that has been successful across multiple geographies with multiple retailing formats." Portsea said its unwieldy multinational business model made Steinhoff "an outlier", and it added: "We do not believe in many retail outliers."

Insiders speak of one incident, shortly before Basson retired in 2016, when he was talking with Wiese about merging Shoprite into Steinhoff. Basson told him: I've built this business for years, and I don't want to put my staff into a structure like that. Wiese replied: Well, if I'm the majority shareholder, you can't tell me what to do with my shares.

I'm not telling you what to do, said Basson. I'm telling you what's best for the Shoprite business and for its staff.

The encounter led to an awkward truce. The two businessmen who'd first become friends at Stellenbosch University five decades earlier weren't keen to bust up their friendship. So Wiese waited it out. He almost had no option. Over the years, he had repeated that "there's not a chance that Whitey Basson would wake up one morning and see that Christo had sold Shoprite to Walmart. That's just never going to happen." Then, in November 2016, Basson retired – and Wiese saw the gap.

On a scale of unforeseen events, revival of the deal at that stage would have been at the very bottom – somewhere between finding chocolate bunnies at Easter and awakening to a hangover after a night on tequila slammers. Within hours of Whitey Basson leaving his office, analysts from Investec Securities published a report saying that such a merger was now "not only likely but could happen in the near term".

Had you been the sort of person impressed by size, the numbers themselves would have clinched the deal: a merged "Steinrite" (or would that be Shophoff?) would have had annual sales of R200bn, profit of R15bn, and a staff complement of 186,000 people. Big, in other words. But other than size, the deal had little going for it. Evan Walker, an analyst at 36One Asset Management, pointed out that Steinhoff knew nothing about Shoprite's main forte – food. "[Wiese] is doing what suits him; he isn't necessarily doing anything that benefits Steinhoff, or Shoprite." Syd Vianello, an independent analyst, was equally scornful. "There's no synergy in buying clothing and baked beans. You don't buy them from the same people. And I don't believe there are many back-office savings," he said. But Wiese only saw the stars.

Speaking today, Wiese says that "Markus was *dead* keen to do this", but quickly adds: "Then again, so was I." The first attempt to merge the companies, in 2016, failed. At the time, Wiese said: "We ran our numbers finally and looked at all the angles and decided there was a difference of opinion on exchange ratios ultimately." Moreover, the deal was unlikely to get the go-ahead. At that point, almost all Shoprite shareholders except Wiese and the Public Investment Corporation, which invests civil servants' pensions, hated the idea.

To the stunned surprise of absolutely nobody, Wiese had another tilt at it a few months later. This time, in August 2017, Steinhoff said it had entered into one of those Byzantine deals that would see STAR end up with 50% of Shoprite's voting rights. In other words, the dreaded takeover was going ahead.

It says much about just how bad the prospect was for Shoprite that on the day the deal was announced, the grocer's share price tumbled 4.3%. It was only good for Steinhoff (whose share price rose 1.8%) and Wiese.

Karl Gewers, head of research at Benguela Global, which held 3% of Shoprite, called it a rubbish deal. "We don't see any benefit for Shoprite shareholders," he said, unequivocally. "If anything, the high-quality Shoprite business will be lumped together with lower-quality apparel, furniture and hardware retail businesses." According to Andreas Riemann, an analyst for Commerzbank, it seemed the deal was only going to happen because "certain investors have an interest and they want to combine certain assets". In other words, Christo Wiese wanted to neaten up his portfolio.

While the deckchairs were being reshuffled, there were rumblings from across the water in Germany. Two weeks after the last Steinrite "merger plan" was announced, the German business publication *Manager Magazin* published a report in which it said that Jooste and a few other former

Steinhoff colleagues, including Siegmar Schmidt, were being investigated for fiddling Steinhoff's accounts. Wiese largely ignored the report. So did most of his directors. When you're big enough, you'll always have *someone* trying to tear you down, said Markus.

*   *   *

In every darkened *kroeg* around Stellenbosch, on the sidelines of every investment conference in Sandton, or during a regulation coffee break at any company AGM, three questions arise, usually in a machine-gun sequence, with almost zero variation. "Did Christo know? Surely Christo *knew*? How could he *not* know?" In numerous interviews with journalists, Wiese could count on those questions being asked. And it began to infuriate him. "It pisses me off, because it's the silliest thing – do people really think I figured out this thing was a rotten fraud and then I wrote out a cheque for R59bn? I'd have to be certifiable." Then he adds: "I'm just waiting for someone to say I *did* know, and then . . ." He doesn't finish the sentence, but you can assume what follows would be a pack of salivating wild-eyed lawyers itching to get off their choke chains and satisfy their bloodlust by disembowelling some thoughtless commentator.

"It's such obvious nonsense. What sane person in the world would know that a barrel is rotten, and then put his life's work into it?" Wiese points out, repeatedly, that he only became chairman of Steinhoff in May 2016 – which meant he was only at the helm for 18 months. He was a non-executive chairman with no management responsibilities, and he chaired exactly four Steinhoff board meetings. "If the CEO does something wrong, how is it that *I* should have picked it up, when it had gone through the internal auditors, the component auditors in the individual countries, through the external auditors Deloitte, and even through the risk committees of all the banks? How come I was supposed to pick it up, yet none of them were able to?" It's a fair point. Though, self-evidently, the failure of one of the gatekeepers doesn't automatically exonerate the failure at the other end.

And if you extrapolate this reasoning, you have to ask: what is the point of non-executive directors at all? Typically, non-executive directors are different from executive directors in that they don't have any management role at a company. They only work part-time, and their job is to oversee what the company is doing, ask the hard questions about the strategy, and keep an eye on the CEO and executives.

In Steinhoff's case, on paper at least, it had a Rolls-Royce board. Three of the directors had a PhD in accounting, and one of them, Len Konar, had even chaired the International Monetary Fund's external audit committee. Johan van Zyl had led life insurer Sanlam with distinction for a decade, while Steve Booysen had been CEO of banking group Absa. Others, like Bruno Steinhoff and Wiese, stood to lose big if anything went wrong. Yet they all missed the fraud. So if they couldn't pick up that something was wrong with Steinhoff, is it not entirely farcical to pretend they're protecting smaller shareholders?

Wiese argues that no director can be expected to be a bloodhound. "To detect fraud in any business is extremely difficult," he says. "When it's at the CEO level, it is actually *impossible*." Mervyn King, a former judge whose name adorns South Africa's corporate governance code, agrees with Wiese that no executive director can be a bloodhound. Rather, he says, with Steinhoff the issue turns on whether the directors were "sufficiently sceptical". "Ultimately, it'll be a question of fact. Did they see things that were red flags? And did they act on it? For example, was the constant growth in revaluation of subsidiaries, of the properties, was that a red flag?"[15] Then again, matters become more complicated when you have a CEO like Markus Jooste, who is so dominant he drowns out other voices. King speaks from a position of some experience. He'd been a director on JD Group's board and, apparently, had raised concerns about Steinhoff's purchase of JD Group in 2011. "When you have a dominant CEO, an intolerant CEO, that wants it his way and no other way, who dominates other executives, that is something the non-executive directors need to look into. I mean, just imagine: if that's what happens in the boardroom, imagine what's happening out there, in the operations of the business."

There are many who would argue that Wiese wasn't sufficiently sceptical of Markus, and hadn't done enough to verify the statements he'd been making. Prudential's Craig Butters says he is struggling to understand how Wiese had no inkling of what happened.[16] "Look, Christo had been warned, even if he doesn't want to admit it. And in my view there was enough out there for him to be more sceptical than he was," says Butters. "Should you as a director know of a fraud like this? Perhaps not in every case, but here it's perhaps too easy to be critical, though I think he could have done more." Butters says what makes it trickier is that Wiese was intimately involved in a number of deals around Steinhoff. "Could this have got in the way of a more sceptical approach to the warning signs, like the *Manager Magazin* article?"

Analyst Syd Vianello notes that Wiese was the chair – and so the buck stopped with him. On this point, Wiese says he never saw any sign that Jooste would have done so much as initial a page in the wrong place. "Every little thing Markus did, he did correctly. What he said, he did, and there was never an inkling of dishonesty. I was worried about the horses, obviously, but he assured me he'd never bet a penny on them." If anything, Wiese says the board did act. "Look, the board was aware of the raid in Westerstede, and we acted – we hired the forensic auditors. Yet, even after that, Deloitte went and signed off the 2015 accounts." As Wiese asks, what more could the board have done than commission a team of experts to examine each allegation? What would somebody else have done? But the auditors will have relied on the board of directors too. If the board wasn't asking the right questions, this isn't an excuse to shift all the blame to the auditors.

*   *   *

Still, for every person who says Wiese *should* have known, there are others who cannot imagine that Wiese would ever have known that the rules were being bent. Rather, they describe him as somebody who trusts too much – and it got him badly burnt.

Speaking today, Renier's son Johann speaks glowingly of Wiese. He says his earliest memories of him were as a regular visitor to the Van Rooyen household. "My father described Christo as his best friend. He was very close to our family, and we'd often visit him when we were young, even during those years when he'd left for the diamond business."[17] Van Rooyen says that even after his father left the business, and emigrated to Europe for about a decade, the bond between him and Wiese remained intact. "Every year, Christo sent flowers to my mother on her birthday. And on my father's birthday, he and Whitey Basson would make a point of visiting him, even in the care facility where he's been the last few years." Wiese, he says, was always highly charismatic – the sort of guy who'll remember the name of everyone in the room.

Today, Johann van Rooyen lives in Vancouver in Canada, where he is watching the slow-motion Steinhoff train crash. "I keep up to date with it, partly because Christo is our family and we want to see what happens, and partly because it involves the fate of Pep, which my dad started."

Friends and colleagues say that since December 2017, there's been a noticeable change in Christo Wiese's demeanour. He is less certain of himself, less trusting of others. It's a step change, considering Wiese's career had largely hinged on trust and confidence. A few years back, he spelt out how, if you want to succeed, "you should believe that if the other guy can do it, you can do it. That's why I have a problem with people who are jealous of other people's success. That's got to be your approach – not begrudge him that he drives a nice car."

For a man who a few years back said, "I literally live as if I'm going to live forever", there's now a realisation that that might not be true.

The sense of betrayal, when he discusses what happened, is evident in his eyes. Whereas in the past, he'd always talk about Markus this, Markus that, now he only refers to the former CEO of Steinhoff as "Jooste". "I've beaten myself up often about this a lot," says Wiese. "People have always credited me with choosing good people – Whitey Basson, Pieter Erasmus, for example. So how did I get it that wrong this time? I really don't know, even now."

Strangely, Wiese was one of the few people who didn't get a personalised SMS from Markus expressing profound regret and sorrow. Apparently

Jooste has told his own friends, often, how bad he feels about what happened to Christo. On this point, Wiese says: "If he feels that, he hasn't told me – he has not once sent me an SMS saying sorry."

What doesn't ease the sense of betrayal is that he now knows that Jooste lied. For example, for years Markus had been telling Christo Wiese that half of the shares under Bruno Steinhoff's name belonged to him. It was all a fib – but he'd relied on Wiese never to raise this with Steinhoff. "The day after we all found out, I asked Bruno about this and he said to me, Christo, that's absolute shit. So, had I ever asked Bruno about this, he would have been exposed as a liar, he would have been unmasked."

So what would he have done differently, had he had the chance? "It sounds horrific to say this, but I have to say I don't know what I'd do differently. All the right structures were in place, the right reporting structures, and the auditors signed everything off. It was the only board I know of where all three members of the audit committee had doctorates in accounting."

Perhaps, if he could turn back the clock, he'd have asked Markus Jooste for a cheque for selling his stake in Pepkor rather than shares in Steinhoff. "But even then, I was 74 – I didn't want to leave my Pep people after 53 years. I didn't want them to think I sold them out, so I told him I'd stay for a few years."

Wiese says when he woke up on 6 December 2017, the morning after Jooste resigned, the chilling realisation of the gravity of the situation came crashing home. He says he looked in the mirror and asked himself: how will I handle this? "I promised three things to myself that morning: first, I wouldn't mourn the loss of money; secondly, I'd count my blessings, particularly that I hadn't put Shoprite into Steinhoff yet; and, thirdly, I wouldn't get bitter about it," he says.

On this last point, in particular, he says he struggles. "There are times when I do get bitter. When I think about how I worked, how my parents worked to build Pep – for someone to come and take it all away . . ." Then he adds: "I promised myself I won't be bitter – but I won't be forgiving either."

10

Rumblings from Lower Saxony

It was the sort of nightmare that would make PR flunkeys wake up scream-
ing for years. In the days before Steinhoff was due for its debut on the
German stock exchange in Frankfurt, after years of carefully scripted planning, a specially trained team of government investigators pitched up at
its Westerstede office bearing search warrants. These investigators were
muttering darkly about fraud, about balance sheet "overvaluation", about
forgery. It wasn't the sort of interaction that does anyone any favours
ahead of a Big Reveal in the largest financial centre in Continental Europe.

It was exactly what Markus Jooste didn't need. For months, Steinhoff
had been planning its bells-and-whistles listing on the Frankfurt Stock
Exchange, one of the ten largest exchanges in the world. The date had finally
been set: Friday, 4 December 2015. When the day rolled around, it all
appeared to go swimmingly, despite the unsettling events in Westerstede
just days before. Publicly, Steinhoff's top brass epitomised the preening,
immaculately tailored entrepreneur for whom a listing in Frankfurt was
the very pinnacle of achievement.

Bruno Steinhoff, Danie van der Merwe, Christo Wiese and Ben la
Grange posed theatrically on the piazza outside the exchange, holding the
horns of the bull meant to symbolise investment fortune – all grand, face-
splitting smiles. Elsewhere in the piazza, Steinhoff arranged a series of
open crates containing furniture from its various brands, to show off
what this South African company was all about. In one crate, a child lazed

on a bed, presumably a model from Kika-Leiner or Poco; in another crate, languid models draped themselves over couches that you could presumably buy from Conforama. At one stage, a choreographed flash mob assembled on the piazza next to the crates, where they spontaneously began dancing to Bruno Mars's "Treasure". Steinhoff's austere white men stood smiling on the sidelines while "Treasure" blared from the speakers, declaring: "You walk around here like you wanna be someone else." Immense flags bearing the company's insignia hung from the exchange's awnings, signs on every pillar declared "Deutsche Börse Welcomes Steinhoff", and even the trading desks on the floor of the exchange were draped in Steinhoff colours.

Then, as the time neared for trading on the exchange to begin, Bruno Steinhoff took the oversized golden bell in both hands, lifted it above his head and rang it with deliberate care, to signal the official start of trading in Steinhoff's shares.

Everywhere you looked, it was Steinhoff, Steinhoff, Steinhoff. Of course, you can see why the Germans would have allowed the retailer to annex the exchange that day: at a value of €19bn, it was the largest listing in Germany in 2015. Only, Markus Jooste, Steinhoff's CEO, wasn't even there. The story was that he had "neck pain" and so couldn't travel to Germany. It was the sort of pain, apparently, that daren't be risked on a first-class flight, with mountains of goose-down pillows, for your big overseas debut. Speaking to journalists remotely from Stellenbosch, Jooste gushed about how it was "an emotional event", especially for Bruno and his family, who were born in Germany. It was, in many ways, a triumphant homecoming. "Europe became the best place for us to list and trade our shares, to have access to all the European investors. It's a big highlight for us, and it made a lot of South Africans proud this morning, on that floor."[1] He said the plan was never to raise European money at that stage for his discount retailer, but rather the listing was "an introduction – not to raise capital". Others believed the motivation, from the outset, was far more sinister. Barry Norris, the founder of British investment company Argonaut, said Steinhoff's "overenthusiastic acquisition policy" was a way for Jooste and Wiese to diversify their wealth away from South African political risk.[2]

However, Jooste's "neck pain" seemed an awfully convenient excuse, given the raid on Bruno Steinhoff's Westerstede office a week before. The prosecutors had even gone so far as to raid Bruno Steinhoff's home, seizing computers, disks and files. Who can blame Bruno for looking "visibly strained" at the Frankfurt listing, as the German newspaper *Handelsblatt* described his demeanour.

At the time, the Oldenburg prosecutors said the raid took place because "there are suspicions that sales were overstated", and that they were looking into the "balance sheet treatment of certain transactions". Prosecutors believed, apparently, that Steinhoff was selling assets to other companies in the group at inflated prices, then declaring these as sales. According to insiders, the prosecutors were also of the view that Steinhoff had set up off-balance sheet companies which were secretly doing deals with the company – and the whole intention was to artificially boost Steinhoff's sales numbers. Conspicuously, Steinhoff's European arm was directly accountable to Jooste for its accounts, not to the chief financial officer, Ben la Grange, as some would have thought more usual.

So, was Jooste's neck pain entirely unrelated to that raid? Wasn't it more likely that he feared a neck pain in Germany from constantly staring over his shoulder, to check he wasn't being tailed by two burly men in blue suits bearing handcuffs? When the *Handelsblatt* asked him about it, he dismissed the question. "That has absolutely nothing to do with it. The neck problem becomes acute from time to time, and my doctor advised me to stay in bed," he said. He'd been in bed for three weeks with neck pain.[3]

With his characteristic phlegmatic fortitude, Jooste brushed off the raid as inconsequential, like so much lint off his starched collar. "It's a local matter, and will be dealt with there." Any transactions between companies in the group would be eliminated when the accounts were all put together anyway, he said. There was no cloud, he said. "It's quite normal to have investigations. We have it all over the world – it's not unique to Germany."[4] Jooste's stoicism calmed the panic that had developed in Stellenbosch over the raid. Relax, Jooste told his fellow directors, the German authorities just don't understand what happened, and they'll soon realise that all the transactions cancel each other out.

At the time of the raid, Wiese was in London, preparing to travel to Germany for the listing. He told the board they needed to hire a firm of forensic investigators to look into the allegations. So, Steinhoff hired Karsten Randt's German law firm, Flick Gocke Schaumburg (FGS). "We asked them to go through each of the allegations by the Oldenburg prosecutors and give us a response on each," said Wiese, discussing this later. "The law firm told us, on each allegation, that everything was in order."[5]

The raids happened on 26 November, but Steinhoff didn't bother telling anyone about it until 4 December. One investor described the eight-day delay as "a bit dubious". But Jooste immediately rubbished that view. "That is [criticism] by people who have no knowledge of the matter. I'm very happy, and the whole board is, that we followed the right procedure."[6]

Then a remarkable thing began to happen. Steinhoff's share price began to slide. It wasn't meant to be this way – becoming a public company in Germany was meant to *enhance* Steinhoff's profile and spark a rush for the shares. Instead, the visibility had the opposite impact. Before the listing, Steinhoff's share price was around R85, and it listed in Germany at €5 per share. But within a month, it had lost 20% of its value. There was a discernible sense that the day the prosecutors walked into Steinhoff's facebrick offices in Westerstede, with the three flags waving outside, the dominoes had begun to fall.

* * *

The tax probe did nothing to diminish Jooste's ardour for deals, however. If anything, the desire to buy more companies, to obscure earnings, accelerated. In the three years from 2014, Steinhoff spent €10bn buying 14 companies, giving it 25 new businesses in all. There were so many moving parts that one of Steinhoff's Stellenbosch employees said he almost expected to arrive in the office every morning and read in the paper how Jooste had just bought some other monstrous retail business in Europe.

After the Frankfurt listing, the pace of deals became particularly ferocious. Firstly, in March 2016, Steinhoff had a tilt for the UK's Home Retail Group, which was owned by Argos, offering to buy it for 175p per share.

The bid pitted Steinhoff against British grocery chain Sainsbury's, which had already put in an offer for 167p per share. Jooste said Home Retail would be a great addition for Steinhoff. "They have taken a traditional mail-order company onto a digital platform but with 1,000 stores for click-and-collect and for service. That is a perfect retailing model for the future."[7] But he soon slunk off, unwilling to top Sainsbury's offer.

Then Steinhoff bid $1.2bn for one of France's best-known brands, electrical company Darty. But there again, it was beaten by the $1.3bn offer from French entertainment company Fnac. Afterwards, Jooste said he'd congratulated Fnac: "I think they've bought an excellent business and I wish them well." Ahead of the deal, Steinhoff had bought 21% of Darty, but because of Fnac's offer, Steinhoff sold it and made a €40m profit on those shares.

Speaking about walking away from both deals, Jooste said: "If you go to an auction and you want to buy a painting or a horse, you must have a price, and if bidding reaches that price, you must have the discipline to walk away. That's what we did with those two deals."[8] But he admitted, "I'm not a good loser – and these are two deals we've lost."

Steinhoff got involved in another bidding war, this time for low-cost retailer Poundland. In the end, Steinhoff paid £466m for Poundland, edging out American hedge fund Elliott. It was a 43% premium to its share price the day before the bid. Quite whether Steinhoff should have been pursuing Poundland so vigorously is debatable. The Brexit vote, for the UK to leave the European Union, had knocked both British growth and its currency. As Steinhoff was buying £120m of goods in US dollars, Brexit was a big deal. Darren Shapland, Poundland's chairman, pointed out how bleak it was on the British high street. "As people tighten their belts we tend to do a bit better, but we are a high street retailer and it's not getting better in terms of footfall."[9] Almost immediately, Steinhoff had to shut 57 Poundland stores and, more symbolically, start selling products that cost more than the eponymous £1.

However, it was the next deal that was to prove the zinger – the feather that settled atop the mountain of suspicion over Steinhoff, and revealed the simmering volcano below, just itching to blow. On 6 August 2016, Jooste announced it would be buying a company called Mattress Firm for $3.8bn. The strange part was that Jooste offered to pay $64 per share to take over Mattress Firm, on a day when the share price was at $29.74 – a massive 115% premium to its share price. In one swoop, Steinhoff had become the world's largest bedding retailer – but at a crippling cost. It seemed, for all the world, that they'd traded in the entire house to buy the bed. Analysts were dumbfounded. "To say we were surprised by this news would be an understatement," said Stifel, a stock brokerage based in Missouri. "Mattress Firm was not exactly hitting on all cylinders in recent quarters."[10] It certainly was an odd deal.

Why, for the sake of comparison, would you walk onto a car lot, see a 1995 Peugot worth R10,000 and immediately offer R20,000? To make the situation all the more confusing, it seemed as if Steinhoff's dealmaking team had walked out of the dealership with the Peugot, and then tried to convince the world it had bought a newly released Maserati. One of Steinhoff's directors says there were some fiery debates at the board about whether to go ahead with the Mattress Firm deal.[11] "We were all shit scared of America – we'd all seen how almost every South African company that went there got hammered. There was Sage, there was Discovery, there were so many. Some of the directors warned against doing this," he says.

This dissension wasn't evident in the gung-ho announcement when the deal was made. In it, Jooste trumpeted how "the boards of Steinhoff and its management team are enthusiastic about the opportunities this transaction creates".[12] He argued that the "synergies" made the deal compelling. Mostly, it seemed about size: it would boost Steinhoff's number of stores globally to 10,372, and its revenue to €17bn.[13]

What not too many people know is that Steinhoff had been itching to climb into the American mattress market for years. In 2012, Steinhoff had its first stab, when it tried to buy Sealy. But it was beaten by Tempur-Pedic International, which offered $229m. This time, Steinhoff wasn't going to risk being beaten.

Mattress Firm had begun life in Houston, Texas, in 1986. But, like

Steinhoff, it had grown suspiciously quickly in recent years. In 2014, it bought Sleep Train for $425m, and the next year it bought the third-largest mattress company in the country, Sleepy's, for $780m. So, when Steinhoff came brandishing a weighty cheque, Mattress Firm had an unwieldy, bulging portfolio of 3,500 stores. It was way too many. As one person said: "I've got two Mattress Firm outlets within a mile of each other. I live in a town of 50,000 people [and I] don't know anyone who has shopped there. About three years ago, I told friends and family it had the classic feel of a private equity pump and dump – build the franchise count with cheap banker funding, then find the greater fool to buy the crap."

Despite the obvious problem with so many stores selling a product that people usually don't replace for a decade, Steinhoff spent all of five days doing due diligence at Mattress Firm, before deciding to pay double the market price. Critically, had Steinhoff's team spent a bit longer investigating, they might have stumbled over the reason for the immense surge in Mattress Firm stores: suspected fraud. This is laid bare in a jaw-dropping lawsuit that Mattress Firm filed against two of its own executives, dated 30 October 2017, in Harris County in Houston. In that 47-page summons, Mattress Firm accused those two senior executives – Bruce Levy and Ryan Vinson – of taking an epic array of bribes from property developers and brokers that caused the company to sign exorbitant leases it shouldn't have.[14]

That story begun in 2009, when Levy was hired as vice-president of real estate to lead Mattress Firm's "national expansion effort". Soon after, Levy hired Ryan Vinson, who became vice-president for growth and store planning. The two of them were the final word on where Mattress Firm would open new stores. Brazenly, Levy even referred to himself as Mattress Firm's "walking real estate committee". The result: "At a time when many national retailers were closing stores in the United States, Mattress Firm, America's largest retail seller of mattresses, was rapidly opening them," the court papers said. In truth, "rapidly" doesn't even convey the full picture of the mattress store deluge. In the seven years that Levy and Vinson were in change, Mattress Firm added 1,500 of its 3,400 stores. You can see why Jooste would have admired their ambition.

The "fixer" who allegedly made the fraud possible was a company called Colliers Atlanta, which was hired as Mattress Firm's "master broker", to act as an intermediary between Mattress Firm and property developers who found the sites for new shops. And the key man at Colliers was its vice-president, Alexander Deitch. According to Mattress Firm's court papers, Deitch and numerous property developers paid "bribes and kickbacks" to Levy and Vinson to get them to open new stores. "The bribes, kickbacks, and fraud . . . affected hundreds of leases, which caused Mattress Firm to pay significantly above-market rents and to agree to other unfavorable lease terms. The bribes, kickbacks, and fraud further harmed Mattress Firm by causing it to misallocate resources by opening unnecessary stores, thereby harming the sales of existing stores nearby." As a result, Levy and Vinson presented "falsely optimistic sales forecasts to Mattress Firm's management to maximize the stores that would be opened and to justify the above-market rents and longer lease terms that were offered to the [developers]". In other words, they lied about the sales.

The court papers say that, just hours before he was fired, Levy admitting to receiving "thousands of dollars in cash, an expensive watch, loans, expensive first-class trips to destinations including Europe, Oregon, Dominican Republic, and Deer Valley, joint investment opportunities, cases of wine, extravagant meals and subsidized gambling". Colliers's Deitch apparently admitted to "loaning" him $120,000 so he could buy luxury cars. And to keep the family sweet, Deitch also gave Levy diamond earrings and a necklace for his wife.

At this point, everyone involved – Levy, Vinson, Deitch – denied Mattress Firm's allegations. Vinson's lawyers claimed Mattress Firm had "unclean hands" – essentially, that it knew what was going on. Deitch, in his legal response, said Mattress Firm's top brass, including CEO Ken Murphy (who resigned in January 2017), knew exactly what was going on, and that it was part of a "brutal and unrelenting competitiveness" to snuff out all competition.[15] He said Steinhoff did its due diligence at the time when "Mattress Firm was most aggressively pursuing its reckless" expansion.

However you look at it, these antics pre-date Steinhoff's offer. The court papers were only filed in 2017, yet all the same there must have been signs and warnings that Steinhoff overlooked. In early September 2016, just weeks after Steinhoff tabled its offer, Mattress Firm admitted to shareholders in a report that "two employees of [our] real estate group had conflicts of interest involving business relationships with certain of the company's real estate vendors".[16] Mattress Firm was "conducting a more detailed investigation into its real estate and leasing practices". But it added that it had "reason to believe that there may have been improper gifts made to certain of its employees from vendors". Had Steinhoff pulled this thread, it would have unravelled the thin covering around Mattress Firm's rotten leases. At the very least, Steinhoff could have argued for a lower price. Instead, Jooste decided to pay double what the market reckoned the firm was worth.

It sounds difficult to fathom, but within a few months of the purchase, the Mattress Firm transaction had become even less compelling. Things first came to a head in January 2017, when Steinhoff's square-jawed bruisers met its largest supplier, Tempur Sealy, at a furniture trade show in Las Vegas, and slapped down a new hardline contract. We won't be paying you what you'd been getting from us, they told them. You need to slash your prices, or we'll walk away. Fine, said Tempur Sealy CEO Scott Thompson, *sayonara*. Thompson was said to be fuming, and within days he'd sent out letters scrapping the partnership. Tempur Sealy wasn't going to agree to Steinhoff's demand for "significant economic concessions", he said.[17]

John Baugh, an analyst with Stifel Nicolaus, attributed the split to "strong egos".[18] Other analysts suggested it was just Jooste, who had swaggered into town and wanted to flex his "reputation as a tough negotiator". As Baugh put it: "We do not see this as necessarily a helpful event for Steinhoff given Tempur's brand strength and premium price points in the Tempur-Pedic brand."[19]

To Jooste, it felt like he had Tempur Sealy over a barrel. But it only seemed that way. Actually, Mattress Firm's top seller was the Tempur-Pedic mattress, a memory foam product that was responsible for its most profitable sales. In all, more than 40% of Mattress Firm's sales came from Tempur Sealy mattresses. Insiders say Jooste reckoned he wasn't going to be bossed around, since he held all the cards as the biggest buyer of mattresses in the country. So, instead, Mattress Firm began stocking Serta Simmons's mattresses.

It was hardly a till-jangling success. As the weeks wore on, it became clear that the springs had given up the ghost in Mattress Firm's sales numbers. For the six months to June 2017, Mattress Firm's sales lost about 8%, while it made a bottom-line loss of $133m. Finally, the fact that there were more places to buy a mattress in the US than to buy a Big Mac burger had come back to bite the industry.[20] In June 2017, Jooste admitted that there had been "complications" at Mattress Firm. Brian Pyle, an analyst at Old Mutual Investment Group, said people were already expecting pretty nasty figures from Mattress Firm, but investors maybe "didn't understand how bad it was going to be". One of Steinhoff's directors, speaking today, says Mattress Firm wasn't just a fraud-ridden disaster in the boardroom, but the company also got it badly wrong in the stores themselves. "For example, they had different brands, Sleepy's and Sleep Train, which focused on different market segments. But they rebranded everything under Mattress Firm, and lost one of those segments." So, whereas before, there had been a Sleepy's, a Sleep Train and a Mattress Firm on three different street corners facing each other, now there were just three Mattress Firms – making it hopelessly clear how overtraded the industry was.

Jooste was undaunted. Still in 2017, when its new US purchase had begun to hit the skids, he bragged that Mattress Firm "will be a game changer for Steinhoff". He wasn't wrong. But the way that Mattress Firm ended up changing the game for Steinhoff was pretty much the opposite of what he would have wanted.

Fraser Perring, the 44-year old British former social worker, who heads short-selling research group Viceroy, says it was the Mattress Firm deal in August 2016 that tipped them off to the rot inside Steinhoff.

"We'd initially looked at Mattress Firm, because we thought it was a candidate for shorting, and then Steinhoff pitched up with this ridiculous deal," he says. "So we looked at Steinhoff, and saw that they were making all these acquisitions at the time, like Poundland. To buy a company like

Poundland, in an environment of inflationary pressures in the UK, was madness," he says.

He likens Steinhoff's mad acquisition dash to someone that loses a job, but decides to max out the Mastercard anyway, confident that they'd get a job next month. "They were buying other companies at such a fast rate that no one could properly analyse the underlying business," he says.

Perring says in every case, Steinhoff pitched these deals as creating "synergies", that they'd save costs by being part of the same family. "Let's say you get married – you get 'synergies' because you move in together and save costs. If both of you have a job, you should be better off, because you're sharing costs, like rent," he says. "But for a company, the only reason you merge is financial: you get economies of scale, future potential benefits, and you can develop brands".

But at Steinhoff, so few of its deals created real "synergies" that people should have been far more sceptical from the start, says Perring.

Viceroy's report was almost complete when Jooste resigned, and the stock began to crater. So, hours later, they released their 37-page report. "We were wrong by about a week. We'd calculated that at the current run rate of the German investigation, they'd hit a wall at some stage," he says.

Like Enron, the details of Steinhoff's accounting chicanery weren't hidden. But nobody bothered checking. "Steinhoff was held out as a prize asset in the South African market. But the reality was, it was just an enrichment programme for certain executives," he says.

* * *

While the headlines around Steinhoff are largely focused on who lost billions – Christo Wiese, government pensioners, the banks – there is a much smaller group who made a mint from the company's collapse. Specifically, those who bet it was going to implode.

Take Barry Norris, an untypical fund manager, if ever there was one. Unlike the squadrons of blue chino accountants who leave university with commerce degrees, Norris graduated from Cambridge with a master's degree in history in 1996. The year after, he added another master's degree in international relations, which he later supplemented with the CFA qualification. He is predisposed to think of things a little differently. In 2005, Norris started a London-based fund manager called Argonaut Capital, attracting more than £1bn of investors' funds. He looks a bit like a TV action hero, which helps when you're a drawcard who is frequently invited onto Bloomberg TV and CNBC as a resident expert.

It was in early 2016 that Steinhoff popped up on his radar. "I work with a South African, Greg Bennett, and we'd noticed how Steinhoff had moved its listing to Frankfurt, and we just couldn't understand why – other than simply as a method of just taking cash out of South Africa."[21] Bennett, Norris's partner, also had an unusual entry into the finance industry. In 1994, he'd gained a science degree from the University of Natal, focusing on agricultural economics. Bennett then moved to the UK, where he managed various funds (also getting his CFA) before linking up with Norris. "Just because you study accounting doesn't make you a great fund manager," says Bennett today, in an accent that still carries with it more than a hint of the sugarcane fields of KwaZulu-Natal. "I'm not a forensic accountant by any stretch, but what we did is look at Steinhoff from a common-sense angle. And this showed that there was no reason why the margins were going to increase every year, as people expected."[22]

Argonaut thought it was fishy that every year Steinhoff had a new excuse for why you couldn't meaningfully compare its accounts with the previous year's. Either they were buying something, selling something, or shifting their year-end. "The building block of understanding a retail business is being able to compare like-for-like sales. At Steinhoff, you'd never be able to do this."

So, those red flags were already rippling in the wind when, within a few months of the Frankfurt listing, Steinhoff took a tilt at Home Retail (and failed), tried to buy Darty in France (and failed), took a dart at Poundland (and succeeded), and then bought Mattress Firm. "Mattress Firm, more than anything else, acted as the catalyst for our short," says Bennett. "This was the point when people said, Hang on a second – it's a declining industry and you're paying a huge premium for what exactly? Why are you doing this?" Norris said that at the time, Argonaut had no idea of the immense, rotting fraud that was slowly poisoning the Steinhoff body. There were just numerous things that didn't make sense, which the market didn't seem to care anything about. "Everyone in the retail industry was struggling. So, you'd have to believe that there was some secret sauce in Stellenbosch that allowed Jooste's team, and them alone, to fix these distinctly average companies. And we soon found out they didn't even know what was happening in their companies."

That myth of Jooste's superior management skills didn't survive long after the Mattress Firm deal. Soon afterwards, Jooste was tackled on a conference call with analysts and asked what was happening overseas in the business. He replied that they had no idea what was going on, but they'd be going overseas soon to find out. "If the myth was that Steinhoff had a highly competent management team skilled at turning companies around, his response in that conference call created the opposite impression," says Norris.

Norris believed that the Mattress Firm deal was "symbolic of the shambolic acquisition strategy which Steinhoff had come to embody". Certainly, Mattress Firm's "dim prospects did not justify such enthusiasm". Thoroughly unconvinced, in March 2016, Argonaut took out a big "short" on Steinhoff, when its share price was €4.77.

If you've no idea what a "short" is, you're not alone. In essence, a "short" is when someone takes a bet on a company's share price falling. Usually, that's because they don't buy the company's story or they reckon the share is overvalued. What happens is that they "borrow" that company's shares, usually from a bank, which they plan to return later when the price is lower. So, to take the example of Steinhoff, when the share price is trading at €5 per share, a "short seller" will borrow 200,000 shares from a bank (worth €1m), which they must return later. Then, they immediately sell those shares for €1m. If the price then falls (as they're hoping) to, say, €1 per share, it will only cost them €200,000 to buy another 200,000 shares to give back to the bank. *Voila!* €800,000 in profit.

Of course, taking out a chunky "short" is always risky, mainly because of the old cliché that the market can be wrong longer than you can remain solvent. "If you'd taken a short position on Bernie Madoff when he first started conning people, you'd have gone bust," says Norris. "These frauds do eventually blow up, but you don't necessarily know what that catalyst will be, or when it will happen."

As it happens, the Steinhoff short was a blazing, high-fiving success for Argonaut. The London investment company got its timing exquisitely spot on, as the share tumbled to €0.53 by early December. It meant that, for the year to March 2018, Argonaut's Absolute Return Fund made a return of 25.1% – more than fivefold better than the wider market's gain of 4.7%. Argonaut told investors, with stiff upper-lip restraint: "In the short book, the biggest contributor was Steinhoff (–90%) whose share price collapsed . . . we had long been suspicious of the company's opaque reporting, disregard for normal standards of corporate governance and value destructive acquisition policy".[23] Norris told his investors that there'd been numerous other red flags, including "breath-taking disregard for disclosure and corporate governance", not to mention widespread talk of its aggressive accounting practices.

Steinhoff's ill fortune contributed to a £16.5m increase in Argonaut's net assets for the year. "What made Steinhoff such a great short is that it was a fraud in a declining industry. And there was no positive scenario on the other side. Obviously, we didn't know how deep the fraud went, but we saw the red flags," said Norris. He reckons that while some analysts bought Jooste's *shtick*, there were countless others for whom the Steinhoff tale didn't wash. "Many fund managers are inquisitive characters. And those who end up shorting companies often have a sensitive antenna for bullshit – and Steinhoff came across as being full of bullshit."

While Argonaut's "common-sense investing" made for a wise decision, there was a catalogue of other hedge funds that had similar instincts – and who also made a killing. The US hedge fund Och-Ziff Capital Management, created by the flamboyant New York investor Daniel Och in 1994, made an estimated €94.5m from Steinhoff. Equally, TCI Fund Management made a more modest €4.3m. Another secretive hedge fund based in London,

Theleme Partners, which manages $1.9bn, took out a short position in Steinhoff at around the same time as Argonaut. "In many cases, Steinhoff paid a high premium for businesses considered to have structural challenges such as Poundland in the UK and Mattress Firm in the USA," said Theleme. It reckoned that many of Steinhoff's deals "look questionable, with a number of connected parties involved in both sales and purchases".[24]

Steinhoff was such an *obvious* short, in fact, that it even attracted the attention of arguably the most lauded hedge fund manager on the globe – Stanley Druckenmiller. Druckenmiller is the sort of guy who, if he casually mentions a stock tip during an interview, you'll see an immediate spike in the trading of that company's shares. For twelve years from 1988, Druckenmiller was the head of the investment funds run by George Soros, the Hungarian-American magnate who famously earned the moniker as "the man who broke the Bank of England" by making a $1bn profit in a single week, when he bet against the British pound in 1992, days before it was revalued.[25] That bet, still spoken of by other hedge fund managers with raised eyebrows and awed reverence, was Druckenmiller's grand idea.

Another grand idea he had was shorting Steinhoff. Speaking on television a week after Steinhoff's collapse, Druckenmiller said: "I was lucky enough to short the stock, because someone was kind enough to explain to me that these guys might be crooks. There was fraud, at best, when you look [at] what was going on . . . and they buy this mattress company in the US for 100% over where it was trading."[26] Druckenmiller said "half the street knew" that Steinhoff was a con.

In South Africa, a number of hedge funds run by Fairtree Capital also made a mint off Steinhoff's collapse. For example, its R635m Assegai hedge fund made a 22.4% return in 2017. It meant Assegai was named "fund of the year" at the HedgeNews Africa Awards for 2017.[27] Jean Pierre Verster, who runs Fairtree's Protea funds, took out a short position on Steinhoff after the first article appeared in *Manager Magazin*. "I'd had long-running concerns, mostly because of their poor cash flows. But after they bought Pepkor, which was a cash-rich business, I felt they'd addressed that."[28] However, after the revelations of its off-balance sheet antics in Europe emerged,

Verster got hold of company records in Europe, and then contacted Stein-hoff. "They couldn't explain this properly. It's at that stage that we took out the short position." As a result, his main fund returned 19.5% for the year to June 2018 – 7% coming from Steinhoff alone. On the R150m capital in the fund, this amounted to a R10.5m boost.

But for every hedge fund manager who made money from Steinhoff's collapse, there must have been fifty funds that would have lost out. Kaizen Asset Management, a small Johannesburg-based investment house which was owned by Ronnie Mazor, a former analyst at Israel's Bank Leumi le-Israel, took such a pounding from its investment in Steinhoff that it had to shut its doors. Contacted today, Mazor says he has "no comment on Steinhoff". But someone who worked there said the Steinhoff position was "one of the factors" in Kaizen shutting down. "It's easy in hindsight to see the red flags, but we got huge confidence when Christo Wiese injected his assets. Sure, Markus was controversial, but there were many CEOs who are controversial."[29]

*   *   *

As it happened, some of the more well-connected hedge funds had managed to get hold of a withering research report into Steinhoff written by Portsea Asset Management. In June 2017, long before the collapse, Portsea published a 32-page report entitled "Steinhoff: The Empire Builder Has No Clothes".[30] As we have seen, it was the first compelling deconstruction of Steinhoff's murky off-balance sheet company Campion Capital, which it said only really existed "as a means of creating non-cash profitability" and to hide losses. Portsea's conclusion was that Steinhoff's earnings were overstated due to an off-balance sheet vehicle that improved earnings and "severe accounting shenanigans".

But there was more to it. Portsea believed another way Steinhoff was fiddling its balance sheet was by "under-depreciating" its assets. It worked like this: every year the accountants are meant to "depreciate" your assets, to fairly reflect what they're worth. For example, if you buy a new car for R200,000, the next year it'll be worth less – say R180,000 – so you have to knock R20,000 off the value of your assets. While most of Steinhoff's rivals reckon their assets (like their properties, factories and equipment) have a life span of 14 years, Jooste's company reckoned its assets could survive for 24 years. This is clear from the fact that in 2016 it put a value of €5.13bn on its property plant and equipment, yet it only wrote off €216.8m of it. Said Portsea, "It is evident to us that Steinhoff's depreciation charge is far too low and that it needs to be adjusted in order to compare Steinhoff's earnings before interest and taxes with peers." If Steinhoff's depreciation was hauled in line with its peers, its earnings would have to drop by €261m, Portsea argued.

Portsea believed Steinhoff was also using "pre-provisions" to bump up its profits. In other words, it would buy a company for, say, R1m, but before the sale went through, it set aside R1.5m as the entire cost of the deal. It could then "leak back" the R500,000 over the next few years, when needed to boost its profits. This was something that Prudential's Craig Butters also believed was happening. "Once the acquisition was concluded, these provisions would be released – but because the purchased company was now consolidated in Steinhoff's accounts, this reversal of the provision would find its way into Steinhoff's profit."

If you're looking to understand the accounting gimmicks that Jooste used to dupe investors, the Portsea report is a tour de force. Any hedge fund that managed to get hold of Portsea's report would have been scrambling to borrow any shares it could, and take out the biggest short position imaginable – to go for the jugular, as Druckenmiller would have urged.

Had Steinhoff's auditors Deloitte seen Portsea's unbridled assault on Steinhoff's accounting (which it didn't), it would have been even less amenable to signing off the retailer's accounts. As it happened, Deloitte couldn't ignore the next revelations. The next artillery fire took place in August 2017, when *Manager Magazin* published an article entitled "Einstürzende Neubauten", which was a tongue-in-cheek reference to a 1980s Berlin band of the same name, meaning, in English, "collapsing new buildings".[31] "The Steinhoff empire is as much in danger of collapsing as some of the cheap pressboard cupboards and drawers sold in [its] discount stores," the article declared. "The company seems to be built on quicksand." To some extent, the *Manager Magazin* article reiterated the story of the Oldenburg investigation, which had been first revealed nearly two years earlier, just before the listing in Frankfurt in December 2015. Significantly, there were a few grains of fresh intelligence. For a start, *Manager Magazin* named the four people at the heart of the Steinhoff investigation: Jooste, Siegmar Schmidt, Alan Evans and Dirk Schreiber. This was the core group accused of cooking Steinhoff's books.

Secondly, the publication revealed how, during the Oldenburg investigation, it emerged that some documents had actually been forged. This allegation was an entirely new dimension in this drama, and no longer involved just a few accounting tricks. This came to light when Andreas Seifert, Steinhoff's former business partner who'd fallen out with Jooste, was asked questions by the police in July 2016. "He was questioned as a witness about various documents in the offices of the police inspectors in Osnabrück, which he was supposed to have signed. 'I have never seen these papers, and did not sign them,' Seifert declared." It was deliberate counterfeiting, Seifert reckoned.

This, now, was an entirely new game. It's one thing to shift your cash into an opaque company in Switzerland to save tax, another thing entirely to magic up evidence for the existence of the cash in the first place. Steinhoff's share price dived 9.8% on the day the *Manager* report emerged, from R66.07 to R59.59. In one day, R28bn had been wiped from Steinhoff's market value. As it turned out, that was only a shallow dip before the rollercoaster took a serious turn around a much steeper corner. In the overall picture, it was nothing.

Markus Jooste sought to defuse the crisis immediately. He fired off an email to all his directors, refuting the article point by point. So why don't we sue *Manager Magazin*? asked one. We can take them to court, force them to apologise since it's obviously bogus. There's no point, Jooste shrugged. They're a rubbish tabloid publication that registers each new edition as a separate company; we'll be in court for years. Ignore them.

Only, the bad news kept coming: *Manager Magazin* kept reporting the case, and Reuters also published embarrassing fresh details of the off-balance sheet deals too. Jooste then told Christo Wiese, Steinhoff's chairman by that stage, that he'd asked his lawyers overseas to begin drawing up a lawsuit against *Manager Magazin*. (No lawsuit was ever lodged, though.)

With blood in the water, the share price continued to bleed. Wiese appeared on radio, where host Bruce Whitfield asked about the allegations. Wiese described them as "drivel" – a phrase that would come back to haunt him. Asked about that response today, Wiese says: "Yes, I did say that, but that's because there were statements in there I knew to be false. And we had several reports from FGS [the German lawyers] that told us all the allegations were false."[32] For example, Wiese said, *Manager Magazin* said Jooste "dare not set his foot in Germany – but I'd been with him in Germany only the previous week. So, I said, this is the sort of drivel you have to deal with."

Wiese's critics would argue that, nonetheless, ignoring a red flag is a top candidate for the wilful blindness award. This criticism gets Wiese hot under the collar. "Look, what more can you do than appoint a firm of forensic investigators to go into everything, and say, tell me what you find? That's what we did, immediately. Nobody was ignoring anything – we acted." Still, as far as missed opportunities go, it's right up there with the Securities and Exchange Commission refusing to take the calls of Harry Markopolos, who first warned them about a charming elderly wealth manager named Bernie Madoff.

11

Leaks

by Warren Thompson

———

As the weeks wore on, the initial shock at Steinhoff's overnight collapse began to give way to anger, as the extent of the con became more evident. Those in the know – fund managers and investment advisers – were obviously aware of the impact of Steinhoff's meltdown on public savings held in retirement annuities, unit trusts, and pension and provident funds that were exposed to the company. But the wider public had no real sense. They'd been blindsided by what happened. This was evident from the reaction to one article I wrote for *Moneyweb* the day after Markus Jooste's resignation, entitled "Collateral Damage: Who Owns Steinhoff". It went viral. It was read, republished and shared like nothing I'd seen before.

The article wasn't long, but it included a table, showing the damage done to each of Steinhoff's largest one hundred shareholders over the course of the previous week, as the stock tumbled 70%. For example, it showed that the Public Investment Corporation, which invests the pensions of government employees, had lost R12.5bn on their Steinhoff investment in the bloodshed; clients of Swiss investment bank UBS lost R3.9bn; and Coronation's Balanced Fund lost R1.38bn. It demonstrated that "we", meaning the broader public, were all poorer thanks to Steinhoff. Almost every institutional investor lost, which meant that every South African with a pension fund lost too. The loss sparked an untypical outpouring of emotion. Soon, calls and emails began to flood in from everywhere – investors, members of the public, former Steinhoff staff and hedge funds from some of the world's largest financial centres.

One person who got in touch was a man called Jan Strozyk. Together with Benedikt Strunz, Jan was an investigative reporter from the German public news broadcaster Norddeutscher Rundfunk (NDR), based in Hamburg. Strozyk wrote: "We approach the story from a German perspective and are in touch with investors who weigh up a compensation lawsuit . . . I was wondering if you were following up on this and would be interested in some form of cooperation?" It was an easy proposition to accept. Opening the channel to Germany would provide much-needed texture and background to what had led to the collapse.

It was this cooperation that led to the leaked Steinhoff emails, between Jooste and Steinhoff's European head, Dirk Schreiber, and Siegmar Schmidt, who had left Steinhoff in 2013 to run Genesis Investment Holdings and Campion Capital. Schmidt was supposedly outside the tent – but the emails would tell another story entirely. It was, in essence, a sequence of emails between those three people from 17 to 24 August 2014. That week was critical, because at that very moment Steinhoff was preparing its financial accounts for the year to June 2014. These financials were ultimately released on 9 September – a few weeks later.

17 August 2014: Dirk Schreiber, writing to Markus Jooste, 9.21 pm

In the initial email, Schreiber attached three files for Jooste to consider. The first file contained the accounts (a balance sheet and profit and loss statement); the second was called "Details Finco Accounts June 2014"; and the third simply "Turnover". These attachments (which we did not have sight of) related to the June 2014 financial year-end of, presumably, Steinhoff Europe – the accounts for which Schreiber was responsible. Significantly, he referred to those accounts as a "proposal", following a discussion he and Jooste had had the previous Friday.

21 August 2014: Jooste replies to Schreiber and copies Siegmar Schmidt, 7.03 pm

It took Jooste four days to review Schreiber's documents before he replied, and this time he included Siegmar Schmidt in the correspondence. The inclusion of Schmidt is bizarre. While Schmidt did once occupy the same role as Schreiber, he'd been out the company for months already. This is evident from the fact that Jooste used his new email address: Siegmar. Schmidt@trimase.com. It was also unethical. The information being discussed was meant to be kept confidential between employees and auditors of Steinhoff. Any leak, and it could provoke claims of insider trading.

In the email, Jooste kicked off by saying: "I have now reviewed all the figures of the group and need some additional entries to balance the final consolidation please." However, he said, "we" have decided to impair JD Consumer Finance's credit book to remove the risk, effectively writing off R3.6bn. "You can understand that put my consolidated results out of balance."

The revelation that JD Group's lending book was breathtakingly rotten wasn't altogether surprising. Furniture sales had flatlined, and a lengthy strike in the platinum industry had hurt companies that sold goods to people at the lower end of the economic spectrum. In fact, just days before Jooste typed his email, African Bank, the largest provider of unsecured credit to the country's working class, had been placed in curatorship by the South African Reserve Bank. So, the days were dark. Jooste surmised that impairing JD Group's credit book would make Steinhoff's auditor Deloitte, and the lead audit partner Xavier Botha, "very happy/comfortable".

In the email, he discussed how French bank BNP Paribas had agreed to buy the JD Consumer Finance loan book for R6.7bn, which would help him recoup R1.85bn in October "when they pay". But the problem was that he couldn't include this number in the accounts for the year as he hadn't got the money yet. So he had to make another plan. (Of course, his claim that BNP Paribas would buy JD Group's loan book was long on hope anyway. For one thing, BNP later said they'd only pay R4.6bn. And, as we have seen, Jooste had already prepared Steinhoff's June 2014 accounts as if JD Consumer Finance was already sold and was a "discontinued operation". But he only got this "offer" on the very last day of the financial year, 30 June, "subject to due diligence and conditions precedent". And then the sale to BNP collapsed.)

But one can see why Jooste was so desperate to have JD Consumer Finance off Steinhoff's books: it was bleeding money. Consequently, with an offer, no matter how preliminary, he wouldn't have to consolidate those losses into Steinhoff's "continuing operations". That way, it wouldn't interfere with any of the ratios Jooste wanted to show.

So the trick for Jooste was how to find extra income to gild the accounts. In the email, he said: "I have nominated Genesis Group to receive €130m commission/fee from BNP because they have facilitated the negotiation on behalf of the whole Steinhoff group and K/L for the exclusivity to provide finance to both Steinhoff and K/L when they pay and execute in Oct." Genesis was controlled by Schmidt, and it would play a key role in the shady deals occurring before Steinhoff's 2015 listing in Frankfurt. Jooste's email implied that he wanted Genesis to receive a commission and then send part of the proceeds back to Steinhoff, where Jooste needed some extra cash to mitigate the knock from the JD Group impairment. Genesis would get the money back later, when BNP Paribas paid. But even that commission deal was odd. After all, why would anyone, let alone Genesis, qualify for such an immense commission – R1.9bn – on the R6.7bn deal? In no rational deal would you pay 30% to a broker.

The K/L in Jooste's email refers to another European company owned by Steinhoff, Kika-Leiner, which would get the "exclusive" rights to provide in-house finance at Steinhoff stores. But it's in the next few lines that Jooste tipped his hand to the game of using "off-balance sheet companies" to manipulate Steinhoff's accounts. Jooste wrote: "Can we please accrue/pay an additional fee/income of €100m from the Genesis group to Steinhoff to reduce cost of sales which will take gross profit to 40% which is in line with our plans/forecasts and pay an additional €30m on all debit loans to reduce nett finance costs to just below the previous year and makes sense because of the growth in investments and short term loans."

Here, he gives the game away. Essentially, he is instructing Siegmar Schmidt to pay €100m from his supposedly "independent" company to Steinhoff, so that it can treat this like a rebate or commission, and reduce its cost of sales. The trick here is that if you can reduce your "cost of sales" by, for example, claiming a commission, you effectively lower your expenses.

Which, in turn, means your profit looks far better. This, Jooste said, would allow Steinhoff to meet its target of a 40% gross profit margin, which it had promised investors. It was classic, overt gerrymandering.

And then, to make Steinhoff's numbers look just that much better, he instructed Schmidt to pay Steinhoff the other €30m as interest on the loans Steinhoff had made to Genesis. The impact would be to lower Steinhoff's net finance costs – again making profits look better. He said it would "make sense" for net finance costs to drop because of Steinhoff's "growth in investments and short-term loans". When Steinhoff eventually released its financial statements for the year to June 2014, one could see what he meant: "investments and loans" made by the company rocketed from R1.1bn to over R10bn. While R3.7bn of this was due to the rise in value of Steinhoff's shares in PSG, another R6bn was simply disclosed as "short-term interest-bearing loans". There was no detail anywhere about who these loans had been made to or at what rate.

Jooste then added: "Genesis will then be in a nil position after receipt of the BNP money and Steinhoff neutral because Europe received it instead of Africa and we have written off the debtors book in this year but achieved our overall group target." At this point, of course, Genesis was meant to be an independent company. About a year later, Steinhoff would merge with Genesis, using it as a vehicle through which to list in Frankfurt. But this paper trail lays bare the fact that Jooste was calling the shots at Genesis, and Schmidt (who had supposedly left Steinhoff) was cravenly doing his bidding. Jooste had manipulated things so that if the BNP Paribas money came, Genesis would get an immense kickback, which it could then use to provide extra padding for Steinhoff's profit as and when it was needed.

It is already evident that shunting around money in this way had little to do with reflecting Steinhoff's true economic position. It was all designed to manipulate the accounts to achieve a pre-agreed result.

21 August 2014: Schreiber to Jooste, 8.32 pm

About ninety minutes later, Schreiber wrote back to Jooste. "I understand the situation but I like to share my view with you: I still have gains of

€82-million from 2011/2012 in my books" – money that he evidently could not recycle back in the previous year. This implied that there were two sets of accounting records. (Like the Mafia.) Schreiber went on to discuss how profits were generated in previous years, stressing the contribution from the foreign exchange gains (in other words, the gain made by translating the euro profits into a weakening rand). This was an important point since many analysts (like Craig Butters) had long believed that Steinhoff was manipulating its foreign exchange numbers to boost profits. Schreiber's email would appear to corroborate that view.

Schreiber then said, explicitly, that for the current year Steinhoff Europe would be getting €500m in profits from turnover, which would be boosted by €90m (R1.2bn) received as "interest" from Genesis and Talgarth Capital, another murky company. In all, this would lead to a bottom-line number of €580m. While this was only 3.5% better than the previous year's €560m, it would mean a 26% improvement on the previous year for Steinhoff, because the rand had weakened from R11.50 to the euro, to R14.1, he said. Schreiber suggested that this could surely be used to cover most of the impairment from JD Consumer Finance, instead of having to resort to the €130m "commission" from the BNP deal.

Tellingly, Schreiber also requested some sort of "confirmation or guarantee letter", presumably from Steinhoff to Genesis, so as not to risk revealing the link between the two. "Otherwise the link between Steinhoff and Genesis is dangerous under IFRS 10", an accounting provision governing the way companies are controlled. While it is commonly accepted that a company exercises "control" if it owns 51% or more of another company, there are also situations where it can own less than 51% but still exercise control – for example, where it is an "off-balance sheet vehicle" set up as a sham.

It seems Schreiber was worried about getting questions about just how independent Genesis really was from Steinhoff. This was for good reason. As the report by the research company Viceroy would later show, many of the loans Steinhoff issued to supposedly "independent companies" like Campion to buy loss-making entities weren't on an arm's-length basis.

Accordingly, these entities should have been consolidated into Steinhoff's books to more accurately reflect the economic control the company exerted. This is painfully clear from the emails: Genesis was being instructed by Jooste.

22 August 2014: Jooste to Schreiber, 11.05 am

The next day, Jooste wrote to Dirk Schreiber and reiterated the problem: how to find a way to plug the hole of the R3.6bn JD Group impairment, while waiting for the R6.7bn from BNP Paribas to come into the bank account. "Thank you for your positive comments which I understand of course. My problem is just trying to match the income from BNP with the write-off of the book in the same year," he wrote. Jooste said that it wouldn't work to just use the impact of the rand's fall, because investors "ignore the currency effect". This wouldn't, in itself, fill the hole. But given Schreiber's concern about having to explain Genesis' independence, Jooste said it was "good advice" to use Talgarth, "who has been involved all the years to receive the €130". Talgarth could then pay the interest back to Steinhoff. This appears to be overt manipulation: at the stroke of a pen, he simply swaps one off-balance sheet vehicle for another, as the preferred way to collect an enormous commission amounting to nearly R2bn.

"These entries do not change our cleaning up for next year," he said. This is a reference to the need to clean up Steinhoff's accounts and get them "ready" for the listing in Frankfurt in December 2015 – a milestone in its history. In the end, Steinhoff would list in Frankfurt by reversing its assets into a Genesis company. Jooste said that before then, Steinhoff would sell its 45% of the industrial company KAP and its 20% of PSG, the financial company run by his good friend Jannie Mouton.

"I and you agreed to meet late Sept to work out the Brand/Property deal to create the right values ... we need to show the right group figure without currency now to lay the table for next year." This, it seems, was a consistent theme in Steinhoff's accounts: recycling Steinhoff's brands and trademarks between off-balance sheet companies like GT Branding and Talgarth, which usually led to a rise in the value of Steinhoff's assets.

He told Schreiber that for the Austrian retail chain Poco which Steinhoff had bought "we show 100% because we have overprovided for the payment of the purchase price". This is interesting partly because, at that stage, Jooste's estranged former European partner, Andreas Seifert, claimed he owned 50% of Poco while Steinhoff owned the other 50%. Here, Jooste appeared to be telling Schreiber to include the full amount for Poco in its books.

This may also relate to another tactic used to boost earnings: pre-provisioning. In this case, when a company was bought for €100m, before the cash was transferred to pay for it Jooste would raise a provision for the acquisition of, say, € 120m. Such a step isn't unusual, given that companies always have advisers to pay. But some companies also do this so that they can "leak back" some of this money later into the profits, to fill a hole or make profits for a particular year look better. While it isn't necessarily illegal, it creates a distorted impression of how well a company is doing that year.

"Please consider my suggestions," said Jooste. "I try to do what is best for the group and to make it possible to clean up in the next 6 months but we need the tools to do that."

22 August 2014: Jooste to Schmidt, 11.09 am

Five minutes after his email to Schreiber, Jooste fired off a brief communiqué to his old colleague, Schmidt, asking him to assist Schreiber with the final entries. "I please need your help to assist Dirk here with the final entries, he now needs your support and guidance again. I will really appreciate if you can do that for us."

22 August 2014: Schmidt to Jooste, 11.45 am

About forty minutes later, Schmidt replied to Jooste. He said he was "always in close contact with Dirk" and added that while he understood Jooste's email, "I also understand Dirk's concerns". According to Schmidt, Schreiber was "fighting with CT to get everything through the books. But your additional entries without any proper documentation will not be accepted by CT. I discussed this with Dirk a few moments ago." Here, he was referring to Steinhoff's European auditor, Commerzial Treuhand (CT), the German tax and auditing firm which employed just a hundred people spread across four cities. This was always one of the weaknesses of Steinhoff's global structure: the relatively obscure CT was auditing one of the most important arms of a global multinational. But, as Jooste's former chief financial officer, Ben la Grange, would testify in the South African Parliament, Jooste wanted it this way. Nonetheless, it is clear from the tone of the emails that CT weren't a complete pushover, and were now demanding documentation for deals. Evidently, manufacturing year-end entries was becoming increasingly problematic.

What is noticeable from the emails is that not once did Jooste mention La Grange, who was, ostensibly, Steinhoff's chief financial officer. In Parliament, La Grange would say there was a "limited sharing of information from Markus Jooste", and the emails appear to attest to that.

In the emails, Schmidt then made references to "old balances" which they had "moved" from Steinhoff to Triton-KLS – the precursor of the Genesis entities, which was also managed by Schmidt. He then referred to all the "balances pushed up in the last years" – and empathised with Schreiber on how to clean this all up.

22 August 2014: Jooste to Schmidt, 12.55 pm

An hour later, Jooste replied to Schmidt. "I did not suggest we do the additional entry without paperwork, that have always to be there, that I understand. Therefore my suggestion that we do that with Talgarth and pay it, and when Talgarth get the fee from BNP in October, you pay it back, and it contras out, so we are in the same position." Jooste assured him that they would all "make sure that all the balances clean out". In other words, Talgarth would pay out the €100m to Steinhoff, and when the money (fingers crossed) came in later from BNP Paribas, Talgarth would be repaid. This was simply an elaborate chain of transactions designed to ensure Steinhoff's accounts were flattered for the year to June 2014, and that no gaping hole would be evident.

Jooste added that Steinhoff's stake in PSG and KAP could be sold "through your structure, before listing, [which] will eliminate a lot of balances". This suggests that when Steinhoff's assets were put into Genesis for the listing, much of these funny accounting entries could be hidden. And he warned Schmidt: "If we stop short [now], my concern is that the rest is then more difficult." Doing it the way Jooste suggested would "strengthen all arguments of the past about the values of these investments and its integrity".

It's clear that all these transactions were meant to cancel each other out at some stage, so that there was no clear trail, but it's also clear that there was no underlying logic to the flow of money between Steinhoff and these off-balance sheet companies.

22 August: Siegmar Schmidt to Dirk Schreiber, 2.02 pm

Amusingly, there followed a series of emails, in German, between Schmidt and Schreiber in which they mocked Jooste's inability to understand what was happening in the accounts. Dirk Schreiber wrote to Schmidt that while he'd been told to book only "100" million" through Talgarth, "we do not have any money, so we have to give loans ourselves". He said that if Jooste sold the shares in KAP and PSG "he has not won anything". "He can not even make €5-million himself", so he charges a €20m surcharge on the head office, "because his people are too stupid". "Sorry, but he does not have things in hand – that's the reality. To overstate the result in the current market, as in the past, brings nothing!"

Schmidt then advised Schreiber to "talk to him about it", but Schreiber said there was no point. "He does not understand how he did not understand everything in the last years! You know him! Just a different opinion is enough reason for him to want it that way," said Schreiber.

Evidently, Jooste's European accomplices were feeling the pressure of having to conjure up numbers from nowhere. And they believed Jooste didn't understand this.

* * **

Two weeks after the trail of leaked emails, Steinhoff published its financial statements for the year ending June 2014, duly signed off by auditors

Deloitte & Touche. But instead of impairing the JD Consumer Finance business, as was indicated, Steinhoff said it had received an offer from BNP Paribas to buy the business on the last day of the financial year – 30 June. In actual fact, the sale to BNP would never go through. Eventually, over a year later Steinhoff would sell the haemorrhaging business to Campion Capital, a Schmidt entity, using money lent to it by Steinhoff. But Campion only "paid" R4.7bn to Steinhoff for JD Consumer Finance anyway – R2bn less than the French bank had apparently been willing to pay.

For its financial year, Steinhoff's gross profit margin remained unmoved at 35%, in line with 2013. But interest income from "loans" and "other" sources rose by R530m over the year. In the annual report, Jooste boasted that while the European market for household goods remained stable, Steinhoff's sales from its international retail activities grew by 4% to €5.2bn, while operating profit improved 22% to €325m. He said this was "due mostly to [a] continuing focus on cost savings and gross margin improvement". There is no mention of Talgarth, Genesis or Siegmar Schmidt anywhere in the annual report.

These emails are a microcosm, all within a week, of the machinations involved in getting Steinhoff's European business to balance its books, and reach a predetermined outcome. All of this was meant to satisfy the expectations of the market. Benedikt Strunz, the journalist from NDR, said it was electrifying to see "the private and innermost details of one of the biggest fraud cases in Germany. You could see the scheming taking place and I never thought you would see how blatant the details looked." The emails indicated too how the thought patterns which underpinned these transactions dated back many years: how to offset losses; how to manipulate income from investments; how to launder profits through different off-balance sheet vehicles. What happened was nothing less than an assault on modern accounting principles.

So why did no one see this? Why did CT allow these transactions, and why did the group auditors, Deloitte, not re-examine what was happening in Europe? And where was Ben la Grange? Finally, how did Steinhoff's board allow one man to treat the accounts of an immense multinational as if they were his personal ledger?

12

Stellenostra

It was a line of five Norfolk pine trees that came to embody the distinction between the older established families of Stellenbosch and the "new money" that many believe has polluted the town over the last decade. Strictly speaking, those pine trees weren't in Stellenbosch, the winelands city that became Steinhoff's headquarters, but about an hour away, in the seaside town of Hermanus. They were planted by someone who'd lost his children in the Great War, on a plot of land just above Grotto Beach in Voëlklip. A house was built on that land in the 1930s. Later, the property (between 143 and 147 10th Street) was bought as a holiday home by Dr Anton Rupert. Dr Rupert was one of South Africa's most celebrated entrepreneurs, the creator of the tobacco company Rembrandt, which owned cigarette brands like Dunhill, Peter Stuyvesant and Rothmans, founder of the company Richemont, which owned luxury brands like Cartier and Montblanc, and a founding member of the World Wildlife Fund.

When he died in 2006, at the age of 89, his son Johann gave a rousing eulogy at his funeral, recalling how Anton Rupert's motto in life was "he who does not believe in miracles isn't a realist".[1] Also, money is like a knife – in the wrong hands, it's dangerous; in the hands of a surgeon, it can save lives.

In 1946, Anton Rupert left Joburg, and moved his burgeoning business to the old Distillers premises in Stellenbosch. When Rupert paid £6,100 for his house in Thibault Street, on the banks of the Eerste River, he became the first of many businessmen who decamped to Stellenbosch, laying the groundwork for an exodus to the small town in later years. As Rupert's biography would put it: "The Ruperts would eventually become one of Stellenbosch's most famous assets, in certain respects more widely known than the university ... he turned the name of this tranquil Western Cape town into a world-famous trademark."[2] Thanks to Rembrandt, the winelands town was visited by global personalities, among them David Rockefeller, Robert Kennedy and Prince Philip. Lord Montgomery, who defeated Rommel's army in North Africa, smoked his first cigarette in Rembrandt's factory.

Rupert's house in Hermanus was, by all accounts, a fantastic seaside villa. Single-storeyed with a colonnaded porch, a thatched roof and solid teak casement windows, it was a classically understated residence that stood in contrast to many of the shinier, glitzier places built in Hermanus after the 1980s. When in 2005 the Anton Rupert Trust sold it to Markus Jooste, the latter soon hauled in the builders, renovated the house and grounds, and razed the pine trees, like confetti being swept off the dance floor on the morning after a wedding. It was the trees that made Johann Rupert, by now chairman of Richemont and Remgro, purple with rage. After all, there'd been an agreement that those trees were to remain. So, he confronted Jooste: civilised people plant trees, he growled; uncivilised people rip them out. Jooste just stared at him, the story goes.

It's a tale that many tell in the winelands, a metaphor of the schism between the elder statesmen of Stellenbosch, the Ruperts, and the interlopers, represented by Christo Wiese and Markus Jooste.

* * *

The one thing that hasn't really changed in Stellenbosch since it was established in 1679 is the miles of oak trees, rustling languidly among the Cape Dutch gables, the art boutiques and *tuisnywerheid* (home industries) shopfronts. It also remains classically, fallibly South African: barely a kilometre outside town, there is a poor township, Kayamandi, where more than twenty-four thousand people are wedged in their corrugated iron shacks, with spaza shops squatting in the dirt selling airtime and oranges, chickens running loose, and anomalous satellite dishes. It's a stark contrast, particularly if one considers that Stellenbosch also happens to be the town in South Africa with the highest growth of ultra-rich dollar millionaires. Over the last decade, the number of ultra-rich in the winelands area of Paarl, Franschhoek and Stellenbosch grew by 20% to 3,400 people – nearly 8% of all the ultra-rich in South Africa. It punches way above its weight, in other words.[3]

Piet Mouton, the son of Jannie Mouton, who created financial services company PSG, describes it as "a great little town". "It's got everything you need, really. It's not far away from the airport. There are enough head offices in Stellenbosch now to make engagements. The restaurants are just fantastic and it's great for outdoor activities. Mind you, it's better when the students are off on vacation, far less traffic . . ."[4] And, importantly for Johann Rupert, it has the oaks.

Rupert, scion of the Rembrandt empire, likes to speak of himself as a "reformed prostitute", referring to his early years as an investment banker in New York. As a young man, he opted not to go into Rembrandt's business, but to launch out on his own. So, he first started working at Chase Manhattan Bank, before switching to investment bank Lazard Frères for three years. In 1979, he came back to South Africa and started Rand Merchant Bank (RMB), using the licence from the spluttering Rand Bank. But Johann's father enticed him back to Rembrandt as vice-chairman in 1983, so he sold RMB to three merchant bankers who were looking to build their own new enterprise called Rand Consolidated Investments (RCI) in 1977: GT Ferreira, Paul Harris and Laurie Dippenaar.

Rather curiously, when Johann returned, he opted not to move back to Stellenbosch, but rather to buy a house in Paarl Vallei in Somerset West. Stellenbosch was too small for all the enormous egos already wedged between the Simonsig Mountains and the Eerste River. And yet, Rupert remains indelibly *Stellenbosch*. He is still the chancellor of the university, and the Rupert Museum is still a well-trampled tourist attraction in town.

Interestingly, Christo Wiese, who is often depicted in folklore as the anti-matter to Rupert in Stellenbosch, also chooses not to live in town. Rather, he lives in Clifton, in Cape Town. This means, ironically, that neither of the two "generals" seen as the faces of the two opposing Stellenbosch factions actually lives there.

When Markus Jooste arrived in Stellenbosch, he slotted neatly into the "new money" faction, the faction that Rupert believes broke the town. Speaking today, Johann Rupert says: "I haven't lived there for thirty years, but I do suppose, at one stage, there was something of a Remgro culture, and then there was another, newer culture."[5] It's not a metamorphosis that he is entirely comfortable with, either. "To some extent, it does disturb me what has happened to my old town. People have cut down trees and built palaces. I felt the culture has changed," he says.

To an extent, the Steinhoff collapse has acted as a lightning rod for those who feel that way, and who believe the company embodied the worst of Stellenbosch's "new wealth". Most people know someone with a sad-sack story of how they'd unwisely had their life's savings tied up in Steinhoff, and lost it all. Well, 98% of their savings at any rate.

It's these losses that rankle with Rupert. "There are people who borrowed heavily, using their shares in Steinhoff as collateral, and now all they have is that debt."[6] You could frame this clash in many ways: old money versus new money; a generational war; or the inevitable power tussle you get when a new, self-appointed sheriff swaggers into town. The Norfolk pines, of course, are just the obvious manifestation of this division.

Outside Stellenbosch, in the hotel bars of Joburg or in the offices of pension managers under the shadow of Table Mountain in Claremont, there's another narrative about the town: the Stellenbosch Mafia; the Stellenostra; or, more common today in the wake of the Steinhoff scandal, Skelmbosch. It's a myth that has been percolating for years, this tale of an organised coalition of Stellenbosch tycoons, who supposedly meet to divvy up deals among themselves, plot assaults on new sectors of the economy, and conspire to keep out aspiring entrants. It makes for snappy headlines, but the reality is depressingly less titillating. Rather, it's a loose affiliation of friends and rivals, who live in the same small town, who drink wine together, who eat at the same restaurants, and some of whom can't stand each other. Some of them don't even live in Stellenbosch.

The truth is that no one has been to swim with the fishes at the bottom of the Eerste River. There are more people wearing posh Australian RM Williams boots in Stellenbosch than have ever ended up wearing concrete boots. A few years back, Jannie Mouton was asked about this myth, and he joked: "We Mafia members don't talk We are friends, we even compete with one another. Do you think, for instance, that they'd share all their transactions with you? It's a small pond, and we are friends.".[7]

Mouton was one of those rare folks that managed, for a time at least, to remain on good terms with the two bulls in the kraal – Christo Wiese and Johann Rupert. He'd also been firm friends with Jooste. They'd bought a wine farm together – Klein Gustrouw – in the Jonkershoek valley. A bit later, Jooste sold his half back to Mouton. According to the label on the bottles of Klein Gustrouw wines, "Established in 1817, this property nestles in the beautiful Jonkershoek valley in Stellenbosch. Owners Jannie Mouton and Markus Jooste have extended their long-standing friendship and partnership into a new venture." The bottle warns that alcohol abuse is dangerous to your health.

With a woolly white beard and a thick, gravelled accent, Mouton is like the Everyman's investor. He's often called the "Boere Buffett", and his decisions are as closely scrutinised in a corner of Stellenbosch and with as much fervour as anything Warren Buffett does in Omaha, Nebraska. If anyone should have been invited into the Mafia, it is Jannie. Though Mouton still appears remarkably sharp, in May 2018 he bravely wrote to staff and investors to tell them he'd just been diagnosed with an early form of dementia. "My short-term memory does not always function as it should, the result being that I sometimes forget people's names, repeat myself or may appear somewhat disoriented. This does not happen every day, but I cannot ignore it."[8] It was a poignant revelation from a man who had climbed to the apex of the country's business sector after famously being fired by his own stock brokerage – Senekal, Mouton and Kitshoff – in 1995. Describing his feelings when he was axed, Mouton said: "You're shocked, you're worried and, to a certain extent, you're ashamed. I thought of keeping it a secret and telling nobody but it was impossible." So, he spent hours at home, thinking about what had gone wrong (he had to improve his people skills, for a start), reading, and figuring out what to do next. Some months later he bought control of a small recruitment services company called PAG for R3.5m. His firing provided the necessary feng shui: PAG became PSG, which was the nursery for such blue-chip companies as banking group Capitec, schools group Curro and agricultural company Zeder. The value of that R3.5m investment in PSG today? Comfortably more than R12bn.

Speaking recently, Piet Mouton, who is now the public face of PSG, laughs when asked about it. If there's a Stellenbosch Mafia, my family's invitation is long overdue, he says.[9] "After the Rembrandt crowd, GT Ferreira was probably the first wealthy person to move down here from Joburg in the mid-1990s. He convinced Jannie to move down here too. He said to him, we've just bought office space down here, and it's a fantastic place to live." According to Piet, while GT and Jannie are fantastic friends and have deep reservoirs of mutual respect, there is still an intense rivalry, given that Ferreira had made his fortune from banking group FirstRand, while a large part of PSG's success is down to their own bank, Capitec. "If there's any commonality, it's that many of these people were Afrikaans businessmen who had studied at Stellenbosch University, enjoyed their time there, and have either stayed or returned," says Mouton.

David Meades, a veteran stockbroker and former journalist who has written a soon-to-be-released book called *Afrikaner Kapitalisme: Van Brandarm tot Stinkryk*, says it's not the Mafia in any real sense. "It's just that there were many influential people, all within the same area – the likes of Jannie Mouton, GT Ferreira and others – all with immense firepower."[10]

Christo Wiese himself has a notable take on why it is that Stellenbosch punches above its weight, and why it's seen as something of a winelands Silicon Valley. "You see an interesting picture emerging as far as the SA business scene today is concerned. The most prominent people, the names you always read about, are 80%-plus Afrikaans. That is a complete reversal from thirty to forty years ago, where there were a few Afrikaans business luminaries but the bulk were English-speaking or Jewish."[11] But today, Wiese says, it is Afrikaans and black businessmen who are making the headlines. To some extent, it is because Afrikaans or black business people are second-generation entrepreneurs, who come from the stock of industrials who made their mark years ago. "They had a good education, were brought up around commerce, and are building on what they inherited."

The casting of the Stellenbosch Mafia as a myth is one of the few points of consensus that you'll find on all sides of the Great Divide – even if the rasping irony of the tales of the Stellenbosch Mafia is that neither of the supposed "two Dons" even lives in Stellenbosch.

So, what is the root of this splintering between the two factions? "The animosity between Johann and Christo was widely known," says one prominent member of the so-called Stellenbosch Mafia. "People were pretty much seen as being part of the Remgro camp or the Wiese camp. And when Markus joined, it was clear where he stood." Those close to Rupert will carp that it's because "Christo has often stepped on the little man to get where he is". (Wiese's comment: "My businesses weren't built by stepping on anyone – rather, we try to build people up and give them jobs.") Those close to Wiese will retort that Rupert still thinks he owns the town, and doesn't realise he's not the big cheese in Stellenbosch that he once was.

David Meades, who covered the Afrikaans business sector as a journalist for decades before turning to stockbroking, says the falling-out between the Ruperts and Wiese dates back decades.[12] "Back in the 1990s, Anton Rupert was a director of the South African Reserve Bank, and when Rembrandt bought one of the banks that would later form part of Absa, he felt he needed to resign. One of the guys who replaced him was the up-and-coming Christo Wiese."

In 1999 Remgro's 50%-owned diamond company TransHex tried to buy out Ocean Diamond Mining (ODM), a company that provided the bulk of De Beers' marine diamonds. But Wiese swooped in and mopped up enough shares in ODM to block Rupert's takeover bid. In 2000, an extensive account in the *Financial Mail* recounted how Wiese and Rupert were "friends and mutual admirers for many years, until the fight for control of

ODM highlighted differences in approach and sundered their friendship".

Just before the vote in June 1999, Wiese told Rembrandt that he wasn't going to vote for the takeover bid. But, he said, Rembrandt could buy his stake in ODM for R8 a share (it was trading on the JSE at R6.50 at the time) and his stake in TransHex for R35 a share (when it was trading at R30). Wiese's reasoning was that he had an offer at the higher price from someone else, but as a courtesy he would offer it to Rupert first. A furious Rupert then accused Wiese of "greenmailing" him – essentially, blocking the bid unless he was paid above the bar for his stake. The contretemps got nastier and nastier, culminating in a series of hearings at the takeover panel, in which Wiese confronted Rupert about being branded a "liar". Rupert's retort was that Wiese's explanation for how the deal went down was just too far-fetched. When something looks like a dog, has hair like a dog, and barks like a dog, it's probably a dog, said Rupert. Well, that dog ended up biting you, didn't it, Wiese retorted. (TransHex's takeover of ODM failed. But in a final irony, Remgro unbundled TransHex, and in 2016 Wiese ended up as TransHex's major shareholder anyway.) "It was really quite astounding," says one lawyer of that meeting. "Both of them, Johann and Christo, were just going at each other. I'd never seen anything like it."

Ask either Wiese or Rupert about this split today, and they'll typically grumble that they don't want to get back into it. But it's evidently still a visceral dislike. As one executive who lives in town says: "You've got to pick your side." Wiese says this isn't how business works. "Of course not. There's no way you can run a personal feud through your companies, and there's certainly no way I'd do that."[13]

What's clear, though, is that while Johann Rupert didn't much like Jooste, he liked Steinhoff even less. Legend has it that when Christo Wiese was trying to shotgun a wedding between Shoprite and Steinhoff, Johann Rupert spent some time examining Steinhoff's financials. Over a weekend, Rupert spent three days going through various Steinhoff annual reports, but he couldn't understand anything. He couldn't understand how Steinhoff made its money, what was happening with its assets, or just what the margins really were in the individual European businesses. It's a sentiment that was apparently shared by Rupert's good friend Whitey Basson.

* * *

If there's one man who could charm both warring camps, it is GT Ferreira. He is one of the first people you'd put down on any list of Stellenbosch royalty. Erudite and cerebral, with a hint of mischief never far from his eye, GT is the epitome of the cultured modern Afrikaans businessman. With a raconteur's sense of wit, you could easily imagine him, in another life, as a suave and skilful diplomat, resolving crippling global crises with the flick of a cufflink.

In 1977 Ferreira, along with his two partners, Laurie Dippenaar and Paul Harris, built the skeleton around which the continent's biggest bank, First-Rand, would later be created, after buying Johann Rupert's Rand Merchant Bank. Famously, they started with just R10,000. Some of South Africa's best companies grew up in the FirstRand nursery: medical company Discovery, short-term insurer OUTsurance and life insurer Momentum are the best known.

In person, usually casually dressed in jeans with stubble, GT has something of the air of a venture capital billionaire, who turfed it all in early to go spend time on a farm, sipping wine. Which is pretty much exactly what he did. That story begins in 1992, when Ferreira was hijacked in Joburg and shot in the chest. The bullet deflected off his ribs, saving his life. (He still keeps the particular necktie he wore that day, branded with a hole in the centre.) But the event made GT reconsider his frantic life in the headlights of Joburg. So, in 1994 he and his wife Anne-Marie moved to Stellenbosch. "Initially, I was just interested in buying a gentleman's estate," says Ferreira today. "You know: a couple of hectares where we could keep a few horses, have a trout dam and all those nice things I'd learnt over the years from the British."[14] They searched, and eventually found a valley, anomalously perched at the crest of the Helshoogte mountain pass near Stellenbosch. Looked at from above, it's almost as if it's a sunken valley at the top of the world. And he was among auspicious company – on the left was the Delaire Graff wine estate, on the right was the Thelema farm built by Gyles Webb, and above him was the Rustenburg wine farm.

In the beginning, GT only bought part of the property, and the original owners still had the right to pump water from the dam. "I saw my trout floundering in the mud, and I figured that was the cue for me to do something about it." So, he bought the rest of the farm. Says Ferreira: "It was my merchant banking background. I figured I'd be really smart: sell off parts of the property in tranches and maybe I'd get it all for free. So, I drove up the mountain and looked down, and thought, do I really need the money I'd get by selling it? And the answer was no. So, the question was: what to do with it." You wouldn't have to search for that answer very long. He had only to look across the fence to realise that his farm lay in the very middle of vine country. He chatted to his neighbour, Webb, who encouraged him to do the maths. "What we wanted was a winery that could still be regarded as a family farm, but which is of a size that could, hopefully, make money eventually. That figure was 800 tons, which we didn't have. So, when the farms around us came on the market, the tradition was you had to buy it because you only get that chance once in a lifetime." So, he bought two adjacent farms, Simonsberg and Kelsey. That was the start of Tokara – the name derived from those of his children, Tomas and Kara.

The first vines were planted in 1998 and, with the assistance of Gyles Webb, the first wine was produced in 2001 under the name of Zonder-naam, until they figured they'd got the quality up to scratch. By 2005, once Ferreira and Webb were happy with what they were bottling, he released it under the Tokara label. Thanks to this ambition, Tokara has since become one of the world's top wines. In 2018, the well-reputed Drinks International listed Tokara among the top fifty wine brands in the world – one of the youngest wines on the list. It was judged by 200 wine masters.[15]

When Ferreira launched Tokara's 2015 Telos in London, he held a tasting with the world's top wine critics, presenting his new red blend alongside six of the best Bordeaux reds ever produced – all rated 100 points by Robert Parker. As Greg Sherwood, a London-based South African wine master who judges the World Sommelier Awards, put it: "Hell, if you are going to go down the whole comparative benchmarking route, why not do it properly and present your wine alongside the best there is! Needless to say, this approach needs more than a little confidence and self-belief." And the Telos didn't fall short of its esteemed peers.

Ferreira may be confident, but he's also disarmingly self-deprecating. He openly mocks billionaires, such as himself, who buy wine farms as simply seeking a "return on ego". But the Telos wine is an embodiment of Ferreira's instinct to either do it properly, or not bother. Right from the beginning, even though Tokara had not produced a single bottle of wine, he hired architects Van Biljon & Visser to design perhaps the most outstanding winery in Stellenbosch. *Financial Times* wine critic Jancis Robinson, who visited Tokara in 2003, reckoned it might just be the most beautiful winery she'd ever seen. "In aesthetic terms, [it is] beyond the wildest dreams of even the most munificent Napa Valley billionaire-vigneron, thanks partly to its breathtaking view from the slopes of the Simonsberg."[16]

It is partly because of Ferreira's rigour and demand for quality that the Steinhoff debacle cut deeply into his sensibilities. It was a painful experience – "It still makes me wince," he says – which cost him and his staff R1.1bn. The story is that back in 2004 Ferreira set up two trusts for the staff of Tokara – a black empowerment trust and a general workers' trust, with the caveat that at least 60% of all benefits from the latter must flow to black staff. About eighty families benefit from these trusts. Using a rough average, these farm workers would have had, potentially, a paper wealth of about R10m apiece before the crash. In the court papers he later filed against Steinhoff, Ferreira said: "The benefits which could (and should) flow from the trusts are capable of influencing the course of generations. Over the last eight years, the two trusts have collectively distributed some R24m to their beneficiaries."[17]

Besides that, the trusts have also bought land for a Tokara "Agrivillage" – a housing project which will be built on the farm. Up to 2015, the biggest asset that the farm workers had in the trust was shares in Jannie Mouton's company PSG. This was no great surprise, since Ferreira and PSG's founder, Jannie Mouton, had been great friends for decades. Both Ferreira and Mouton share offices in the same building at 35 Kerk Street, called Ou Kollege. "It was GT who decorated these offices," said Mouton, pointing to the paintings on the walls around his office and the wooden panels.[18] Ferreira had held shares in PSG since 1995, and that's why, when he set up the Tokara staff trusts, he bought shares in PSG and donated them to the trust. "I considered the PSG Group to be an excellent medium- to long-term investment for the trusts. I was also the holder of a number of PSG shares in my personal capacity," he said.[19]

But, as talk of Steinhoff began to infiltrate dinner-time conversations at Helena's Restaurant in Church Street, or at breakfast at Meraki down the road, Ferreira began to take an interest. Since Mouton co-owned Klein Gustrouw, they all spent a lot of time together. Then in May 2015, Jooste made a fateful approach to three of Stellenbosch's elite – GT Ferreira, Thys du Toit, and PSG Konsult's former chairman, Jaap du Toit, who all had shares in PSG. "Jooste approached me with the proposal that entailed a swap of those PSG shares for shares in Steinhoff," says Ferreira. "Jooste told me that he also approached two other well-known businessmen, Thys du Toit and Jaap du Toit, with a similar proposal."

Ferreira wasn't entirely sure why Jooste wanted to do this. Perhaps, he figured, it was because Jooste sought "negative control" of PSG – in other words, if he could push Steinhoff's shareholding in PSG to 25.1% (by buying the interests of GT, Thys and Jaap), he could block any PSG deals. Nonetheless, Ferreira was keen. He'd be swapping his shares in an entirely domestic company, PSG, for those in a company five times larger, with international exposure. It would also be far easier to trade the Steinhoff shares if he wanted. Of course, GT had heard the rumblings about Steinhoff – the dodgy tax deals, the shady European purchases, and talk of parlous ethics. But, he says, Jooste had "always dismissed these as unfounded allegations made by an erstwhile business partner" (the well-trodden Blame-It-On-Andreas-Seifert path).

Then Ben la Grange appeared in the picture. La Grange was another slick Stellenbosch resident, who'd rapidly become part of Markus Jooste's inner circle. After studying at Stellenbosch University (where else?), La

Grange had worked at auditing firm PwC for nearly three years, before joining Steinhoff as a manager in its corporate tax division. (A cynic might regard that division as the real engine room of Steinhoff.) Anyway, it was La Grange who handled the technicalities of the share swap. He sent Ferreira the documents, discussed the tax consequences and told him he'd be getting 2.65 Steinhoff shares for each of his PSG shares. GT agreed – but only if Jannie Mouton sanctioned it.

Thys du Toit tells the same story. He says Jooste walked into his office, and told him it had to be all three of them, or none at all.[20] "Markus explained that Steinhoff currently had 20% of PSG, and if they could take this to 25%, they'd get a massive tax advantage. I told him, It sounds attractive, let me evaluate it, and speak to the others and Jannie first. He replied: 'No, just do everything through me. I'll speak to Jannie.'" This is a central part of the story. All three of them were great friends with Mouton and none of them wanted to jeopardise that.

But a few days later, Jooste came back and told them all that he'd spoken to Jannie Mouton, and that Jannie was "fine with it". Even then, it wasn't easy. As Ferreira puts it: "I found it very difficult to inform Jannie Mouton, a good friend and chairman of PSG, about my [intention] even though Jooste assured us that Jannie Mouton did not have a problem with the proposed exchange of shares."[21] Only, it seems Markus had lied. He'd only casually mentioned the share swap – and Jannie was anything but "fine" about it. Insiders say that it was only late one night, after a dinner at Mouton's house in Stellenbosch, as Jooste was leaving, that he mentioned the swap. Jannie was apoplectic with rage. "Jannie felt very hurt and betrayed," says one of his friends. "He'd been one of Markus's biggest supporters for years, and a close friend, and then this share transfer was snuck in through the back door. It left a really bad taste."

So Jannie called a full meeting in Stellenbosch attended by Jannie's son Piet, Jooste and La Grange. And he left nobody in any doubt about how angry he was. Why weren't you honest and open about these plans? he asked. Why did you hide it? Jooste scrambled to apologise. He claimed he "forgot" to speak to him. Jannie was still sore, however – not because he believed Ferreira and the others weren't allowed to sell their PSG shares, but rather because Jooste had gone behind his back to do the deal.

Piet Mouton says Markus told him that Steinhoff wanted to boost their stake above 25% for tax reasons. Obviously, it also gave Steinhoff "negative control", but Markus had glossed over this. The nagging discomfort, however, was the way in which it was done – not notifying Jannie beforehand – and it made PSG's brains trust worry that Steinhoff might have ulterior motives. In the worst case, they worried, Steinhoff could even mount a hostile takeover of PSG.

Mouton must have forgiven Jooste, to some extent. Mouton stayed on Steinhoff's board for a number of months after that, before resigning in March 2016. Jooste remained on PSG's board, too, and chaired their remuneration committee. "Markus was a very good director," says Piet Mouton. "He read and studied all the board packs, he contributed to every discussion, and is obviously highly intelligent. He also acted independently, and never asked us to do transactions with Steinhoff. You don't get many better."[22]

In March 2016 Jannie Mouton resigned from Steinhoff's board. Quite fortunately for him, he sold all his shares in Steinhoff over the next year. The obvious question is: did he see something that caused him to lose faith? "No, not really. Jannie remained positive, and watched with intrigue as Markus continued to build his global furniture empire," says Piet. "The reality is, Jannie hates travelling, and after the listing in Frankfurt, their head office moved to Amsterdam, where their board meetings were held. And Jannie was turning 70 that year and had no further appetite to travel extensively to meetings abroad." A couple of months later, Jannie decided to "de-risk" himself. He owed quite a lot of money, and the only assets he could sell easily (beside his PSG shares) were his shares in Steinhoff. And he used part of the proceeds to fund his charitable foundation.

Since Steinhoff's crash, Jannie hasn't spoken to his former wine-farming partner. He, like the others, got the text message from Jooste saying "sorry" for what had happened. Unlike the others, Mouton's prescience meant he escaped without losing his shirt.

* * *

By contrast, GT Ferreira, Thys du Toit and Jaap du Toit would rue their share swap. When Steinhoff capsized, Ferreira felt particularly angry. "At first, when I found out what happened and the share fell, I went through so many emotions," he says today. "Shock, disbelief, disappointment, disillusionment, anger – but, mostly, self-doubt and self-recrimination. You start to ask yourself how it is possible you hadn't seen what was happening."[23] It wasn't as if he'd listened to Jooste and La Grange and just swallowed what they told him. He considered himself a reasonably astute investor, so he did a deeper due diligence – looking at all the accounts dating back to 2010. "After what happened, it makes it difficult to trust anyone around you, especially the auditing profession." In his court papers, he says he felt "duped out of the valuable [PSG shares] which the two trusts and I held".

On 12 February 2018, Ferreira wrote to Johan van Zyl, who was then a director of Steinhoff, and told him how disappointed he was that he'd been coerced by Jooste and La Grange into swapping his shares on the basis of lies. "I can . . . say that, without a shadow of a doubt, our decision to accept the Steinhoff share exchange proposal was based on misleading financial, as well as other, information that was available to us at the time," he wrote.

Nobody responded to him. So in May 2018 he lodged an immense R1.1bn claim against Steinhoff. It's some degrees less than Wiese's R59bn claim, to be sure, but Ferreira has the easier case to argue of the two. In his court papers, Ferreira says he was aggrieved to learn that the accounts he'd relied on were now "demonstrated to be untrue, unreliable and misrepresentative of Steinhoff's true financial position". Of course, people may struggle to have sympathy for a billionaire, especially one with hundreds of litres of the country's best wine at his fingertips. But this isn't how it is for Tokara's employees and their families, who have effectively lost a potential benefit of R760m within a year – on average, nearly R10m per family. "I set those trusts up about twelve years ago for the benefit of the Tokara employees," says Ferreira. "I funded the trusts myself with my own money, and we started investing on behalf of the trust in a variety of investments. They were mostly successful – especially the investments we made in the PSG

Group." The employees' investment was split into two: 5.2m Steinhoff shares in the Tokara BEE Trust, and 4.9m shares in the Tokara Employees Trust. Those shares were worth R787m when they were bought in 2015 – and just R18.9m today. Says Ferreira: "It's not the end of the road for those trusts, though – this wasn't their only investment. There are one or two other investments there that are quite valuable." But he adds: "It is indeed a sad story, because we shall never be able to recover what we have lost."

The Steinhoff collapse has been equally scarring for Du Toit, who, despite an unusual route into investing (his first degree was in science), is still spoken about in some circles as one of the founding fathers of South Africa's modern investment industry. Not only was Du Toit one of the founders of South Africa's fourth-largest fund manager, Coronation, in 1983, but he also convened the Investment Managers Association of South Africa. "Look, the whole thing has polarised Stellenbosch to some extent," Du Toit says. "There are still those people loyal to Markus in Stellenbosch, and there are others who are furious at what he did. So it's created a very poisonous dynamic."[24]

Financially, it would seem that Du Toit wasn't as badly hurt by the whole episode as Ferreira was. Steinhoff's unaudited half-year results, released in 2018, revealed that both Thys and Jaap had "derivative agreements" to protect themselves against adverse movements in Steinhoff's share price. This agreement meant that if Steinhoff's value fell below PSG's value, then Steinhoff would pay out the difference or give those PSG shares back. Which was just as well. As you can imagine, when Steinhoff's shares crashed, the company owed a fortune to the Du Toits. Steinhoff's accounts show that the Du Toits, between them, got a "settlement" of €700,000 and 2.3m PSG shares (worth R510m), in exchange for 6.2m Steinhoff shares (worth about R15m). "It now appears that Steinhoff's accounts were vastly overvalued at the time Markus spoke to me about swapping the shares," says Du Toit. "He must have known this. He must have known he was swapping shit for ice cream."

It's another illustration of the fact that the severity of the knock was directly proportional to how close you were to Markus. While South Africa's civil servants and pensioners took a heavy knock, Markus' friends were swiped the hardest. That's probably why some people like Thys du Toit got an SMS saying "sorry" for what had happened.

* * *

Roll a rock down Church Street in Stellenbosch today, and odds are you'll hit someone who lost at least something in Steinhoff's fall. Some, of course, never invested. Many Stellenbosch alumni found Jooste's showmanship too crass and ostentatious from the outset, and steered clear. "He'd go to one of those auctions at Stellenbosch University to raise money for something, but he'd end up paying a hundred times what was being asked. It wasn't because there was no other way to make a donation – it was because he wanted to show the younger guys just how much money he had," says one university alumnus.[25] To some, this suggested that money bought impunity, a sense that the normal conventions don't apply to you. Which brings us to another story.

Some of the Steinhoff top brass tell of how, at one point, a striking, self-confident blonde began appearing alongside Jooste with some regularity. Her name was Berdine Odendaal. "I met her with Markus in an airport lounge," says one of the Steinhoff directors. "Afterwards, I thought there had been something odd about that encounter, because he specifically didn't introduce her to me. It was only later that I figured out it was her." Another tells of how a white Ferrari pulled into the Steinhoff parking lot in Stellenbosch. "Who's that?" he asked. The secretaries who were watching the same scene just rolled their eyes: ask Markus, they said.

Soon after the Steinhoff bubble popped, newspaper headlines revealed Berdine Odendaal to be Markus Jooste's mistress. Pictures of Odendaal, with short-cropped hair, languid and glamorous, were suddenly hot property. Journalists Angelique Serrao and Pieter du Toit reported: "Those who know Odendaal saw her drive a customised silver Bentley and white Ferrari and they spoke about her two Argentinian polo ponies."[26]

Today, Odendaal refuses to speak to anyone. Her old cellphone number has been disconnected; her Facebook profile, from where those pictures originated, has been disabled. Her friends talk of how she's "been under siege and just wants to be left alone". For a long time, she was holed up indoors – some reports say with her parents. Every now and again, people would see her at the odd event – a polo meeting or the theatre. Haven't you heard, she supposedly told someone at one such event, I've become famous. Some of her friends, like Pretoria architect Carlu Swart, say she's "been through a hard time, but she's a lovely woman". Swart was hired to design and build a house for Berdine at the Mabalingwe Nature Reserve in Limpopo, but those plans seem to have been scuppered.[27]

What is remarkable is that Odendaal appears to have been kept by Jooste, in a way more evocative of an eighteenth-century courtesan than a modern twenty-first-century woman. She lived in one of Cape Town's most exclusive apartments, the Bantry. But that apartment was owned by Coy's Properties, whose only director was Markus Jooste's British associate, Malcolm King. Stefan Potgieter, Jooste's son-in-law, supposedly "managed the apartment" for King. When it all fell apart, the Bantry apartment was sold for R57m.

Odendaal is actually listed as the owner of six properties at Val de Vie. This includes a 109m^2 unit at the Polo, bought for R3.3m in 2016. But she's also listed as the owner of two properties in the Mabalingwe Nature Reserve, presumably where the building was halted.[28] The dates of many of the Val de Vie purchases, in her name, go back to the beginning of 2016. This suggests her relationship with Jooste was fairly recent.

Christo Wiese says he never had a clue about Berdine Odendaal's existence. "If he'd had a girlfriend that his wife didn't know about, it would have been a red flag to me," he says. "Because, if he could lie to his wife for years, why couldn't he lie to me?"[29] About a year before the implosion, one of Wiese's friends from Pretoria said to him: Christo, do you know Markus has a flat in the Bantry? And do you know he keeps a girlfriend there? Wiese was taken aback. Surely he'd know about this, especially since Wiese's own son has an apartment there? I mean, Markus wasn't obliged to mention it, but surely he *would* have? So, a few weeks later, Wiese asked him. You know, Markus, someone tells me you have a flat in the Bantry?

Ja, said Jooste, it's an excellent investment.

Wiese replied: Well, why don't you let one of your children live there? It's a really beautiful place to live. They'd like it.

No, no, said Jooste. It's far too luxurious for a child to live there.

Wiese persisted: Markus, someone tells me you keep a girlfriend there.

Jooste's reaction: Christo, you must be mad, man. Where would I find time for a girlfriend . . .

To Wiese, this made sense. It takes time to run a girlfriend. And that's the one thing Jooste didn't have . . .

*   *   *

In the five years up to Christmas 2017, Steinhoff pretty much *owned* Stellenbosch. Its distinctive maroon branding was all over the rugby posts at the Danie Craven stadium, on the scoreboards, the tickets and the players' kit. But in December 2017, everything changed. Suddenly, Steinhoff's money wasn't welcome anywhere. The billboards bearing the slogan "Adding value to your lifestyle" were ripped up, and stashed in a pile out of eyesight, at the back of a shed. On the bridges over the stadium, masking tape was used to black out Steinhoff's name. And when first-year students arrived in February 2018 to be officially welcomed by the rector, a black cloth was thrown over a Steinhoff sign at the cricket field.[30] A noticeable pall descended over the town.

Up on the hill above the Jonkershoek valley is the farm that Markus Jooste shares with two of his long-standing Steinhoff confidants, Danie van der Merwe, the current CEO, and Frikkie Nel. In 2003, the three of them bought the farm, called Bengale, together for R31m. After a while, Danie van der Merwe moved into the old farmhouse, which he fixed up, while Frikkie Nel built a new barn-style house, which has a dam out front. Both Danie and Frikkie are irredeemably unpretentious: for years, Frikkie drove an old bakkie, the sort you'd often see rumbling down Stellenbosch's farms road. Jooste also built a house, but his was a contemporary Cape Dutch construction, with a few glitzy trappings, like a jacuzzi, a sauna and an indoor pool.

The three Steinhoff musketeers called their new farm Jonkersdrift. By all accounts, it's an impressive oasis, even by the standards of Stellen-bosch's exalted wealth. There's only one entrance ("for security reasons"), and as you drive in on a wide, gravel road, there are wide, open paddocks, set far back on either side behind a split-pole fence, where horses graze. There's a rocky river that ripples through the middle of the farm. So perfect is it that it could easily be the opening shot of a Stellenbosch real estate commercial. "It was great for them when everyone was getting on. It's one of the safest places in the world," says one family friend.

Though Danie, Frikkie and Markus lived separately, they'd occasionally have braais together and they knew their colleagues were never further away than a brisk walk. Now, Steinhoff's collapse has strained this relation-ship. "A lot of things must still be proven – I cannot judge anyone," says Frikkie Nel today. "I obviously have to communicate with Markus about issues on the farm, but I've only seen him twice since December. But otherwise, I'm living the same way I have for the last fifteen years."[31]

With Markus Jooste effectively banished to Hermanus, it means that if there's a problem on the farm – like a fire – they communicate largely through SMSes. Supposedly, Rian du Plessis, the CEO of Phumelela, who is one of Markus' oldest friends, acts as a go-between if there are any problems on the farm.

Both Nel and Van der Merwe would be justified in being furious. Both are interwoven into the fabric of almost every decision Steinhoff has taken for the last two decades. Yet, between them, Frikkie and Danie will have lost a fortune of more than R400m. Nel, the last time it was disclosed in 2015, had 1,952,735 shares in Steinhoff – a paper fortune equivalent to more than R109m. The crash seared that to human proportions. It meant that by August 2018 those shares would have been worth R5.4m.[32] Van der Merwe, at last count, held 6.1m shares in Steinhoff, which he'd accumulated over the years. Before December's crash, they would have made him fan-tastically wealthy, with stock worth R345m. By September 2018, Van der Merwe's shares were worth just more than R15m.[33]

Not many people can look at the loss of more than R320m and know it's largely thanks to your neighbour, on the other side of the porch. Worse:

any forensic investigation into fraud at Steinhoff would almost have to contort itself to avoid questions over Van der Merwe's and Nel's role in what happened. Van der Merwe, now acting CEO, was the man who brokered that first deal with the shady Alan Evans, inserting Fihag into the deal to buy the forests – a deal that was never disclosed as a related party, but from which Markus Jooste scored millions. Van der Merwe, amiable and pugnacious, is no fool. He was first admitted as a lawyer in 1986 and was Steinhoff's chief operating officer from 2013. But insiders close to the PwC investigation say that at this point there's nothing that implicates him in any accounting manipulation. "Danie was an operations guy, more than a finance guy. So if this is an accounting problem, it isn't really something laid at his door," says one.

Nel, earnest and grandfatherly, must be just as disappointed. For years, he was the man closest to Steinhoff's accounts and, arguably, the closest to Jooste. In fact, Frikkie is godfather of Jooste's children. Back in 1993, he'd taken the role of Steinhoff company secretary. Up to 2015, when Steinhoff listed in Frankfurt using Mickey Mouse accounts, Nel was Steinhoff's finance director. Its prospectus for that listing says the preparation of Steinhoff's historical accounts was "supervised by: Frikkie Nel CA(SA), Financial director". In Steinhoff's 2015 annual report, Frikkie Nel and Ben la Grange together wrote a cock-a-hoop eight-page financial report, gushing about how "our experienced management team remains optimistic about the future". At that stage, La Grange was the chief financial officer for just Steinhoff's southern hemisphere operations, before taking over Frikkie's role. Now, of course, each page of Nel and La Grange's report carries a bright red stamp, warning that "information can no longer be relied on". The question is, could it ever have been relied upon.

Speaking today, Frikkie Nel is philosophical about what happened. "I have also lost wealth, lots of potential wealth, but so have many people," he says. "Things happen over which I have no control. I can be disappointed about what happened, but what would it help to be cross?"

13

The Gathering

In August 2017, an anonymous package arrived at the Dutch headquarters of the auditing firm Deloitte. Inside was part of the whistleblower's report on Steinhoff – the same document that had earlier landed up with the Oldenburg prosecutors in Germany. Supposedly compiled by lawyers, the content was explosive: it detailed a trail of fake documents, allegations of artificially boosted profits, and balance sheet manipulation. Deloitte's auditors were understandably astounded. After all, they were Steinhoff's auditors, and had signed off the retailer's accounts the previous September. Now it seemed, if the whistleblower's report was true, the accounts were riddled with errors.

The auditors took out the contracts in the report, and compared them to the ones they had on file for the same transactions. "The ones we had on record were different," says someone at Deloitte. The auditors, in other words, had been given forged documents. The revelation spooked the audit firm. "That's when we resolved that we needed a proper forensic investigation. To assess what was true, what wasn't, what deals were above board, what weren't." (In Parliament later, Jooste would say that Andreas Seifert's lawyers had given the documents to Steinhoff. But that's evidently not what Deloitte believed.)

A few weeks later, after receiving the documents, Deloitte sent a letter to Steinhoff, addressed to Dr Steve Booysen, who chaired Steinhoff's audit committee. Stehan Grobler, the man in charge of Steinhoff's treasury, told

Booysen about the letter, and what was in it, on 25 September 2017. But don't worry, he said, we're addressing all the issues they've raised.

Grobler knew how serious the matter was. As someone who'd been a lawyer (and remained a partner at Hoffman Attorneys) until he met Markus Jooste at Gomma Gomma and become Steinhoff's company secretary a year later in 1999, he was waist deep in the matter himself.

Booysen would have been startled when he opened the letter. Inside, Deloitte had set out a long list of questions, mostly around the issues raised by *Manager Magazin*, to which they wanted answers. They were questions around the revaluation of properties, around the "off-balance sheet companies" like GT Branding, and of whether sales had been inflated. And, Deloitte said, we need you to commission a forensic investigation.

So Booysen called an urgent audit committee meeting the following week, in early October. It was attended by Dr Len Konar and Theunie Lategan, but he also invited Jooste and Dirk Schreiber. Schreiber's position was that of head of finance for the European business.

At the meeting, Booysen told them about the letter and Deloitte's demand. Markus shook his head with mock exasperation: Deloitte, they just don't understand what's going on. The Dutch guys are new to the audit and it's all one giant misunderstanding. And besides, they signed off the audit last year, and they didn't raise any of these issues. So it means all the documents they're asking for in this letter should be in their files.

Everyone else agreed. Well, yes, Markus is right – it *should* be in their files. Why would they sign it off last year if this stuff was an issue?

Len Konar then said, Look, we can't afford to miss the date to sign off our financials for the year to September. We've only got about eight weeks left – so we have to put pressure on Deloitte to sort themselves out.

Markus, as ever, was entirely convincing. But on the way back from Stellenbosch, Deloitte's letter still niggled with Booysen – a forensic investigation is a big deal, and if Deloitte was demanding that, could everything *really* be kosher? And why was Markus *so* resistant to a forensic investigation, anyway? If everything was above board, what could he possibly lose?

The next week, Booysen arranged to go and see Deloitte in Amsterdam, to sit across the table and discuss the wall they'd hit. Jooste was clearly not keen for this to happen without him: I'm coming with you, he said.

12 October 2017

Steve Booysen decided to fly to Amsterdam separately, a day earlier than Markus. He clearly wanted to hold a separate meeting with Deloitte's partner Patrick Seinstra, without Markus's presence, given how central the CEO was to the allegations.

Deloitte's fifteen-storey office in Amsterdam bills itself as the greenest building in the world. Green is probably an apt description of how Booysen felt as he walked into that meeting. He told Seinstra that he was no friend of Markus Jooste and was willing to take him on if need be. But what proof did Deloitte have? If there was any evidence, he said, he'd pull the trigger immediately.

Seinstra replied that Deloitte didn't have evidence yet; only allegations and plenty of concerns. And plenty of questions.

Booysen asked: Well, do you think Markus is unethical, then?

No, replied Seinstra, we don't. (This clearly was a little too coy: pretty clearly, the auditors had their own thoughts on the matter, even if they didn't want to share them just then.)

That afternoon, Booysen again met with Deloitte, but this time with Jooste and Dirk Schreiber present too. Markus trotted out his story, and stuck to the same line: it's all a big misunderstanding. There's no related party deals. It's all Andreas Seifert's fault. All those deals that Steinhoff has done with the likes of Campion, involving the trademarks and lending books, are at arm's length and with independent parties. Steinhoff isn't Campion's only customer, and these guys – Pasquier, Schmidt and Evans – are millionaires in their own right.

Jooste, as usual, was silky smooth, with answers for everything. He didn't break a sweat. So, Deloitte agreed to go and meet with the law firm that had scrutinised all the Oldenburg allegations, Flick Gocke Schaumburg (FGS), and its principal, Dr Karsten Randt. In numerous (expensive) reports, FGS had said it had found zero evidence. In the end, Booysen would have left Amsterdam convinced things were moving, that he'd opened the channels, that perhaps it was just one giant misunderstanding, and it would all be cleared up. Which, of course, wasn't what happened at all.

14 November 2017

At about 11 am on 14 November, Booysen got a call from Deloitte's Amsterdam office. We need to speak to you, one of the auditors said, *without* Markus being present. It turned out that Deloitte had met with FGS, but weren't convinced that the law firm had done a proper job. And Deloitte's own forensic team had done an exploratory probe into the whistleblower's allegations. While they hadn't uncovered any smoking gun, there was a pretty strong circumstantial case being built. In the light of all this, Deloitte told Booysen, we now have a longer list of questions we need you to answer, a list they would email to him.

Booysen was quite frustrated by this slow dance, especially since Deloitte had nothing concrete. So he told them: Guys, you ask a lot of questions. Go and do the audit: find the accounting entries, and follow the cash flows, check the journal entries, and if you find something concrete, then bring it to me and I'll act on it.

Well, sure, Deloitte replied, but Markus isn't cooperating with us. He isn't giving us any of the documents that we need to do the actual auditing work.

Immediately, Booysen called Jooste. Why hasn't Deloitte got that information yet? Didn't you say you'd get it to them after the meeting in Amsterdam? Anyway, they've now sent another long list of questions, which you have to answer.

After he emailed the list to Jooste, Markus called him back. Of course I'll answer them, but it's quite an extensive list and it'll take me a few days to put all the documents together.

Booysen evidently did not realise it at the time, but this was how Jooste had played the bluster game for years. He would withhold information from the auditors until the last possible minute, perhaps betting that they'd blink first and shelve their concerns and then sign off the accounts anyway.

Or, perhaps they'd have a day to scan through the numbers before panicking and, with an eye on the clock, accepting what they had to sign off.

But Booysen wasn't going to wait around. He called another audit meeting for 20 November. It was time to get to the bottom of the problem once and for all.

20 November 2017

This time, everyone was in the room at Steinhoff's Stellenbosch office. Jooste was there, Stehan Grobler, Deloitte's auditors and FGS's lawyers. Also, Steinhoff's audit committee members, Konar and Theunie Lategan. Even Timo Cybucki, the managing partner of Commerzial Treuhand (CT), which audited Steinhoff's European business, was there.

Again, the issues raised by Deloitte were tabled, and again Jooste trotted through his answers (it's a story he stuck to consistently, throughout). The FGS documents – weighty lever arch-files – were tabled too.

The audit committee then asked Jooste's management team to leave. Then they grilled FGS: Deloitte seems to believe you're influenced by management and aren't independent – is this accurate? How thorough were you in this report?

FGS went through their *schpiel*: Our firm is 45 years old, we provide legal tax advice to 2,000 companies from our 119 partners, and most of the firms listed on Frankfurt's DAX use us. Then the focus shifted to CT, the German auditor. Tell us what you did to check the "related party deals", tell us about your quality controls, and what questions you asked.

On the face of it, it seemed everything had been done as it should have been. As a result, Len Konar reckoned Deloitte was just messing everyone around. We need to tell them to finish the audit, he said.

23 November 2017

That day, 23 November, was meant to be the day on which the audit for Steinhoff's European was to be completed. Consequently, Deloitte was sitting with Booysen, Dirk Schreiber and CT's Timo Cybucki in Stellenbosch, trying to pull everything together. They were wrestling with the accounts, and why it was that the European company was pushing through such huge numbers for "cash and cash equivalents". How could it be that the cash number was so large, when the actual operations, with the odd exception (like Pepkor Europe), didn't appear to be thriving?

At every turn, they kept coming back to the *wechsels* – the German guarantees that had been provided which, according to German accounting rules, can be included under a company's "cash and cash equivalents". Not many companies use these *wechsels* in their accounts, so it wasn't exactly as if everyone was completely au fait with how they worked. What were these *wechsels* being used as a guarantee for, anyway? And why were there so many of them in the European accounts?

Finally, at this meeting, the exact, circuitous route of these *wechsels* was plotted. And Booysen and the others began to realize what was happening: people who owed Steinhoff money, its debtors, had been given a *wechsel* as a guarantee by Steinhoff itself. And the effect of this, they figured out, was that it made a debt look like actual cash on Steinhoff's balance sheet. This was alarming. It meant that the money Steinhoff was owed by outside parties, like Talgarth, was being guaranteed by Steinhoff itself. What if Talgarth defaulted on this debt? The consequence was that Steinhoff would become liable for this debt – so its liabilities were understated. (The reality was actually worse. What nobody realised at that meeting was that those debtors appear to have been fictitious anyway. In other words, they seemed to be "fake debts" cooked up by Jooste and his overseas accomplices to make it seem as if Steinhoff had way more cash than it really did.)

There was a long silence in the room when the reality of what had happened sank in. Then Booysen spoke: Right, let's take five of these items flagged by Deloitte – including the property valuations, Talgarth, the *wechsels*, the off-balance sheet companies, and the deal with Serta Simmons – and let's prepare a report for the chairman, Christo Wiese. We'll go see Christo, and lay out where the problems are.

At that point, the realisation began to crystallise: Deloitte hadn't been fretting for nothing. Perhaps the glass cladding around Steinhoff's swish

Stellenbosch office really had been constructed out of precarious playing cards all along.

Then the dominoes began to tumble: the meeting between Wiese and Deloitte (described in chapter 1); Jooste's broken promises to fetch the documents from Germany; his tears, his sudden resignation, his vanishing. And, lastly, Steinhoff's long overdue reckoning with the fury of the stock market.

14

The Reckoning

———

Heather Sonn could almost taste the sour vapour of dread that hung over Steinhoff's glass-fronted De Wagenweg Office Park in Stellenbosch the day after Markus Jooste's resignation. There was no real sense, back then, of who exactly could be trusted. Deciphering who'd been "in on it" became of pressing importance for Sonn and the remaining directors, who had to step over the debris and pilot a way forward.

The realisation of what had happened, says Sonn, was like having cold water poured down your back when you were looking the other way. "Basically, it was your worst nightmare," she says. "It's not something I'd wish on anyone – to have that sense of betrayal of trust from senior members of management is just horrible."[1]

The first goal was just to find out what happened, what was real in Steinhoff's accounts, and what was a mirage. For this, auditing firm PwC bused in sixty forensic auditors, who split off into fourteen work streams and were given the run of the place. Every file, every hard disk, every scrap of information was fair game for them. They hoovered up more than 4.4m files. It was, as Sonn would later say, like finding herself in a burning building. "When in a burning building, you run out. Some stayed – we are happy some stayed in the burning building to help out."

Nine days after Jooste quit, Christo Wiese also resigned as chairman, after Steve Booysen approached him about it. Booysen told him: "Christo, I think you need to resign. You're the largest shareholder, and you'll probably end up with massive claims against the company, and there'd be a huge conflict of interest." So, Sonn became the chairwoman, and the focal point of the brains trust, consisting of herself, Booysen and Sanlam's former CEO, Dr Johan van Zyl.

Booysen told her it was the sort of opportunity you only get once in a lifetime.

"I said, Heather, you can read about this sort of thing in a hundred textbooks, but the lessons you'll learn right here, over the next few months, you wouldn't find that in any textbook – it's invaluable."[2] For a company largely dominated by elderly white men, most of whom had been accountants, Sonn's appointment was like stepping into another dimension. "I'm a coloured woman, and I'm younger than most [46 years old when she took the job, thirty years Wiese's junior], so it's been a challenge in many ways. But luckily, all I really could do was put my head down, and go to war every day, then do the same tomorrow."

She'd had tough jobs before. Back in 1997, Sonn had worked sixteen-hour days at brokerage company Merrill Lynch in New York. There, the stories were legion of how interns kept a roll-away bed next to their desks, because they never dared leave the office. Heather had returned to South Africa and worked at various brokerages, like Legae Securities, as well as other financial services companies like Sanlam. Then, her father Franklin Sonn, a respected academic whom Nelson Mandela picked as his choice as ambassador to the United States, resigned from Steinhoff's board, and nominated his daughter to take his spot. It was Steinhoff's gain. Heather, compact and wiry, with luminous eyes and a broad disarming smile, is sharp and confident enough to tackle anyone – even a bruiser CEO with a propensity for smacking down anyone who challenges him.

Until December, Heather had been a part-time Steinhoff director. The rest of the day, she devoted to her own company investment, Gamiro (its motto: do well, do good), and had even done a spot of guest lecturing at the University of Cape Town. As it happened, about a week before Steinhoff's collapse, she'd been lecturing accounting students, when one of them asked her to what extent a board of directors should place unqualified trust in a company's management. "I told them there was no option, a non-executive director just has to trust the CEO. If you don't, if you think there's some major fraud going on the whole time, you can't operate. There's no point being there."[3] It was a prescient question, as it turned out.

Sonn could never have known then that just a few days later, she'd be propelled into a real-life case study on exactly this question, where she'd also have the unenviable task of overseeing South Africa's largest-ever multinational fraud probe. "It's been a peak experience," she says. "There hasn't been much time to reflect on what was happening – it was just about fighting this fire, then moving to the next one."

Booysen was equally sapped by the experience. "I'd get to Steinhoff early in the morning, work until after it was dark, then go home to sleep, and all I'd do was roll in my bed for six hours thinking about what I had to do the next day."[4] The hours were uncompromising. Within three months of Jooste's resignation, Steinhoff's board committees met 63 times. Yet the whole of the previous year, the board had only met four times.

As PwC's team combed through every entrail and every scrap of paper with a euro sign on it, the portrait that began to take shape was particularly unsettling. It provided grim corroboration of everyone's worst fears, and the particularly bad news was that it dated back far longer than anyone suspected. As one person close to the investigation said: "It seems there were about three or so basic recipes used often to paint a misleading picture of the accounts – it was repeated when it came to property transactions, branding transactions, and a few others." What Markus Jooste did, it seems, was to find a way to boost Steinhoff's sales by creating "fictitious debtors" – in other words, companies that supposedly owed Steinhoff money that could be used to create false sales and cash flow. It seems that Jooste set up a network of companies, like Talgarth and GT Branding, that were theoretically "independent" but, in practice, were run by his accomplices, like Siegmar Schmidt and Alan Evans, who were working with Dirk Schreiber, seemingly to fiddle the books.

Take the intriguing tale of Talgarth Capital. Talgarth is another of those opaque companies registered in the British Virgin Islands. Thanks to being in this tax haven, where there is virtually no transparency about who actually owns anything, money could swish through Talgarth like waves across a beach, without anyone having any sense of where it came from or where it was going to. Jooste had told Steinhoff's top brass that Talgarth was a "global brand company with many clients", which would buy brands from Steinhoff and would help promote those brands. "The way Markus explained it to us was that Steinhoff was a manufacturing company, and it couldn't risk suppliers thinking we were competing in the retail space, or they wouldn't supply us," says one insider. "So, he proposed that we get an outside third party to build brands for us. And the company he proposed that could do it for us was Talgarth."

Essentially, Talgarth would carry the "costs" of finding these brands, but provide the revenue to Steinhoff. The only problem was that a lot of these brands didn't really exist, or were traded back and forth from a bunch of companies owned by Jooste's associates, so as to push up the purchase price and inflate Steinhoff's assets. What seemingly happened is that Steinhoff would lend money to Talgarth, and Talgarth would then drip-feed "interest repayments" back to Steinhoff. But take a peek inside Steinhoff's accounts, and you'll see why this was such a poisonous deal.

Firstly, Talgarth was a "debtor", as it owed money to Steinhoff, but Steinhoff provided a *wechsel* to Talgarth, which acted as a "guarantee" for this debt. In other words, Steinhoff was guaranteeing its own debt. But because Steinhoff was now owed money that was backed by a guarantee, it would classify this debt as almost equal to cash – a "cash equivalent", in other words. This artificially boosted Steinhoff's cash flow and it gave Steinhoff "income" from the repayments, even though Talgarth was never going to repay the debt.

Nobody knew it, but Talgarth's contribution to Steinhoff's profits had crept up to grotesque proportions. It was at €600m by 2015; and by June 2016 Talgarth was secretly boosting Steinhoff's accounts to the tune of €1.2bn, say company insiders. It was a staggering revelation – not just for the size of the amount or for the fact that nobody picked up that it was, for all intents and purposes, no real profit at all. Rather, it was simply paper money that had originally come from Steinhoff and was simply shifting back to Steinhoff in a haze of artificial deals. It looked like a fake deal, creating fake sales and fake profit. Talgarth seemed to be just as hollow as Campion, GT Branding and so many other Jooste vessels.

Then in 2017 Steinhoff "bought" Talgarth, shifting it back onto its own books. The move was ingenious. It meant that the massive debt Talgarth owed simply vanished (or was "consolidated out"). And the amount that Steinhoff paid for Talgarth would be hidden in Steinhoff's books as an "intangible asset". In this way, Jooste appeared to be trying to cover up Talgarth's role in boosting profits. He'd just make it vanish into Steinhoff's accounts. (Remarkably, this was a similar pattern to those transactions that Craig Butters had first flagged to Wiese, back in 2009. It suggests the problems had begun years before.)

But Markus Jooste didn't just have one ball in the air. There were a range of other such "off-balance sheet companies" recycling paper money back into Steinhoff to make its accounts look better. And, at the same time, Steinhoff was "buying" other companies, which meant, on its books, it had a debt it owed to those sellers. In Steinhoff's own books, those fake companies were included as "assets", typically as "intangible assets" once it had been bought. "Primarily, it was about manufacturing a false picture of Steinhoff's performance and earnings to perpetuate this story about phenomenal growth," says one insider.

*　*　*

But perhaps the most audacious swindle that Jooste appears to have pulled off was convincing his directors that he was part of a massive "buying group" that swung rebates for the company. Jooste would tell everyone that he was jetting off overseas to go and meet the other retailers who were part of this "TG Buying Group". As the story goes, they'd meet somewhere exotic in Europe, form a consensus bargaining position, then engage in brutal mouth-to-mouth combat with suppliers that would last for hours. In the end, Jooste said, they'd get "rebates" and "bonuses" that would ultimately benefit Steinhoff's profit numbers. "He would tell us how there was blood on the floor after these negotiations. He talks of how they wrestled all night, and how hard it was," one Steinhoff director recalls.

Only these "buying groups", in all likelihood, never even existed. In the end, it was all just a sophisticated scheme to fiddle the accounts. By claiming "rebates, bonuses and marketing contributions" from this murky, poorly defined "buying group", Steinhoff could reduce its "cost of sales". In other words, the arrangement would lower Steinhoff's expenses, and make its profit look much better. It was also, of course, convenient cover for any money that Jooste wanted to circulate through Steinhoff via those off-balance sheet vehicles run by Siegmar Schmidt and others in Europe. "It would never have been easy for anyone, including the auditors, to trace this flow of money. Often cash would move through about three or four European companies, before it would re-emerge in Steinhoff's books," says a source close to the forensic investigation.

The question, of course, became how to present this in Steinhoff's accounts without the auditors realising what was happening. Deloitte, it turns out, wasn't so easy to dupe. In Steinhoff's 2016 annual report, Deloitte had flagged "vendor allowances", supposedly paid to Steinhoff as a member of the "buying group", as a "key audit matter". The auditors said that Steinhoff received various "vendor allowances", including "buying group bonuses, rebates and marketing contributions", which helped reduce Steinhoff's cost of sales.

The problem, as you'll have realised, is that often accounting is more art than science. In some cases, accounting rules give a lot of scope to a company's top brass to insert their own "judgement calls" about certain values. The value of property, for example, is often dictated by what a company's CEO says, rather than by the accounting rules. This is all fine, until you encounter someone intent on cooking the books.

In the case of the "buying group", Deloitte warned in its 2016 audit report that "significant management judgment is required to estimate the value of the significant vendor allowance receivable". In other words, Deloitte had to rely quite heavily on Jooste's word for where these "rebates" came from.

The auditors tried to do more: they said they had tested "management's controls around the completeness and accuracy of the contractual arrangements in the accounting system" and "challenged management's assumptions used in determining the unrealized vendor allowances through discussions with management". They'd also taken "samples" of the contracts in respect of the buying group and "confirmed the related positions and terms with the vendors".

But just because there *was* a contract doesn't mean it was real. One person close to the forensic investigation says they have since discovered that if an auditor wanted a contract, it would magically appear, having apparently been created in Germany or in Stellenbosch. "If you, as an auditor, wanted a document – no problem. It would appear. Whatever you wanted, you could get it," he says. "But just because it appeared doesn't mean it was legitimate."

In a development that would have washed over the heads of most of his audience, Steinhoff's former finance czar, Ben la Grange, alluded to how the "buying group" would operate when he testified in Parliament in August 2018. "We were all led to believe there's an external buying group – it would take volumes of product, and someone would negotiate with suppliers to give additional rebates," he said. But, according to La Grange, it turned out that this buying group was "non-existent". "It looks like it was funded by loans from Steinhoff. It made a loan to the buying group and it then paid money to Steinhoff."

La Grange, in particular, must be irked by this "buying group". In August 2018, his contract with Steinhoff was suspended when investigators from PwC apparently came across a "fake buying group". And among the contracts and invoices used to justify this move was an invoice that La Grange had sent to the buying group, from Steinhoff's African arm.

What had happened, according to those close to La Grange, was that on a plane trip back to South Africa, Markus Jooste had told him he needed an invoice to give to the "buying group". La Grange played it by the book: OK, fine, but give me the contract. Jooste then produced a contract to justify this. La Grange then said: OK, now I need to see the cash that we got as a rebate. Again, Jooste made this happen. He managed to get one of his off-balance sheet companies – such as Talgarth – to hand over enough cash to make it believable. Satisfied, La Grange then gave him the invoice. Nonetheless, the PwC investigators weren't impressed. How could he not have seen through this? they asked. Perhaps. But, then, how come nobody saw through any of it?

*   *   *

When Ben La Grange finally appeared in Parliament in August 2018, he cut an impressive figure. Unlike the stubble-shaded, open-collared hipster in all the photographs prior to Steinhoff's crash, La Grange appeared clean-shaven in a pinstriped suit and a blue-checked tie, speaking crisply with wide eyes. He talked of how he was "deeply saddened" by what had happened, but protested repeatedly that he'd been duped by Jooste, who hid information from him.[5] "There were certain relationships between him and third parties [that] were not disclosed to the company or me. Had I known that relationship was one whereby he controlled those parties, I would have accounted for it differently." In other words, those "off-balance sheet" companies like Campion were hardly independent third parties. "I thought it involved valid third parties. Now it seems these parties were in fact related to the previous CEO or, rather, were influenced by the previous CEO."

The members of Parliament present oozed frustration. After all, if you can't pin accounting shenanigans on the company's financial supremo, who *can* you pin them on? Yet, at each turn, La Grange had a slick answer – even if not always an entirely compelling one. How was it that you missed this whole thing? he was asked. Were you too gullible? How is it after the *Manager Magazin* came out that you can still claim you were taken by surprise? At the very least, surely the German police raid in 2015 worried you?

"I got a lot of comfort from my verbal engagement with [Jooste]," said La Grange. "I also got comfort from the fact that even though [he] was being investigated, the reporting [by] the specialists was not going via [Jooste] but through the board." In other words, La Grange bought Jooste's spin, that it was all some giant conspiracy theory cooked up by the Austrian evil genius, Andreas Seifert. His answers "were plausible", La Grange said. Instead, La Grange skilfully shifted the focus to the auditors. He argued that had there been one set of auditors handling all of Steinhoff's companies throughout the world, the outcome would have been a different story. As it was, Commerzial Treuhand (CT) audited the European companies, while Deloitte audited the overall holding company. Deloitte's duty was to review CT's working papers, however, and dig deeper if there was anything that didn't make sense. One parliamentarian asked La Grange why he then hadn't suggested letting one auditor handle the entire thing. "It was raised," said La Grange – but Jooste shot it down. "We had an internal meeting with the head of the audit committee [Steve Booysen] and [Jooste] convinced [us] that in certain places, we should retain these small firms because of the language barriers and the relationships they had with the staff internally," La Grange said.

So why did you step down if you weren't responsible? he was asked. "People were so angry at Steinhoff – if they were to see my face, they would want to hit it," he said. La Grange testified that the con appeared to have begun years before. "So, this false profit was in the [accounts] way, way, way back. If you grow this profit every year, no person, no auditor, no analyst will, just by looking at the numbers, tell you here's something that changes this year, [that this is] false income.

Remarkably, the parliamentarians bought his testimony as if it was a quaintly gift-wrapped parcel of soil that could be spirited into gold. None of them asked him what responsibility he himself took for signing off the Mickey Mouse financial statements since 2013. Yunus Carrim, the veteran ANC politician who chaired the session, said La Grange provided the "best response we've got from Steinhoff as a whole". He'd learnt more from La Grange in ten minutes than he'd got in months from Steinhoff, he said. La Grange, contrary to all expectations, skipped out of Parliament smelling of roses.

*   *   *

Ben la Grange was actually right in one respect: having numerous sets of auditors made it easier for Markus to get away with his schemes. The way it works is that a multinational company like Steinhoff has what are called "component auditors", which audit specific countries or regions. Here's a practical example: a company called Commerzial Treuhand (CT), based in Germany, audits the European businesses, and hands its audit findings to Deloitte, which does the final numbers for the whole group. Of course, Deloitte is meant to check that there's nothing odd or worrying in CT's audit; so it will review CT's working papers, and then consolidate all those audits from other countries into one final result, which it signs and presents to investors.

In Steinhoff, of course, it all went wrong. Just to recap, the apparent fraud here was that Jooste created fake debtors – companies that supposedly owed Steinhoff money in Germany. But, in a circuitous web, Steinhoff would also provide a "guarantee" for that debt – a *wechsel*, in German law. This would allow that debt to be reclassified as a "cash and cash equivalent" that ended up on Steinhoff's balance sheet. In other words, thanks to fancy footwork, a made-up debt owed to Steinhoff was converted into actual cash in its accounts. And since investors tend to look at cash flow as the ultimate litmus test of the health of a company, and one of the fundamental ways to assess its value, this manoeuvre ended up hiding the true picture.

As one accounting expert close to Steinhoff explained: "What should have happened is that in the audit pack that CT gave to Deloitte, it should have included a list of all the guarantees it relied on. Then Deloitte would have seen that the guarantees came from Steinhoff itself, and reclassified this as a debt, and tested to see if it was recoverable." In other words, Steinhoff should never have got away with including those debtors (and any other fake income) as a positive cash inflow in its accounts. Especially since those fictitious debtors were never likely to repay anything to Steinhoff.

At one point, of course, the process just looks like numbers moving on a spreadsheet. The con is that this is meant to represent actual money. But once in the white-hot centre of an accounting fraud, the link to real cash has long since vanished.

Of course, for thousands of people across South Africa, the inevitable collapse in Steinhoff's share price did have a rands-and-cents impact. The immense losses splashed all over the JSE's trading screens, in grizzly, luminous red technicolour, hurt people's pockets. In all, more than half of the pension funds in South Africa had exposure to Steinhoff and would lose some money, at least, from the collapse. But then there were the people who chose only to invest in Steinhoff shares, who also lost, and, also, some of South Africa's largest banks.

*   *   *

On 6 December 2017, Sanlam's Tony Gouveia had just woken up on the third day of his year-end leave. As the executive head of finance at Sanlam's capital markets division, he'd had a tough year. He was looking forward to recovering during the holiday, before setting foot back in the office in the new year. Then Steinhoff happened. "I was going to take December off. But the minute I heard 'accounting fraud', I figured the price was going to go to zero, so we had to decide what to do. So, I had to cancel my leave and come in," he says.[6] At the time, Sanlam had more than R1.4bn worth of exposure to Steinhoff – R800m which it had lent to Markus Jooste's company Mayfair Speculators, R370m in terms of offshore bonds to Steinhoff directly, and another R395m for Steinhoff bonds. Of course, it wasn't as if Sanlam had cavalierly handed over a cheque without receiving any security: it's just that the security it had for that loan was shares in Steinhoff. And those shares had just tanked.

"When the news broke, Steinhoff's share price went into freefall," says Gouveia. "When fraud happens, alleged fraud, the price just tanks and goes quite close to zero – that's normal. In our lending business, it's only ever happened three times, so it's very rare, but the results are usually severe." Only, it wasn't just Sanlam. Overall, Mayfair had borrowed more than R1.2bn from various banks. Besides Sanlam's R800m, Absa had lent it R266m and Investec lent it R256m. But the really sneaky part was that less than a week before the Steinhoff bubble popped, while Jooste was already in meetings with Deloitte that he must have known could end badly, he convinced Investec to lend Mayfair more money. In an unusually fiery affidavit filed in mid-December, Absa manager Hester van Niekerk said there was "little doubt that the conduct of [Stefan] Potgieter and Jooste, in inducing Investec to advance a further amount of [R93.5m] . . . was also nothing less than naked fraud".[7] It was just another step "in the fraudulent course of conduct".

But if you think that's shifty . . . A few months before, in August 2017, Mayfair Speculators had secretly shifted all its R1.5bn in assets to its holding company, Mayfair Holdings, in what was called a payment of a "dividend in specie". In other words, its loans to property companies, its investment in a food and branding company called Lodestone, and about R200m in cash were all smuggled out. Other things were happening at that exact time: the *Manager Magazin* reported that the German police were investigating Jooste for accounting fraud. It seems hardly much of a coincidence. The upshot was that the banks were left holding a huge amount of debt from a company that now, technically, owned almost nothing. Absa's Van Niekerk said: "Jooste and Potgieter knew that when the [irregularities] came to light, Steinhoff's shares would plummet, the loans to Absa, Sanlam and Investec would become due and . . . [Mayfair] Speculators would not have sufficient liquidity to discharge those debts." Shifting those assets, she said, was "nothing less than a fraud" aimed at denuding Mayfair Speculators of assets, "so as to benefit Mayfair Holdings and the Silver Oaks trust and its beneficiaries, which are, in all likelihood, Jooste and his family".

Actually, what many people don't know is that a week before the Steinhoff house of cards collapsed, Investec had lent Jooste another R93.5m and R26m to a company called Ruby Street, whose sole director was Danie van der Merwe (Steinhoff's current CEO). The backstory is that Investec had a long-standing relationship with Jooste. Not only was Bernard Kantor, Investec's co-founder, his racing partner, but the bank had been lending to Mayfair since 2012. But Jooste played a sneaky trick on Investec in November 2017 – by far the dirtiest he'd pulled on any of the banks.

In court papers that haven't yet been reported on, Investec's legal adviser

Avrom Krengel revealed that on 20 November – about three weeks before the crash – Jooste's son-in-law Stefan Potgieter contacted Asher Levien, a consultant in Investec's corporate and investment banking department.[8] Potgieter wanted to know if Investec could put together some structures for Mayfair (hedges and options) around its Steinhoff shares. The aim was "to provide Mayfair Speculators and Ruby Street with downside protection in the event of a collapse in the value of Steinhoff shares". This suggests, overwhelmingly, that Jooste saw the tornado approaching in the distance, and wanted to put in place a beachhead when the stock price collapsed. Krengel said that at the time Investec had no reason to be suspicious of Potgieter's request. In retrospect, he says, the "inescapable inference to be drawn from this is that Jooste and his son-in-law knew that Jooste was about to resign as CEO of Steinhoff and what effect this, together with the other revelations of the alleged accounting irregularities, would have on the share price".

On 23 November Potgieter called Levien back. Actually, we've changed our mind, he said. What we want to do now is borrow more money, using those shares as collateral. Krengel reckons they only did this because they realised that, given what would come out, they would be exposed to charges of "insider trading" – essentially, looking to benefit yourself on the basis of inside knowledge that you have but other investors don't. Like, for example, knowledge of a giant fraud that is likely to emerge. Instead, they chose to "extract value . . . at the expense of Investec," Krengel says.

On 28 November, Potgieter wrote a remarkable email to Levien, saying "the deals are off . . . it feels wrong, there is a lot going on at the moment". Levien then reassured Potgieter that if he was worried about insider trading, he needn't be – this was just drawing more money from an existing loan facility. This seemed to put Potgieter's mind at rest. So, on 29 November, Investec transferred the money. It meant that Investec's exposure to Jooste's company and Ruby Street rose from R136m to R256m. (From the outside it seemed that Jooste had ludicrously easy access to finance.)

The bank would have felt assured, however, since it had Steinhoff shares as collateral worth R473m, which more than covered the loan. Of course, one week on, and those shares would only be worth R84m. "There can be no doubt that Jooste ... must have been aware of the [accounting irregularities] long before the approach was made to Investec for the additional loans in November 2017," says Krengel. Nobody had even told Investec about the hassles with Deloitte, and that the audited accounts weren't likely to come out during the first week of December.

Of course, if Jooste was hoping that the fancy shuffling of assets between the Mayfair companies would protect him, he'd underestimated the bank and, it seems, his own son-in-law. When Jooste resigned as a director of Mayfair, Potgieter took over all the negotiations. And he immediately agreed, effectively, to recognise the banks' debt in Mayfair Holdings too. "Stefan was true to his word at every point," says Tony Gouveia. "He said that he wanted to see the lenders being settled. And his actions in the past nine months or so were indicative of this."[9]

In the end, Potgieter struck a deal with everyone to whom Mayfair owed money. There would be a "scheme of arrangement", whereby Mayfair's assets would be sold off slowly, before the end of 2018, and that money would be split up between the creditors. Since then, nearly all Mayfair's horses have been sold, and negotiations are taking place to sell the stake in Lodestone. Fingers crossed, the banks won't lose a thing.

There is, of course, the curious case of a claim lodged against the estate by Malcolm King, Markus Jooste's shady British associate. Only, for some bizarre reason, King agreed to "subordinate" this debt to everyone else – in other words, he agreed that everyone else who was owed money could get paid first. Hardly anyone understands why he did this. One of the Mayfair creditors says: "Subordinating a loan like this doesn't make economic sense to us, but perhaps there's a method to it somewhere."

Whatever the outcome, it's been another brutal reminder of how even South Africa's biggest banks, with high-powered and overqualified risk management teams, can get duped. Gouveia, for one, reckons the whole Mayfair order has led to a rethink of how Sanlam lends money to people using shares as collateral. "We've adjusted our approval frameworks," says Gouveia. In the past, Sanlam required someone who borrowed from it to give it collateral, such as shares; and when the collateral fell below a certain level, it would ask for extra cash. The Steinhoff experience showed that in some cases the multiple was not high enough. Now Sanlam is far more conservative. It will ask for extra cash collateral at an earlier stage. "These things happen from time to time. There'll always be fraudsters. It's only happened to us three times over the last decade or so. Hopefully, it'll be a long time before it happens again," Gouveia says. And, hopefully, he can get to take that Christmas holiday next time.

* * **

There's more than one hardened entrepreneur who might liken a board of directors to tonsils: largely useless, mostly harmless, but best ignored. Dealmakers often dislike having to explain themselves to a bunch of sceptical greybeards who did business in a different era.

At Steinhoff, as people began to pick through the wreckage, the public focus shifted to the board of directors. How could they *not* have known what was going on? And, if they hadn't known, what then is the *point* of even having a board? some asked. There were three directors who had doctorates in accounting – Dr Len Konar, Dr Steve Booysen and Dr Theunie Lategan. And yet this was a company that was involved in an accounting scandal. Almost everyone was embarrassingly overqualified. Dr Johan van Zyl, the former CEO of Sanlam, had a PhD in economics, Claas Daun was an accountant, and Thierry Guibert of Conforama had an MBA. There was a full alphabet of degrees there. Had there been an Olympic medal for board qualifications, Steinhoff would probably have won by a mile.

In Konar's case, he'd not only lectured in ethics, but was also, at one stage, the head of the International Monetary Fund's external audit committee.

Konar says much of the criticism of the board was unfair. "We were misled, we were lied to. We asked for information and either it was not forthcoming, or [it was] presented in a way that wasn't representative of the truth," he says.

Many of the directors, in fact, personally held shares in Steinhoff, and experienced "catastrophic losses and reputational damage". For example, he said, Konar, Booysen and Lategan's personal shareholdings in Steinhoff fell in value from R40m to R3m within weeks.

To many outside critics, the key issue is whether the directors were sceptical enough.

In the end, in so far as the epic scale of the fraud was designed to deceive anyone in an oversight position, Steinhoff's directors will be judged on whether they asked the right questions.

In June 2018, the University of Stellenbosch Business School published a case study pointing to the weaknesses of the board. "The Steinhoff board was dominated by white males in the period 1999 to 2015," it said. "Many of the [directors] served on the board for extensive periods of time and the possibility of a group-think culture having taken root cannot be ruled out."[10] And, obviously, if you're a director for too long, you can hardly class yourself as an "independent" director – someone well placed to exercise real oversight. In fact, most of the members classed as "independent" had either been on the board longer than nine years (which is globally considered the maximum tenure) or had such a vast stake in Steinhoff that they were hardly impartial.

The day before its share price collapsed, Steinhoff had eleven directors on its supervisory board and three on its "management board": Jooste, Danie van der Merwe and Ben la Grange. Since December 2017, eleven of those fourteen people have resigned or retired. They include Christo Wiese, Jacob Wiese, Jayendra Naidoo, Thierry Guibert, Claas Daun, Theunie Lategan, Len Konar, Bruno Steinhoff and Dr Johan van Zyl.

Dr Johan van Zyl seems particularly scalded by the ordeal. For years, Van Zyl was an academic, the dean of the Faculty of Biological and Agricultural Sciences at the University of Pretoria, before becoming the institution's principal in 1997. Then in 2003, there was plenty of consternation in Sanlam's head office in the Cape Town suburb of Bellville when he, an academic, was picked as the next CEO of Sanlam. But it proved a masterstroke. The share price of Sanlam went from R6.26 when he started in 2003 to R75.60 by the time he retired in 2015.

Then in 2016, he joined Steinhoff's board. "When Christo became chairman, they needed more independent directors. And for me, I figured it would be great to be involved in a company which had such international exposure," he says.[11] At the time he joined, the net was already closing in. Steinhoff had already been raided by the German police, and the dispute with Andreas Seifert was becoming increasingly bitter. "I can tell you, at every single board meeting, the directors grilled management on the progress on this and the investigations. We also insisted on reports from and discussions with the auditors and the law firms. But the fact is, we were simply lied to." If you're a part-time board member, and someone is spending twenty hours every day scheming to deceive you, he'll probably get away with it, says Van Zyl. "A board works on trust between the management and the board. So, when you find out that there is an entire other 'inner circle' of people doing deals you're not seeing, and there have been goings-on to mislead the board, shareholders, analysts and auditors, you stand no chance." These off-balance sheet entities were "set up deliberately to bamboozle the governance structures, including the supervisory board and auditors". In hindsight, Van Zyl says that perhaps the board could have done more when it came to the individual deals. "We could have interrogated the purchases of things like Mattress Firm more, perhaps. But we saw the plans, and the returns, and it looked good."

Another weakness, he says, is there were too many people on the board with deep, entrenched relationships with Jooste and his management team, and with a vast personal investment at stake. "In addition to Christo and his son Jacob, there were others, like Claas Daun, Bruno and Angela Steinhoff, and Jayendra Naidoo, who were also heavily invested. And guys like Len Konar and Theunie Lategan had been there since the beginning. So, it perhaps wasn't as independent as it should have been," says Van Zyl. After Jooste's surprise resignation, this lack of proper independence at the board became a sticking point that had to be fixed.

The other problem, of course, was group-think because of the board's stunning lack of diversity, as the University of Stellenbosch case study illustrates. As Heather Sonn says: "Almost everyone you ever met at Steinhoff was an accountant. There was only one perspective."[12] Even Mariza Nel, who was head of investor relations, was an accountant.

It also didn't help that Steinhoff used a Dutch model in which there was a "supervisory board" of non-executive directors and a "management board" led by Jooste. This meant that Jooste's management team was entirely split off from the overseers. "In hindsight, this is where many of the issues arose," says Van Zyl. Directors weren't often able to look management in the eye, to divine the nuance of issues.

The Stellenbosch University case study is less forgiving. It says Steinhoff's "weak accountability and a culture of highly creative accounting" meant that many dubious investment deals, excessive debt levels and poor financial performance went undetected for a long time.[13] "Either the truth was hidden, or responsible parties (including the board) were not paying enough attention, or both," they say. This allowed Steinhoff to perpetuate the "myth of unprecedented financial success" for far too long.

At this point, some people might ask: if the Steinhoff board couldn't pick up what happened, what is the *point* of having a board of directors at all? Nick Binedell, an eloquent and highly rated professor at the Gordon Institute of Business Science, says that "many boards have stopped many Steinhoffs". "You generally don't see it publicly when this happens because it's taking place behind closed doors, but many South African companies have had pretty solid governance standards. In many cases, all you'll read about is of a CEO leaving."[14] Having said that, Binedell says it is incredibly difficult for any board to detect sophisticated deception. "At all the boards I've been on, you can ask all the questions, but the managers have the ability to mislead the board – not even always by lying intentionally, but by being less than forthright."

Of course, it is equally true that there are probably many boards that operate far worse than Steinhoff's board, with far less diligence. But their directors just happen to have been lucky enough not to have got involved with con artists. All the same, the Steinhoff debacle has definitively punctured the myth of the omniscient board of elders, impermeable to any trickery. Nicky Newton-King, the CEO of the JSE, comments that she can't say if Steinhoff's board fluffed its duties. "But I will make a few points: first, no amount of rules or policing will stop somebody who is intent on creating a fraud. But if you have an ecosystem of the guardians of governance – such as a strong board, auditors, analysts, pension fund trustees – it makes it more likely that someone will get caught."[15] Secondly, says Newton-King, the more diverse a board is, "the less they are beholden to each other and the more likely it is they are having proper conversations".

In the case of Steinhoff, the fallout has savaged the reputations of some of South Africa's most respected businessmen, who were chewed up and spat out. Few struggled to buy Christo Wiese's argument in Parliament that the scandal was a "bolt from the blue". Surely there were signs? they'd ask.

Steve Booysen says unpicking accounting irregularities isn't a binary process where, one minute, there is no awareness and, the next, full awareness. "It is a process of escalation. First, you have concerns. Then there are questions, then an examination of the answers and more questions, and so on, until finally all the pieces fit together."[16] In the end, he says, when you finally have all the information, and piece the puzzle together, "it *is* a bolt from the blue – even if you'd been working on it for a while".

Just before Steinhoff's AGM in April, Dr Johan van Zyl resigned from Steinhoff's board. The demands on his time, especially as he was trying to build his new company, African Rainbow Capital, were crushing. And that's before you mention the stress. You can ask, rightly, about what more the board should have done to detect the scandal, and you can ask how Steinhoff could have been structurally stronger. And the answers would probably have to involve admitting that the board fell short. But says, Van Zyl, nobody expected what happened. "The magnitude of what was taken, and the extent people went to, to hide everything was alarming. Nobody could say, within or outside the company, that the extent of what was happening wasn't a shock."

15

Barely Concealed Contempt

Ten months after Steinhoff's crash to earth, the hermit of Hermanus was smoked out of the soft cotton wool of his villa into the camera flashes of a world he'd pretended had ceased to exist. Three times, Markus Jooste had been summoned to address South Africa's Parliament, to explain to the country what had happened to Steinhoff. Three times, Jooste had grimly tried to extinguish these requests on the advice of, he said, "my lawyers". First asked to testify on 31 January 2018, Jooste said "no thanks" – and clung to that position when was invited again on 28 March. Had he got his way, he would never have appeared in September either.

But the lawmakers got wise to Jooste's tactics. After Jooste had declined the first invitation in January, the chair of Parliament's standing committee on finance, Yunus Carrim, wrote to him saying his excuse was "very lame". So, on 22 August, Jooste was served with a "summons", demanding that he appear before Parliament to "give an overview of the circumstances that led to the collapse in the value of the share price and to answer related questions".[1] The summons added that, if he didn't show up, he could be convicted and end up in jail for a year. With so many other apparent reasons for him to fear jail, it seemed an unnecessary aggravation to be jailed just for not showing up.

So, Markus Jooste went to court to argue why it was so unfair to force him to testify. In his court papers, citing Carrim and the Speaker of Parliament, Baleka Mbete, Jooste resorted to every arcane technicality he could think of.[2] This included arguing that the summons he had been served with was "facially invalid" (because it didn't describe the documents he needed to bring) and "the name and designation of the person who must serve the summons was not specified". Not that he was disputing that he had received the subpoena, mind – just scraping for any half-palatable excuse.

Also, Jooste argued, it would be "oppressive and unfair" to force him to come. Especially as the Constitution gave him "the right not to be compelled to give self-incriminating evidence". Not to mention, he said, that he'd been given "so little time to prepare". (Could he not have anticipated, over the previous ten months, that he'd ever have to explain what happened?) Just imagine, Jooste argued, if his version of events were "pitted against" that provided by Ben la Grange "in an attempt to ascertain the truth". Quite what the exact horror of this scenario was, he didn't say.

Either way, it didn't wash. Parliament had already got a legal opinion from one of the country's best advocates, Wim Trengove, which said it had the power to "summons and question private sector witnesses on any subject of legitimate interest".

When it was clear Jooste wasn't going to win, he struck a deal with the parliamentarians. They would withdraw the summons and he would appear, in public for the first time since December 2017, to answer questions so as to help Parliament "identify any institutional flaws and challenges" in the regulations that might have led to Steinhoff's collapse. The framing seemed farcical. It's as if the fox were to lecture the farmer on the weakest links in the wire facade around the henhouse. Or, as the Democratic Alliance's David Maynier portrayed it, "It's rather like asking King Herod to assist in identifying flaws and challenges in the regulation of child care facilities."

So, on a rainy Wednesday morning, Jooste, flanked by four lawyers, including his heavyweight attorney, Callie Albertyn, emerged, blinking, into a thousand flashlights. Journalists, posted at every corner of the parliamentary complex, scrambled for the bragging rights of who'd spotted him first. John Lennon and Paul McCartney, landing at New York's JFK Airport in 1964, must have felt more guaranteed of anonymity.

Evidently, the months of solitude hadn't changed Jooste much. Other than being slightly trimmer and noticeably greyer, there appeared little tangible difference. The mountain-man beard described by people who'd spotted him in Hermanus was nowhere to be seen.

At 9.30 am, Jooste entered the small room in Parliament's old wing, ringed by his legal team, and scrupulously avoided eye contact with reporters. Just after 10 am, Markus Jooste held up his hand, took an oath to tell the "whole truth" and began to present what Carrim would later describe as an "incredulous" story.

* * *

Jooste began by giving a prosaic thirty-minute rundown of how Steinhoff was organised, and how "reporting of accounting and accountability of the group was managed during my time". He spoke of how Steinhoff had been split into three – Europe (including Asia Pacific), Africa and America. And he spoke of how there were layers and layers of "committees" all tasked with ensuring the numbers were right. The local management in each country was in charge of finalising numbers, he pointed out.

Then, perhaps pointedly, he detailed how many auditors Steinhoff had employed in its various operations across the world – Deloitte in South Africa and elsewhere, the Austrian firm Rödl & Partner, Commerzial Treuhand (CT) in Germany, KPMG in the UK (for Poundland) and PwC (for Poco in Germany, the Australasian cluster and Pepkor). That was just the introduction.

Then Jooste began building the story, setting out the narrative he'd revert to repeatedly. Unsurprisingly, that story immediately turned to the man on whom he would try to pin the blame: Dr Andreas Seifert. "In 2007 Steinhoff formed a joint venture, strategic partnership with Dr Andreas Seifert of Austria, a huge retailer in Europe with a considerable footprint [in] mass discount brands. The vision between Steinhoff and Seifert was to form a large European household discount chain that could compete with Ikea."

To Jooste's former colleagues, this was no dramatic surprise. Whenever questions arose about the German investigation in the months leading up to Jooste's resignation, he'd trot out the Seifert bogeyman. The backstory is that Seifert and Jooste met in 2006, when Steinhoff took over the Austrian discount chain Poco. Seifert, at the time, ran Austria's third-largest furniture retailer, XXXLutz, along with his brother Richard, and was similarly hell-bent on expansion. Newspaper reports at the time say that Steinhoff's purchase of Poco took Seifert "by surprise", but in the end they decided to "work together" to tackle Ikea. It also led, according to some Steinhoff insiders, to the scrupulously media-shy Seifert becoming one of Jooste's closest confidants. As thick as thieves, they say. (Richard Seifert, apparently, never trusted Jooste.)

In Jooste's telling of the story, back in 2007 it was a natural partnership: Steinhoff was a manufacturer without a shopfloor footprint, while Seifert's experience as a retailer made him "a competent retail partner". It was with Seifert at his side, as a 50/50 joint venture partner, that Jooste struck the Conforama takeover in 2011. "Like most relationships, the beginning is always the best," said Jooste. "Unfortunately, it turned out that Dr Seifert was the wrong person to go into business with." The breaking point, Jooste said, came in 2013, when Steinhoff dared to buy Austria's third-largest retailer chain, Kika-Leiner. "It was the first time we made an acquisition in his home territory where he was the king," he said.

Seifert, of course, would tell the story a different way. He'd say that the troubles began when he exercised his right to take 50% of Poco in January 2014, which infuriated Jooste. At the time, Steinhoff needed Poco. It was a critical arm of the story that Jooste had been flogging to investors ahead of the 2015 listing in Frankfurt. To suddenly drop to just 50% ownership would have looked pretty careless.

In Parliament, Jooste painted his troubles with Seifert as primarily a money dispute. He said Seifert hadn't been able to come up with his share of the money for any of the deals in Europe. Initially, Jooste saw this "as a cash flow issue, not an integrity issue". But later, he says, he realised Seifert "never had any intention to pay for any of the acquisitions".

Then, towards the end of 2014, things really got nasty. So poisonous, in fact, that by March 2015 Steinhoff cancelled its joint venture deal with

Seifert, sparking a rash of bad-tempered court battles. Jooste then claimed that Steinhoff owned 100% of Poco and Conforama, saying that Seifert had been stripped of any rights to any shares because of "serious violations" of his "fiduciary responsibilities". A stand-off, in other words.

A few months later, Jooste said that when he and several colleagues were raided by the German tax authorities, it became clear to him that Dr Seifert was behind this "witch-hunt". "It was Steinhoff's and my view that Seifert was attempting to use public prosecutors, capital market regulators and the press to assist him in his unfounded attempts to obtain information and to influence the outcome of the courts in ongoing civil litigation [and] proceedings at that stage between us and him in Germany, Austria and the Netherlands."

Soon, the allegations began mounting in Germany: of manipulating Steinhoff's balance sheet, manipulating profits and inflating assets. So, Jooste said, Steinhoff hired the German law firm FGS to probe the claims of fraud. FGS, remarkably, found everything was entirely kosher. "We have not found any evidence that would cause us to conclude that the accounting for the referenced transactions was not in compliance with applicable [accounting standards] for the Steinhoff Europe group of companies," it said. Also, "we have not found evidence that would cause us to conclude that counter parties to the transactions were not independent parties". In other words, Campion Capital, Talgarth and similar companies in Switzerland, FGS reckoned, were entirely independent.

But Deloitte, commendably, wasn't convinced. Patrick Seinstra, Deloitte's partner in the Netherlands, said he wanted "additional audit procedures" because he didn't believe that FGS was properly independent. Jooste said that Seinstra told him Deloitte had obtained information "from Dr Seifert's lawyers" about the German investigation. These issues, he said, were mostly "tax planning, non-compliance of tax planning, potential incorrect application of accounting principles – specifically referenced as revenue recognition and transactions with related parties". (Somehow, Jooste managed to avoid using the word "irregularities" at all, not to mention the word "fraud".)

In October, Jooste wrote to Deloitte and told them Seifert's allegations weren't news to him, but that in any case Deloitte needn't worry – FGS had already investigated and found nothing wrong. On 19 November, Deloitte received the whole FGS report – "a huge document, with every issue and every query raised by Deloitte". Deloitte, as is now clear, didn't buy it. They needed a brand-new investigation anyway.

Then the session in Parliament turned to the white-hot hours around Jooste's resignation in December. Jooste described how, when he returned from Germany (where he'd supposedly gone to "get the documents for Deloitte"), he "discussed the developments with Dr Wiese and I shared his view that a further investigation at that late stage, two days before the results must be announced, would be ridiculous". Doing this, he said, would "delay the finalisation of the 2017 financial statements indefinitely and that would put the group in dire consequences from a cash flow, a credibility, an investor's perception and credit lender's point of view". When that happens, he said, a company loses the faith of its investors. And, inevitably, its share price will collapse.

According to Jooste, he then argued that Deloitte should be fired, new auditors hired who would sign off the results, and unaudited results published that week. If that didn't happen, he said, banks would cut their credit, and investors would lose faith in Steinhoff. "I made it very clear [that] if that is not the way the board would want to go, I don't see my way forward to go through this, after I've been through it for three years of my life, fighting and explaining the transactions and having received the reports." He said to Parliament that he was told the next day, Tuesday, 5 December, that PwC had been hired to start another forensic investigation, and "my proposal was not accepted by the board". Jooste added that when he left Steinhoff on 4 December, "I was not aware of any accounting irregularities."

* * *

Needless to say, there were various problems with Jooste's evidence. Firstly, Jooste claimed to have spoken to Christo Wiese, Steinhoff's chairman, on that Monday when he landed from Germany. Only, Wiese didn't speak to him. All that happened was that Jooste left a voicemail on Wiese's phone.

Secondly, his explanation for his resignation was that, in essence, he took a point of principle that he'd "had enough" of all the investigations, and he'd presented an ultimatum to Steinhoff's board: fire Deloitte, or I go. But the timeline of what actually happened, as reconstructed in chapter 1 with the help of a number of sources, paints a very different picture. Conveniently, for example, Jooste utterly failed to mention the fact that he'd promised, on landing from Germany, to bring all the documents with him to the meeting with Steinhoff's auditing committee that Monday, 4 December, and that he hadn't pitched. And that, instead, he had sent a lawyer to Wiese and Booysen as an emissary, who told them how a sobbing Jooste was offering his resignation and saying how he'd screwed up.

Thirdly, Jooste seemed to see no problem in relaying that, because Deloitte didn't agree with him, he wanted the auditors fired. Presumably, new auditors would be more willing to toe the line. As far as moral relativism goes, it's one for the textbooks. Bernard Agulhas, the CEO of the Independent Regulatory Board for Auditors (IRBA), speaking afterwards, said that a CEO obviously shouldn't try to fire an auditor simply because he doesn't like their findings.[3] "Anyway, it wouldn't help to fire an auditor who detected an irregularity, as the outgoing auditor would have to report any problems to the new auditors." And that auditor also has a duty to tell the regulator, IRBA, too.

Overall, the MPs who'd listened to Jooste's speech were deeply sceptical. "I'm not convinced," said Mkhuleko Hlengwa of the Inkatha Freedom Party. "After 29 years of service, just on the basis of one decision, you literally threw your toys out the cot? I'd like you to be frank about the reasons you left."

Jooste argued his corner. He said he resigned to "force [Steinhoff] to take the right decision for the company" and boot out Deloitte. Any other decision, he said, would have led to massive delays in the accounts. "Why would [a new investigation] be completed quicker than two years if all the other people have taken two years? And therefore I knew that the company will be left in absolute limbo with no financial figures and with no investor confidence and, obviously, pointing fingers at me as the CEO."

The Democratic Alliance's David Maynier was even less impressed. What about that text message you sent to your former colleagues? asked Maynier. You know, the one in which you said: "I have caused the company further damage by not being able to finalise the year-end audited numbers and I made some big mistakes and have now caused financial loss to many innocent people." In that message, Jooste also said he would "take the consequences of my behaviour like a man", and vowed that "none of Danie [van der Merwe], Ben [la Grange], Stehan [Grobler] and Mariza [Nel] had anything to do with any of my mistakes". What "mistakes" are you referring to here exactly? Maynier asked.

Jooste didn't miss a beat. "The mistake that I refer to was the choice in 2007 [of] Seifert [as] our strategic partner, [which] had failed and that has cost the company since 2015 all the drama that we went through: the fights, the financial losses and also that led to this perception of accounting irregularities." It was all Seifert, he argued implausibly. It was Seifert who had made his "dream come true" collapse.

Now, how likely does it sound that *that* was Markus Jooste's "big mistake"? Was Jooste seriously suggesting that La Grange, Van der Merwe, Grobler and Nel shouldn't be blamed for his "mistake" made more than a decade earlier? At that stage, after all, Mariza Nel wasn't even a Steinhoff director – so why would she be liable?

It seemed like an overly lawyered response – and it didn't escape anyone's notice. As Yunus Carrim asked him: "Mr Jooste, if you have nothing to hide, why do you have a battery of lawyers?"

It is "in my interests", Jooste replied.

Maybe it was, given Ben la Grange's testimony the previous week, in which he had painted a picture of Jooste as the puppet master, pulling the strings of a series of increasingly Byzantine cons. One prime example was pretending there were buying groups that didn't exist. Speaking in Parliament, Jooste said he could reassure everyone: those buying groups really did exist. "Steinhoff were a member to various buying groups all over the world," he said. "The buying groups had other retail members. Some of them were partnerships, some of them were companies and certainly when I left on the 4th of December, there were a buying group at Steinhoff. These buying groups were audited in the previous years."

He was also asked about Campion Capital, the off-balance sheet vehicle, run by the shady Alan Evans and Siegmar Schmidt, which had "bought" JD Consumer Finance and Capfin from Steinhoff. Jooste responded entirely unfussed: Campion was a "private equity group in Switzerland" that had "done business with Steinhoff", while Evans was one of Campion's partners.

Are you saying you don't know Evans? David Maynier asked him.

"Of course I know him," Jooste replied. "We've done business for years, but I have no financial interest with him . . . we dealt as counter-parties to each other." ("Counter-parties" seems an excruciatingly dispassionate way of describing Jooste's relationship with a man instrumental in most of the shady offshore companies that were used to pump up Steinhoff's earnings. But then, the term "co-conspirator" doesn't sound great either.)

At odd instances during his testimony, Jooste did *try* to suggest that he was, at some level, sorry for what went on; that it "saddened" him. But even then, the expression of regret was often framed within the context of his own loss. "I worked 29 years for this company, every day of my life to build it, and to travel all over the world, travelling 200 days a year into different countries, and therefore it saddened me what has happened to Steinhoff and the circumstances that led to it, and the losses incurred by pension funds, banks, colleagues and people."

At one point, Jooste was asked by one of the MPs why he came across as if he had zero contrition for what had happened. Jooste appeared confused by the question: "I don't understand that last point," he said.

In some ways, Jooste stuck to the script with impeccable precision. He reframed each awkward point adeptly, twisting it to shine the light on a decoy who could conceivably absorb the blame. As for himself, well, the picture he sketched was that of a simple retailer with a dream that had been cruelly snatched from his hands by a venal, scheming former partner who had, in a final twist of the knife, duped Deloitte into destroying a business he'd built over 29 years.

As for accounting gimmicks, perish the thought. "This company wasn't about accounting," he said. "It was a business with 12,000 stores, 50 factories around 30 different countries in the world, giving employment from when we started to a couple of hundred people to 130,000 people." In the final analysis, his only mistake was to have ever got close to Seifert and "to have grown too fast, too quickly, into too many countries".

In a technical sense, Markus Jooste had ticked all the boxes of a workable defence. But still, for those who watched his performance, it left a bad taste in the mouth. Still, the MPs, technically ill-equipped to properly engage Jooste and circumscribed by the court agreement that he couldn't be pushed to incriminate himself, were reluctant to press too hard. Had they pressed deeper, perhaps, the outcome might have been very different. After all, at times Jooste appeared barely able to suppress his seething contempt for the parliamentarians. Once or twice, it seemed he might crack – such as when one MP compared Steinhoff to a Ponzi scheme (it is a real business with shops and staff, he said), and when another MP suggested its accounts weren't up to the standard of a spaza shop.

David Maynier was sitting perhaps the closest to Jooste throughout the hearing, about one and a half metres away. He noticed, during the hearing, that Jooste's demeanour shifted. "He was becoming more confident *and* more exhausted," he says. "Which could have proven fatal because, had the cross-examination continued for a couple more hours, Markus Jooste would, almost certainly, have dropped his guard and blown himself up."[4] Only, it didn't happen like that, because one of the chairmen, Themba Godi, adjourned the meeting at lunchtime. So, Jooste didn't end up cracking. "Markus Jooste survived to fight another day because of a built-in tactical advantage – which is that members of Parliament are always reluctant to miss lunch," says Maynier.

* * *

There was an incident, as Jooste was walking out of Parliament, that few people noticed. A trade union member of the Federation of Unions of

South Africa (Fedusa) managed to push through the scrum of Jooste's legal team, and get close enough to yell in Jooste's ear. "How do you feel?" he yelled. "We lost billions because of you, how do you feel? And you come here and act is if nothing is wrong. You must be ashamed of yourself." As he has done for months, Jooste set his jaw and ignored the heckling, just as he'd iced out the throngs of journalists the whole day. He kept walking, as if nothing had happened, out into the street where bulging, stern-eyed men shepherded him into the back seat of his car.

Dr Dennis George, general secretary of Fedusa, said he found Jooste's performance unconvincing. "Jooste doesn't want to take responsibility. When you're the CEO, the buck has to stop somewhere. For him to try to put the blame on someone else is totally unacceptable."[5] You could understand George's frustration. After all, his union members – the civil servants who belonged to Fedusa, whose pensions were invested through the Public Investment Corporation – had lost plenty of money. Before Steinhoff's crash, those civil servants had a R5.7bn stake in Steinhoff; by early September, when Jooste appeared in Parliament, their shares were worth R667m.

It's a similar story for pension fund members around the country. Nearly two-thirds of South Africa's pension funds had some kind of exposure to Steinhoff, and some got hurt worse than others.

In most cases, though, the fact that pension funds had plenty of other assets staunched the bleeding to some extent. Far worse were those closest to Jooste who had invested pretty much *everything* in Steinhoff. One former member of Steinhoff's executive committee, who lost more than R180m but who doesn't want to be named, says he never sold a share in his life. He explained it was an unspoken rule that you didn't sell – that it was somehow "disloyal". But, since anyone who exercises share options still has to pay tax on those shares, he even borrowed more money to pay the tax. Today, he still owes money for the transaction, while his shares are worth just R5m. "I believed the story. I thought Markus was the cleverest guy I'd met." Jooste, he believed, would Midas his wealth into multiples of what it was. Then the opposite happened. "It made me incredibly bitter initially," he says. "I had to come to terms with it. I woke up one night and thought about it, and figured, if all those stories are true, then I'm actually glad I never sold a share, because it would be the proceeds of crime."

After Markus Jooste had appeared in Parliament, this Steinhoff executive remarked that it made his stomach "churn to watch it".

16

Trapped

———

"Markus Jooste is a great person, I'm telling you," says Thembinkosi Sobazile, who has the unique distinction of holding a job title that nobody else
across the globe can boast of. Sobazile, known to those around town as
"Bravo", is the official "Whale Crier" of Hermanus, the Western Cape seaside
hamlet about 115 kilometres from Cape Town. Sobazile is only the fifth
man to hold the kelp horn, which he sounds whenever he sights a whale
from atop the coastal cliffs.[1]

He's been doing the job for three years, and until recently he'd often
speak to Markus Jooste, who is perhaps even more famous today than the
Hermanus whales. "I haven't seen him this year. But he has a warmth, the
sort of person who can give you confidence when you speak to them. He's
not like others – people who're untouchable or ruthless." (Other Hermanus
residents, especially those who invested in Steinhoff, may beg to differ
with Sobazile's assessment.)

In Zakes Mda's lyrical novel *The Whale Caller*, he tells how Hermanus
has been swallowed by the rich. The double- and triple-storey houses belong
to "rich people from as far away as Johannesburg, who spent part of the
year enjoying the spoils of their wealth in the laid-back ambience of the
village". Hermanus has always been a refuge for the wealthy. Particularly
from the mid-1900s, well-heeled businessmen from Joburg or Pretoria
would frequently make the long trek down to Hermanus for the Christmas
holidays. The list of people with a soft spot for the town includes former

Anglo American chairman Gavin Relly, Dr Anton Rupert and Markus Jooste himself.

While the lesser-spotted Markus has become almost a mythical character in Hermanus these days, for more than a decade he was *the* big shot. He'd bought vast wedges of land, including the old Post Office. Back in 2005, when Markus Jooste bought Anton Rupert's old house in Voëlklip, he asked the local master builder, Lourens Theron, to create his new villa. It was a handsome job he did too: wooden shutters, and an understated, elegant open-plan design inside with low-hanging chandeliers, an indoor pool and wooden floors. (Markus took out some of the old Norfolk pines, infuriating Johann Rupert in the process.)

Just more than a decade later, in 2016, Jooste called Lourens again, and asked him if he could build something far more elaborate – a villa on the shorefront on East Cliff, between his current house in Voëlklip and Hermanus's old harbour. It was to be an immense and complicated job, situated on the water's edge, on part of the property known as Owl Rock, once owned by Gavin Relly. After Relly and his wife died, the property was subdivided. Jooste's company Erf 2825 Hermanus Pty Ltd paid R36.5m for his subdivided 7,441m² section, according to Deeds Office records.[2]

Speaking today, Lourens Theron says: "It was going to be an ambitious, upper-class project. But we had all the knowledge of the previous one we built for him, so we assembled our team and we started on the property."[3] It wasn't easy. The ground sloped dramatically towards the sea, and there were numerous ageing trees, a swimming pool, and a crumbling cottage towards the bottom. The trees were taken out, and some boulders moved, before the ground was levelled. "Under the whole site, we found fragmented rock at different depths, which had to be cleared and excavated," says one person who worked on it. At the top level, there was to be one garage and one immense house. Architect Rossouw Theron (no relation of Lourens Theron), who designed the house, said it was a tricky site, partly because there was a lot of rock that had to be moved, as well as the usual underground water you'd expect near the coast. "We had to create a platform for the house to be on. It was difficult," he says.[4]

Then, 5 December happened. Three days after Jooste's resignation, Rossouw Theron says he got an instruction: stop everything you're doing. The whirr of bulldozers that had penetrated neighbours' ears for months finally fell silent. "We're in the process of making it safe now," Theron says. But he's hoping that, at some stage, the project can be completed.

If it does go on, it won't be with Lourens Theron. Once he got the instruction to stop, he decided to retire completely. "Ja, it wasn't just the building – I also had Steinhoff shares, unfortunately," says Lourens. "I had those shares through my retirement annuity, which paid out recently when I retired. In the end, the fall in the Steinhoff shares ended up costing me R140,000."

Eward Grobler, who runs a consulting engineering company called Grobler & Associates, had also done work on the property, and he took Jooste's firm to court to recover his costs. "We were told the day before Jooste's resignation as Steinhoff CEO to stop all work, and that we should send accounts for all the work we'd done to that point. But they didn't pay anyone, which is why I told them I had no option but to go to court." Finally, in April, Jooste's company apparently sold a flat in Hermanus and used the proceeds to pay the contractors like Grobler. It wasn't a big amount of cash for Jooste, but for a small business the amounts were pretty substantial.

* * *

Today, Markus Jooste's ambitious beachside villa remains a forlorn building site. Mounds of compacted sand remain, and the chunky rectangular concrete slabs, meant to filter water away from the foundations, stand as a monument of Jooste's stillborn seaside dream. The odd strand of red-and-white barrier tape hangs, disembodied, along the wire fence. On any given day, voyeurs will stop and gawk at the abandoned site – a freeze-framed postcard from the Steinhoff crash site.

Not that Markus Jooste was ever keen to share his dream, mind. The complex was one of a bunch of properties which stand in the way of plans by Hermanus residents to build a continuous twelve-kilometre-long cliff path, from Voëlklip to the old harbour. Debora Wynn, a member of the

Cliff Path Action Group, says that about ten families are fighting efforts to have the cliff path extend past the bottom of their properties. "They don't want to accept that. So it means that over this entire twelve-kilometre stretch, there's just this one 800-metre stretch where you can't walk, and you have to return to the road."[5] The families – including Markus Jooste – have resisted efforts to build the path, claiming it will "restrict their privacy". Jooste, before his fall, apparently said that over his dead body would he let anyone build a path across the front of his property.

Jobre Stassen, who has a holiday house in Hermanus and is part of the Cliff Path Action Group, says Jooste had often enjoyed walking on the cliff himself. So it came as quite a surprise that he was unwilling to compromise on the path. "For someone who'd lived there twenty years, perhaps you can understand it. But Markus was only in the building phase, and he was totally uncooperative. It seemed utterly selfish not to let people walk on the shorefront in front of his property," she says.[6]

It wasn't the sort of posture that endeared Jooste to many of the residents. Nor, in fact, was the collapse of Steinhoff, in which many of the residents themselves had money. There was plenty of anger initially, says one resident, who asked not to be identified. "But people's attitudes have probably softened over time – I don't think there's much ill will towards him anymore," he says.

Stassen, however, says: "What we do understand is that we have a judicial system that doesn't put the *skelms* in jail. So why should it be that the guys who steal cellphones are jailed, but the big guys aren't?" She says the Steinhoff collapse had a knock-on effect for the people of Hermanus. "If you look down 10th Street in Voëlklip where Markus lives, almost every second person had shares in Steinhoff. He had an ability to involve those closest to him in the business, and now they've lost a lot of money." Which is probably why, as the whale crier Sobazile will tell you, it's been a lot easier to see whales in Hermanus this year than it has been to spot Markus Jooste.

* * *

If you're looking for losers from the Steinhoff debacle, few come larger than Braam van Huyssteen. Van Huyssteen's story dates back to 1989, when he opened his first clothing store (called Tropika) in the southern Cape town of Mossel Bay with a loan of R20,000. This small beginning led, after more than a decade of wheeling and dealing, to the opening of the first Tekkie Town store in 2001, in swish Somerset West.

As you'd expect from a man whose nose has seen more insoles than is probably good for anyone, Van Huyssteen has always been a heart-on-the-sleeve operations guy. Unencumbered by subtlety or the oily skills of corporate diplomacy, he's the sort of man you'd expect to be standing in shorts, roasting boerewors over a grill and debating the finer points of Velcro straps. Bernard Mostert, who was Van Huyssteen's MD at Tekkie Town, describes him as "the simplest man", but with the sort of steely nerve under pressure that he's never seen elsewhere. "If I had to make a six-metre putt on a golf course, I wouldn't hand the club to anyone who'd won a major championship like Tiger Woods. I'd give it to Braam, because, when the pressure is on, he doesn't miss."[7]

At any given time, you'd expect to find Van Huyssteen on the floor of one of his stores, testing a new trainer for flexibility, rather than behind a desk. Still, he'd find time to haggle mercilessly on leases and barter for hours with the suppliers of branded shoes. It was a formula that worked. By 2014, Tekkie Town was one of the largest suppliers of Nike, Adidas, Puma and Converse shoes in the country through its 265 stores. That year, the World Economic Forum named Tekkie Town as one of six South African companies, alongside Capitec Bank, law firm Webber Wentzel and Growthpoint Properties, which had what it takes to become a global heavyweight.

Soon afterwards, in November 2014, a private equity firm called Actis pitched up, and snapped up 42.5% of Tekkie Town for R724m. It was around that time that Van Huyssteen met Markus Jooste on the racecourse. (Braam is also an avid owner of racehorses.) "I'd just done the Actis deal when I met him. And Markus asked me what my plans were for Tekkie Town. We spoke about Africa and he said, Don't worry about Africa. Instead, he invited me to Poland after the World Cup in 2015 and he'd show me what they're doing there."[8]

Van Huyssteen went and saw the Pep & Co. stores, which were thriving in Poland. Jooste asked why they couldn't replicate the Tekkie Town model in Poland. Van Huyssteen loved the idea. So, in September 2016, Steinhoff bought the whole of Tekkie Town for R3.25bn: Actis was paid R1.5bn for its stake, and the rest went to Braam van Huyssteen and his five managers. "They weren't just buying a business with earnings of R289m," says Van Huyssteen. "They were buying the ability to replicate this model across the world in places like Poland, and they were buying our skills, to help them fix the speciality part of Pep's business, which had Shoe City in it."

It won't surprise you to learn that rather than getting paid cash, the Tekkie Town management were paid with Steinhoff shares. And, worse, there was a "lock-in clause" preventing them from selling any of these shares within three years. So, when the crash happened, it meant that the Tekkie Town management, including Van Huyssteen, had only R50m of their R1.75bn left – scant reward for three decades. "Look, there are some of my managers who've lost everything, who'd taken out debt against those shares that they couldn't sell, and are now bankrupt," says Van Huyssteen. He, at least, got R724m in cash in 2014 from the Actis deal. So while he took a R1.6bn knock from Steinhoff, it was not as crippling as it was for his managers. He still has a home in the luxurious Fancourt golf estate, a boat in Turkey, and some cash in the bank. "Remember, I also had debt as well. But at least I did have some other shares I could sell. Of course, it's much easier for me, because I'm probably still worth R1.5bn or so. It's not the R3.5bn I had before Steinhoff's collapse, but it's a lot."

What made it worse is that Steinhoff struck a deal with Tekkie Town's management for a profit-sharing deal called an "earn out", which, Van Huyssteen says, would have given his staff at least R800m. Tekkie Town was then injected into STAR, where Van Huyssteen's crew had to answer to many of Pepkor's top brass – who clearly despised him. "There was massive jealousy from the guys in Pep. Pieter Erasmus [Pep's former MD] would ask me, how's that deal you did on the racecourse going? My answer was, Look at the results. We were doing great, up 15% every year. But they couldn't wait to get rid of us."

In January, with Jooste out the picture, relations became even frostier. At a meeting on 31 January, STAR CEO Leon Lourens asked Van Huyssteen to resign. He refused. Then in April, at another meeting, Van Huyssteen called Lourens a "liar". "The cultures were like oil and water," says Van Huyssteen. Lourens agrees, saying that "from a cultural point of view, maybe things didn't work out very well".

But it was more complicated. The 44 top Pepkor old guard, many of whom had disliked the 2014 Steinhoff deal anyway, were furious at being bankrupted by the scandal. They'd also received Steinhoff shares in that process, and were spitting mad about losing it all on a deal they despised in the first place. Throw in the fact that Van Huyssteen was seen as "Jooste's guy", and it was a relationship that was never really likely to thrive anyway.

Then in May, with the cold war many degrees below freezing, Lourens booted Van Huyssteen off STAR's executive committee. Van Huyssteen resigned, claiming his contract had been breached. A month later, more than a hundred Tekkie Town staff followed him out of the door. Almost inevitably, in August 2018, they set up a rival company, Mr Tekkie. "We're starting from scratch again," Van Huyssteen says. "I can honestly tell you, this whole experience made me realise that I'm not really that materialistic. I came from nothing, from a small town, Parys, in the Free State, so I believe we can do it again."

Remarkably, given what has happened, Van Huyssteen has been one of Jooste's stoutest defenders, and remains so even today. "I wasn't his house friend, but I haven't seen with my own eyes what he did yet. Where are the specifics? So, without that, how can I join the peanut gallery?" His experience of Jooste, in every business context, was always positive. "He was very cordial, and from what I saw at board meetings, he always acted in the company's best interests," Van Huyssteen says.

There are others who're also sticking by Jooste. Rian du Plessis, the former CEO of the betting company Phumelela, still speaks to Markus often. "He has given me the assurance that he'll stand and be reckoned for what he has done. He hasn't left the country. He hasn't gone anywhere. So I believe him."[9] It is quite brave of Du Plessis to admit to his continued friendship with Jooste. Many other firm friends have frozen him out completely. But Du Plessis says this is a reflection of a friendship that dates back forty years. "If he has done something wrong, it doesn't mean I'm condoning that. If my brother did something untoward, or something criminal, would I abandon him? No, of course I wouldn't. It would be the easiest thing to walk away, but also the wrong thing."

As for why Jooste has frozen out the world, Du Plessis says this is because of the legal advice he'd received. "Look, in all likelihood, he will be prosecuted both criminally and civilly, and he'll have to answer in those forums. His advisers are telling him not to say anything until then."

*   *   *

Speak to any of Markus Jooste's former colleagues, and none of them can get a fix on his motivations. Quite clearly, it wasn't the money. Besides the 68.9m shares in Steinhoff which he'd accumulated, and besides the secretive proceeds from the forestry deal and Unitrans deal, he'd made an absolute fortune just in his salary and bonuses. From 2003, Jooste took home R492.7m – including R212m in "bonuses". Even after tax (of which he seemed furiously and philosophically opposed to paying), Jooste would have got more than R300m over those years.[10]

In Parliament, Jooste made much of the fact that he had 68.9m shares and "had never sold a single share". The implication, of course, was that he had suffered along with everyone else from the cliff-top plunge of Steinhoff's stock. In one way, it is true: those 68.9m shares were worth R3.5bn before the fall; but just R320m afterwards, when they were sold by Mayfair Speculators. Only, Jooste appears to have *caused* this crash. And anyway, his gargantuan salary shows that it's not like Markus Jooste lost everything. Besides, there was also the money he got from Kluh Investments for the forestry deal, and the Unitrans motors deal. And who knows what else? (For example, did any of the proceeds from the loans to the likes of Campion, Talgarth or the "independent buying groups" find their way into Jooste's hands?)

So, if it wasn't for the money, why would he have done it? There are, of course, numerous theories. For example, Christo Wiese has spoken of how in 2014, when he did the deal that saw Steinhoff buy Pepkor, he made Jooste promise to ensure Steinhoff kept its debt at manageable levels so that it always had an "investment grade" credit rating. Could it be that Jooste was so desperate to keep the rating that he conspired with Siegmar Schmidt and people like Alan Evans to shift assets off Steinhoff's balance sheet to keep that rating? Could it be that he was so desperate for vindication of his strategy of buying assets in Europe that he created companies run by friends who could "leak back" profits, so that Steinhoff showed growth? Could it be that when the auditors began pressing for evidence of contracts and invoices, Jooste, Schmidt and others reacted to this pressure by doing the wrong thing? Or could it just have been ego: the desire to be seen as one of South Africa's most successful businessmen, a high-profile racehorse owner and possibly the largest property owner in Hermanus?

Some believe that Jooste fell prey to the same affliction that saw many other executives succumb to the dark side. It's a playbook that goes like this. At first, a small problem arises – like not being able to recognise a sale in the present financial year. So you fudge it: shift money from another company to "cover it" this year, while telling yourself you'll repay that amount as soon as you get the cash. All you need, you tell yourself, is a bit more time, a bit more luck, or a turn in the market. But the problem doesn't disappear. If anything, it gets worse. So now you have to cover up the last hole, with a new turn . . .

Bernie Madoff, in letters he would write from jail after being convicted of running a Ponzi scheme that swindled investors out of $64bn, described a similarly constricting turn of events. In some cases, he said, someone sets out to steal. But in other cases, he "finds himself trapped in a business situation and makes a tragic mistake that he believes will eventually work itself out".[11]

Mark Dreier, an American lawyer who ended up swindling $113m from clients including Bill Cosby, Tim Burton, Bon Jovi and Justin Timberlake, says he started this way too. "I did not set out to steal hundreds of millions of dollars, but ended up doing so incrementally, after crossing a line I could not retreat from."[12]

Of course, if you believe Jooste's testimony in Parliament, he didn't do anything wrong. According to those who know him, it's possible that Jooste actually *believes* this too.

* * *

Three months after Steinhoff's collapse, Harvard Business School professor Eugene Soltes was part of a panel at the Gordon Institute of Business Science. discussing why white collar criminals do what they do. Soltes told the story of how, one night, flipping through TV channels in the mid-2000s, he'd come across a documentary of regular convicts describing what drove them to break the law. In most cases, it was grim circumstance: drug addiction, money problems or gangs.

But what about the well-heeled executives from Tyco, Enron and World-Com who'd ended up behind bars, Soltes wondered. They had had relatively luxurious lives, draped in privilege. So why did they do it? As a result Soltes began writing letters to those fallen CEOs in prison: Enron's former chairman Kenneth Lay, Bernie Madoff, WorldCom's ex-CEO Bernie Ebbers. Many of them wrote back to him. And their letters were intriguing.

"None of the former executives I spoke with saw himself as a fraud," writes Soltes. "Some, of course, clearly recognized that they had committed a crime, but the person they saw in the mirror was successful, entrepreneurial and ambitious."[13] In their minds, they were victims. In reality, says Soltes, they were "victims of their own self-deception".

Professor David Solomon, who teaches finance at Boston College in Massachusetts, told Soltes in various emails that "nobody is ever the villain in their own narrative". Rather, he says, if somebody does something that paints them as a bad person, "they are more likely to change their opinion of what's right and wrong than change their opinion of themselves".

In some cases, there seems to be something deeper at play – an emotional distance from the consequences of their behaviour that speaks to a certain kind of pathology. There's one moment that Soltes describes, a conversation with Madoff, that implies the former investment manager operates on a different emotional wavelength from most people. It was September 2014, and Madoff's second son, Andrew, had died the previous day of cancer. As Soltes was reading the email informing him of Andrew's death, his phone rang, and it was Bernie Madoff. Madoff had just heard the news of Andrew's death on the radio, and asked Soltes to read the obituary to him. Soltes said he tried to describe the news "in the most compassionate way I could". At the end of it, he asked Madoff how he was doing.

"I'm fine," Madoff replied, and he then asked Soltes a favour.

"I thought he might want me to send a copy of the obituary to him, or deliver a message on his behalf to someone. It wasn't that. Instead, he asked me whether I'd had the chance to look at the Libor [London interbank interest rate] we'd discussed in a prior conversation," says Soltes.

It was an arresting moment for Soltes. Madoff went on to hold an entirely fluent conversation on the arcane technicalities of interest rates. "Madoff interprets and responds to emotion differently from most people. Regardless of how close he got to investors, his personal limitations enabled him to continue his fraud without remorse or guilt."

Dr Giada Del Fabbro, a Johannesburg clinical and forensic psychologist, says that in her career, she's seen numerous businessmen who've bent the rules – and when it gets to that stage, it's never really about the money. "For a certain type of person, it's really about the power, and getting a 'fix' of sorts by getting away with something," she says.[14] Del Fabbro knows what she's talking about. With a master's in forensic psychology from Kent University, and a subsequent doctorate in psychology, she has often worked with the South African Police Service in criminal cases and has lectured on personality disorders. She's always been fascinated with what first turns someone down this road ever since her childhood crush, the South African cricket captain Hansie Cronje, astounded the country by admitting to taking bribes from Indian bookmakers to influence cricket matches.

"It got me thinking, though, what causes someone to go down this path in the first place?" says Del Fabbro.

In Parliament, Democratic Alliance MP David Maynier proposed one reason why Jooste would go down this path: Maynier quoted one of Jooste's former colleagues as saying he was a "fucking psychopath", and asked Jooste for his thoughts on the sentiment. The former Steinhoff CEO was, as you'd expect, entirely unfazed. "I am not in a position to comment on that last question, because I am not aware about the statement or have ever heard it," he replied, his voice not dipping an octave.

But, he added, "I would like to say that I never lied about the activities of the company."

Of course, the term "psychopath" is much abused, appropriated by pop culture and used as a slapdash back-of-matchbox diagnosis for everyone from knife-wielding murderers to genocidal leaders. But in some cases of fraud, Del Fabbro says, it is entirely the right description. "In many of the fraud cases I've seen, it would probably be the correct diagnosis," she says.

The definitive academic work on this subject was captured in the book *Snakes in Suits*, written by two psychologists, Paul Babiak and Robert Hare, who had interviewed two hundred high-potential executives.[15] Babiak and Hare classified 3.5% of them as fitting the profile of corporate psychopath – more than three times what you'd expect in the wider population. "All had the traits of the manipulative psychopath: superficial, grandiose, deceitful, impulsive, irresponsible, not taking responsibility for their actions, and lacking goals, remorse and empathy." Moreover, corporate psychopaths lie with impunity, have a sense of entitlement, and have clear dictatorial tendencies, which often manifest in bullying. Now, you might think that most corporate leaders fitting into that category would actually have quite clear goals. But often they act opportunistically, rather than to reach some defined, long-term strategic vision. For example, they'll buy a company that comes onto the market, rather than because it's the right acquisition. "Yet they can weave compelling stories about situations and events of which they know very little into surprisingly believable visions of the future," say Babiak and Hare. "They will not only blame others, but also create 'evidence' that others are to blame."

As *Snakes in Suits* puts it: "The economic and emotional impact of their selfish behavior on others is irrelevant to them, in part because they believe everyone in this dog-eat-dog world is as greedy and unfeeling as they are . . . people do not exist in their world except as objects, targets and obstacles." But corporate psychopaths aren't great with emotion. As the experts put it, they "hear the words but not the music" of normal emotion. The limbic region of their brains fails to ignite the way other people's do when processing emotional material.[16]

Take Jack Abbott, a man who served plenty of time behind bars for manslaughter and robbery. In the late 1970s the writer Norman Mailer encouraged him to write about his experience, which led to Abbott writing a book called *In the Belly of the Beast*.

In one revealing passage, Abbott says: "There are emotions – a whole spectrum of them – that I know only through words, through reading and in my immature imagination. I can *imagine* I feel these emotions, but I *do not*."[17]

Snakes in Suits shows how corporate fraudsters initially come across as ambitious and enthusiastic, competent, loyal, likeable and "open and honest". They blame any stories to the contrary on "envy of their popularity, a simple misunderstanding, or the failure to know them well enough". And they also rationalise that they're "entitled" to what they're taking.

There's a revealing anecdote in *Snakes in Suits*, recounting the story of Joyti De-Laurey, a 37-year-old personal assistant at the British arm of the famous investment bank Goldman Sachs. Over three years, De-Laurey pilfered more than £4m from her three executive bosses, which she parlayed into a fabulous string of assets, including a seaside villa in Cyprus (£750,000), Cartier jewellery (£300,000), a speedboat (£150,000) and, magnanimously, a £10,000 donation to a charity for sick children.[18] Her lawyer not only blamed the bosses for not noticing that money was going missing, but then argued she was guilty of nothing more than "honest greed". And a dash of entitlement. She wrote a message to God in her "Bible of daily thoughts", saying, "I need one more helping of what's mine, and then I must cut down and cease in time all the plundering."[19] Initially, after she was caught, she signed an affidavit admitting that what she had done was "completely wrong" and saying she wanted to "make amends".

By the time she went to trial, the story had flipped. Her lawyers argued that the three Goldman Sachs MDs she stole from were "fully aware" and, in one case, she said it was "hush money" to cover up an affair. It was a "reward for me being me", she argued. The judge didn't buy her story – and in April 2004, she was convicted of twenty counts of fraud and sentenced to seven years in prison.

What was significant, besides the lying, was that De-Laurey had entirely justified this as her due. Speaking to *The Guardian* newspaper in 2005, she recalled how people would cheer her to court, saying "good on you" and "serves them right". "They could afford to lose that money . . . I am being punished because I dared to take from people like them," she said.

Her case would appear to fall squarely within the *Snakes in Suits* definition of a "corporate psychopath". But this is how it is: if challenged or caught in a lie, the fraudster suffers no embarrassment. Rather, say Babiak and Hare, they "simply change or elaborate on the story line to weave together all the misarranged details into a believable fabric". The motive: to avoid responsibility at all costs.

In many corporate scenarios, "the goal of their game is to set up a scam within the organisation's structure that can fulfill their need for excitement, advancement and power – all without concern about the harmful outcomes to others. Winning almost always involves financial and power rewards."

Babiak and Hare say that corporate psychopaths are particularly attracted to businesses that are constantly in flux, whether it be through mergers, takeovers, joint ventures or constant facelifts. It allows them to cloud the difference between "good" and "bad" leadership, and the constant shifting of the deckchairs enables their tactics to go undetected for longer. "The fact that the psychopath's efforts rarely result in long-term business improvement is clouded by their self-serving bravado and the mystique that follows them." Eventually, when things fall apart, the people who trusted the corporate psychopath realise they've been manipulated. "They feel cheated, defiled, and often incredulous that the person they liked and trusted betrayed their trust."

Speaking today, Del Fabbro says another characteristic of the corporate psychopath is that they believe they're far smarter than anyone else. Their actions, in this sense, are a manifestation of how little respect they have for others. "Often, psychopaths will do horrendous things that you or I couldn't imagine, but it's partly neurological – their baseline levels of what causes anxiety are often a lot higher than other people's. So they tend to take higher risks that would cause other people to crack."

Much of their action is underpinned by a deep level of insecurity. They seek to make themselves look better in the public eye, and can't stand any sort of public humiliation, like being seen to run a failing company. They'll do anything to maintain their standing and prevent anything that they believe would make others lose respect for them. When they get away with it the first time, this emboldens them, "vindicates their sense that they're far smarter than anyone else, and are entitled to this". Of course, when it does all go wrong, and they are caught, it's entirely inevitable that they will seek to shift the blame to others, so that it's not they who're responsible for any failure.

Many of these corporate psychopaths will serve their whole careers without being detected. As Del Fabbro says: "There are some really perceptive people, who're really smart or work in places where they're in charge, and they can last forever. And it's a gradient: for some people, these symptoms aren't that pronounced."

This is a critical point, here. Just because one of Markus Jooste's former colleagues described him as a "psychopath" doesn't mean he is indeed one. For one thing, as the experts say, a few trees don't make a forest. Just because someone has one or two characteristics that might make him a candidate for the title doesn't mean he has all of them. And, anyway, it's the sort of diagnosis you'd like to leave to the experts.

What's clear from Eugene Soltes's research is that all the executives who bent the rules had created their own version of reality, their own narrative of what took place. Speaking at the Gordon Institute, Soltes said that many of the traditional explanations, like greed or some sophisticated cost-benefit analysis, were frustratingly inadequate. "Instead, what I saw was not a failure of reasoning but a failure of intuition. That is, they didn't see the harm associated with their actions at the time." The cognitive dissonance was striking. They saw no "victim" in what they did, and they rationalised their actions. "The problem is, very few people who graduate from top business schools that are sitting comfortably in some of the world's largest organisations, who engage in very serious misconduct, in criminal misconduct, actually believe they're going to be held criminally accountable." Rather, they just didn't see themselves as criminal, as the sort of person who'd get sent to prison.

This dissonance is clear from all the case studies. Take Sam Waksal, a biotech billionaire convicted of insider trading in the early 2000s in the US. Talking about his conviction later, Waksal said: "I could sit there at the same time, thinking I was the most honest CEO that ever lived. And at the same time, I could glibly do something and rationalize it [when] I cut a corner."

*   *   *

After his testimony in Parliament, Markus Jooste melted back into his compound in Hermanus, spanning a whole block on 10th Street above Grotto Beach. If you visit the house, his staff are wary about giving away any information as to his whereabouts. Understandably. One afternoon when I was at the house, two bruisers in vests drove slowly past twice, then doubled back and asked me, standing at the gate, if "the owner" was around, as they'd been asked to come "fix something". It seemed entirely menacing. Reason enough, perhaps, for Jooste to employ the army of bodyguards that rumour suggests he has.

The walls around the house – effectively, at this point, the walls of Jooste's private prison – betray the trauma of 2017. On each one, there are visible signs of the frequent whitewashing that took place over Christmas, as painters were deployed to erase the words "Thief" and "Con artist" that had been daubed on the walls. There were others too: "Pants on fire" and "Psychopath".

It remains unclear to what extent this bothers Markus Jooste. Lawyers who've sat with him during the past few months have said privately that he is in high spirits, jovial and apparently unconcerned, as if nothing was wrong. It speaks to a level of disconnection from the world crashing around his ears. (In Parliament, when he had finished testifying, he jokingly asked his grey-haired advocate, in Afrikaans: Old chap, can I help you with all those papers?)

Elsewhere in Hermanus, tales abound of "Markus spotting". Some talk of him filling up his Bentley at a service station nearby; others say they've seen him at the local OK MiniMark, or during one of his frequent Friday lunches at the Burgundy restaurant at the Old Harbour. "When he's there [at Burgundy], he keeps a low profile," says one of the patrons who has seen him frequently in town. "In the old days, he'd chat to everyone, he was very friendly. But he's no longer like that."

Instead, Jooste is often seen walking, chin set rigidly to avoid meeting anyone's stare, on the cliff paths – thin trails that wind around the coast – with his wife. He flatly ignores neighbours when they greet him. It is as if they don't exist.

The lights flicker on in the evenings, as he swaddles himself behind the high walls and wooden shutters. Markus Jooste may not have been arrested and the final verdict will be that of a court. Given the ineptitude of the country's prosecutors, there's even a real prospect that he might never have to answer to criminal charges. But it doesn't really matter. Frozen out of his community, he's a prisoner already.

Notes

CHAPTER 1

1. Abram Brown, 'The billionaire African behind the continent's greatest retail empire', *Forbes*, 1 March 2016.
2. Elisabeth Dostert, 'Aufgewachsen im Möbelhaus', 17 May 2010, *Süddeutsche Zeitung*, http://www.sueddeutsche.de/wirtschaft/das-unternehmen-xxxlutz-aufge-wachsen-im-moebelhaus-1.772489.
3. Von Henryk Hielscher, 'Prozess um Möbeldiscounter Poco startet im Juli', *Wirt-schaftsWoche*, 26 May 2017, https://www.wiwo.de/unternehmen/handel/steinhoff-prozess-um-moebeldiscounter-poco-startet-im-juli/19849978.html.
4. Ursula Schwarzer and Sven Clausen, 'Einstürzende Neubauten, 24 August 2017, *Manager Magazin*, https://heft.manager-magazin.de/MM/2017/9/152773870/.
5. Paul Theron, interview with author.
6. Interview with author.
7. Interview with author.
8. Bethany Mclean, 'The smartest guys in the room: The amazing rise and scandalous fall of Enron', *Portfolio Trade*, 2003.

CHAPTER 2

1. Interview with author.
2. Jonathan North, 'Soviet prisoners of war: Forgotten Nazi victims of World War II', *World War II* magazine, January 2006.
3. Ibid.
4. H. Giliomee, *The Last Afrikaner Leaders: A Supreme Test of Power* (Tafelberg: Cape Town, 2012).
5. Transcript of recordings made in 2013 to celebrate Steinhoff's 15-year anniversary of its JSE listing, in possession of author.
6. Ibid.
7. Kerstin Schumann, 'Sie geben Westerstede ein Gesicht', *NWZOnline*, 26 February 2016, https://www.nwzonline.de/ammerland/wirtschaft/sie-geben-westerstede-ein-gesicht_a_6,1,506044866.html.

8. Heiner Otto, 'Hard-working: Via Bremerhaven to Sylt', *NWZOnline*, 18 June 2018, https://www.nwzonline.de/bremerhaven/bremerhaven-riesen-radtour-fleissig-treten-ueber-bremerhaven-nach-sylt_a_50,1,3311206954.html.

CHAPTER 3
1. Alec Hogg, "Markus Jooste – on losing bids, building Steinhoff and drawing inspiration,' BizNews.com, 3 June 2016.
2. Ibid.
3. Thys du Toit, interview with author.
4. Author discussion with Rian Oberholzer.
5. Adele Shevel, 'Following in the steps of a master deal-maker', *Business Times*, 24 May 2015.
6. Interview with author.
7. Alec Hogg, "Markus Jooste – on losing bids, building Steinhoff and drawing inspiration,' BizNews.com, 3 June 2016.
8. David Meades, interview with author.
9. Michael Delport, interview with author.
10. Companies and Intellectual Property Commission (CIPC), directorship records for MJ Jooste and MM Delport.
11. Transcript of recordings made in 2013 to celebrate Steinhoff's 15-year anniversary of its JSE listing, in possession of author.
12. Ibid.
13. Ibid.
14. Ibid.
15. Terence Craig, interview with author.
16. Author interview with former Steinhoff colleague, who spoke anonymously.
17. Author interview with Cape Town businessman, who spoke anonymously.
18. Christopher Rutledge, interview with author.
19. Christopher Rutledge, 'The seagull's name was Markus: Steinhoff and the Stellenbosch Mafia', Huffington Post, 12 December 2017, https://www.huffingtonpost.co.za/christopher-rutledge/the-seagulls-name-was-markus-how-a-patriarchal-culture-at-steinhoff-allowed-it-to-hide-the-losses_a_23303325/.
20. Christo Wiese, interview with author.
21. Fredrick Kunkle, 'Here are some takeaways from the Uber founder's departure', *Washington Post*, 20 June 2017, https://www.washingtonpost.com/news/tripping/wp/2017/06/20/here-are-some-takeaways-from-uber-founders-departure/?noredirect=on&utm_term=.0862061ab77c.
22. Dr Mary Lamia, 'The psychology of a workplace bully', *The Guardian*, 28 March 2017.
23. Christopher Rutledge, interview with author.
24. Transcript of Steinhoff's 15th anniversary recordings.
25. Ibid.
26. Abbigail Chiodo and Michael Owyang, 'The case study of a currency crisis: The Russian default of 1998', November 2002, Federal Reserve Bank of St Louis,

https://research.stlouisfed.org/publications/review/2002/11/01/a-case-study-of-a-currency-crisis-the-russian-default-of-1998.

27. Ibid.
28. International Monetary Fund, 'The crisis in emerging markets', from *Spillover Effects among Emerging Markets: The Extent of Differentiation.*
29. Transcript of Steinhoff's 15th anniversary recordings.
30. Steinhoff pre-listing prospectus, 9 September 1998, p. 27; and for comparison, Steinhoff annual report 2000, p. 44.
31. Interview with author.
32. Ibid.
33. Transcript of Steinhoff's 15th anniversary recordings.
34. Ibid.
35. Author interview with former Steinhoff banker.
36. Allen Swiegers, interview with author.
37. David O'Sullivan, discussion with author.
38. Author interview with Rutledge.

CHAPTER 4
1. Knysna Woodworkers, http://knysnawoodworkers.co.za/articles/knysna-wood-cutters-3/.
2. 'Barloworld sells timber stake to Steinhoff', *Fin24*, 5 July 2001, https://www.fin24.com/Companies/Barloworld-sells-timber-stake-to-Steinhoff-20010705.
3. Judgment by Judge Owen Rogers in the Western Cape High Court, *Kluh v SA Revenue Service*, 9 September 2014, paragraph 11.
4. Steinhoff annual report 2002, pp. 81 and 100.
5. *Kluh v SA Revenue Service*, judgment, paragraph 12.
6. Ibid., judgment, paragraph 34.
7. Ibid., judgment, paragraph 19.
8. Forestry South Africa, statistical data industry facts 1980 to 2016, http://www.forestry.co.za/statistical-data/.
9. *Kluh v SA Revenue Service*, judgment, paragraph 19.
10. Moneyhouse Swiss company records, accessed by author, https://www.money-house.ch/en/company/fihag-finanz-und-handels-13199007851/messages.
11. Affidavits, obtained by author.
12. Stehan Grobler, interview with author, 2011.
13. Rob Rose, 'Taxman targets the rich', *Sunday Times*, 9 October 2011.
14. Blog post on African Betting Clan, 10 October 2011, https://www.africanbetting-clan.co.za/index.php/kunena/abc-forum/13805-the-tax-man-cometh.html.
15. David Clegg, 'Do SARS and the courts have a Kluh?', *Tax Talk* magazine, March 2017.
16. Adele Shevel, 'Steinhoff ready for European retail takeover', *Sunday Times*, 27 February 2011.
17. Transcript of recordings made in 2013 to celebrate Steinhoff's 15-year anniversary of its JSE listing, in possession of author.
18. Ibid.

19. Ibid.
20. Steven de Bruyn, interview with author.
21. Ibid.
22. Former Unitrans executive, interview with author.
23. 'The dangerous race to the bottom on corporate tax', Oxfam policy paper, 12 December 2016.
24. Danny Hakim, 'Europe takes aim at deals created to escape taxes', *New York Times*, 14 November 2014, https://www.nytimes.com/2014/11/15/business/international/the-tax-attraction-between-starbucks-and-the-netherlands.html.
25. Jeremy Kahn, 'Google's "Dutch sandwich" shielded 16 billion euros from tax', *Bloomberg*, 2 January 2018.
26. Alec Hogg, 'Markus Jooste: On losing bids, building Steinhoff and drawing inspiration', *BizNews*, 3 June 2016.
27. Presentation by Stehan Grobler, 'Will we see a return of traditional financing structures?', Karlsruhe, Germany, October 2010.
28. Steinhoff 2011 annual report, p. 12.
29. Announcement by Steinhoff, 'Hemisphere real estate valuation', 3 April 2018. Andrew Cuffe, interview with author.

CHAPTER 5
1. Craig Butters, interview with author.
2. JP Morgan equity research by Sean Holmes, 'Steinhoff: flatters only to disappoint', 3 April 2007, in possession of author.
3. Andrew Cuffe, interview with author.
4. Ibid.
5. Greg Davies, interview with author.
6. Steinhoff Africa Retail pre-listing prospectus, 4 September 2017, accessible from https://star-group.co.za/2017-listing/, p. 30.
7. Miles Johnson and Ben McLannahan, 'JP Morgan reveals paper Steinhoff loss of $143m', *Financial Times*, 12 January 2018.
8. Ibid.
9. Mark Baker, 'US banks face more taxing issues than meets the eye', *Euromoney*, 26 January 2018, https://www.euromoney.com/article/b16ngtvd4gkysq/us-banks-face-more-taxing-issues-than-meets-the-eye.
10. Hanna Ziady, 'How Steinhoff made Wall Street banks bleed', *Financial Mail*, 25 January 2018.
11. Alex Morrell, 'A single client is blowing a hole through Wall Street bank earnings', *Market Insider*, 17 January 2018, https://www.businessinsider.com/steinhoff-international-is-blowing-a-hole-through-bank-earnings-2018-1?IR=T.
12. Matt Taibbi, 'The Great American Bubble Machine', *Rolling Stone*, 9 July 2009.
13. Terence Craig, interview with author.
14. Interview with author.
15. Prinesha Naidoo, 'Steinhoff slams German fraud allegations', *Moneyweb*, 25 August 2017, https://www.moneyweb.co.za/news/companies-and-deals/steinhoff-slams-german-fraud-allegations/.

16. Craig Butters, interview with author.
17. Andrew Cuffe, interview with author.
18. Thomas Friedman, 'Stampeding black elephants', *New York Times*, 22 November 2014, https://www.nytimes.com/2014/11/23/opinion/sunday/thomas-l-friedman-stampeding-black-elephants.html.

CHAPTER 6
1. Hamilton Sayer, 'Sir Abe Bailey: His life and achievements', University of Cape Town research thesis, 1974, https://open.uct.ac.za/bitstream/handle/11427/21508/thesis_hum_1974_sayer_hamilton.pdf.
2. 'Who's who in the thoroughbred zoo', *Summerhill*, 9 October 2015, http://www.summerhill.co.za/blog/2015/10/9/markus-jooste.
3. 'Markus Jooste', *Sporting Post*, 5 March 2011, https://www.sportingpost.co.za/profile/markus-jooste/.
4. Ibid.
5. David Mollett, 'Jooste's shrewd move on National Emblem', *The Herald*, 26 May 2002.
6. 'John Koster', *Sporting Post*, 20 January 2016.
7. 'Jooste makes huge investment in racing', *The Herald*, 30 September 2005.
8. 'Just get Jooste it', *Sporting Post*.
9. Brett Maselle, interview with author.
10. Ibid.
11. Mike de Kock writing on his blog, 21 November 2014, http://mikedekockracing.com/wp/index.php/2014/11/to-whom-it-may-concern/.
12. Angelique Serrao, 'How the Markus Jooste scandal may impact SA's biggest horse racing auction', *News24*, 19 January 2018.
13. Stafford Thomas, 'Jooste's horses: Shutting the stable door ...', *Financial Mail*, 21 December 2017.
14. 'Just get Jooste it', *Sporting Post*, 20 December 2012.
15. Stafford Thomas, 'Jooste's horses: Shutting the stable door ...'.
16. 'Jack the lad v the Markus cavalry', *The Times*, 7 October 2016.
17. Ibid.
18. 'The Juliet Rose provides a first European group for Mayfair Speculators', *Courses and Elevage*, 5 June 2016.
19. Brett Maselle, 'NHA: rules or guidelines', open letter published in *Sporting Post*, 12 March 2018.
20. Hassen Adams, interview with author.
21. Michael Leaf, interview with author.
22. Bernard Kantor, interview with author.
23. Transcript of recordings made in 2013 to celebrate Steinhoff's 15-year anniversary of its JSE listing, in possession of author.
24. 'Straight-shooting Van Niekerk buries ghosts', *Sporting Post*, 20 January 2018.
25. Interview with author.
26. Dave Mollett, 'Call me Robin Hood of Epsom, yells Markus Jooste from top of the Hill', *Business Day*, 30 May 2017.

27. 'Epsom to feature Poundland Hill as part of Derby festival sponsorship', *The Guardian*, 11 May 2017.
28. Dave Fraser, 'In for a penny ...', *The Sun*, 12 May 2007.
29. *Kenilworth Racing v Gold Circle*, Competition Tribunal ruling, 7 February 2013, http://www.saflii.org/za/cases/ZACT/2013/6.html.
30. 'Phumelela responds to Jayes', *Sporting Post*, 26 August 2011.
31. John Koster, interview with author.
32. Joey Ramsden, interview with author.

CHAPTER 7
1. Giulietta Talevi, 'Jooste's deal making', *Financial Mail*, 12 October 2017.
2. European Union, GDP growth year-on-year, from World Bank data, https://data.worldbank.org/indicator/NY.GDP.MKTP.KD.ZG?end=2017&locations=EU&start=1999.
3. Transcript of recordings made in 2013 to celebrate Steinhoff's 15-year anniversary of its JSE listing, in possession of author.
4. Ibid.
5. Craig Butters, interview with author.
6. Rob Rose, 'Credit crunch', *Financial Mail*, 31 July 2015.
7. Ibid.
8. Rob Rose, 'Don't call us, we'll call you – at a price', *Business Times*, 8 June 2014.
9. Ibid.
10. *Credit Bureau Monitor*, March 2018, published by the National Credit Regulator.
11. 'Long walk to financial ruin', *The Economist*, 18 January 2018.
12. Ibid.
13. Rob Rose, 'Steinhoff shows how little style costs', *Business Times*, 18 March 2012.
14. Steinhoff 2015 annual financial statements 2015, p. 55.
15. Steinhoff 2015 annual report, p. 54.
16. Ibid.
17. Steinhoff 2016 annual report, p. 25.
18. Rob Rose, 'How Steinhoff got JD Group for a steal', *Investor's Monthly*, 28 March 2012.

CHAPTER 8
1. 'Steinhoff: The empire builder has no clothes', report by Portsea Asset Management, June 2017, in possession of author.
2. 'Viceroy unearths Steinhoff's skeletons', report by Viceroy Research, 6 December 2017.
3. Steinhoff director, speaking anonymously, in discussion with author.
4. Preston Smith, 'Where the money went', *Poland Monthly*, September 2004.
5. Will Maydon, interview with author.
6. Tom Bergin and Alasdair Pal, 'Steinhoff didn't tell investors about nearly $1bn in deals', *Reuters*, 8 November 2017.
7. Markus Jooste, 'Steinhoff's GT Branding Holding investor information correct

and in line with IFRS requirements', Steinhoff stock exchange news announcement, 8 November 2017.

8. Southern View Finance, pre-listing statement, 23 September 2013, in possession of author.

9. Christo Wiese, interview with author.

10. 'National Credit Regulator issues a compliance notice to Southern View Finance', National Credit Regulator, August 2014, http://www.ncr.org.za/press_release/aug2014/Capfin.pdf.

11. Michael Jacks and Sa'ad Chothia, 'Steinhoff: Off balance-sheet offsides', Arqaam Capital investment research in possession of author.

12. Transcript of recordings made in 2013 to celebrate Steinhoff's 15-year anniversary of its JSE listing, in possession of author.

13. See www.attheraces.com, ownership statistics of Jim Maxwell, Malcolm King and Markus Jooste, http://www.attheraces.com/form/owner/Jim-Lewis,-Markus-Jooste,-Malcolm-King/1226185.

14. 'Jooste and I are friends', *Sporting Post*, 10 May 2018, https://www.sportingpost.co.za/2018/05/rian-du-plessis-markus-jooste-jooste-and-i-are-friends-rian-du-plessis/.

15. Luca Casiraghi and Janice Kew, 'Meet the investors snapping up scandal-racked Steinhoff', *Bloomberg*, 14 March 2018.

16. Gaby de Groot and Jan Braaksma, 'Steinhoff creëert op Bahama's mistbank rond Brits vastgoed', *Het Financieele Dagblad*, 9 April 2018.

CHAPTER 9

1. Christo Wiese, interview with author.

2. Christo Wiese, interview with Bruce Whitfield, 24 June 2016.

3. Johann van Rooyen, 'Renier van Rooyen: Founder of Pep Stores', ebook, updated 2018.

4. Ibid.

5. Whitey Basson, interview with author.

6. Ibid.

7. Van Rooyen, 'Renier van Rooyen'.

8. Christo Wiese, interview with Bruce Whitfield, 24 June 2016.

9. 'Steinhoff recovers after Frankfurt listing', BusinessDay TV interview with Giulietta Talevi, 7 December 2015.

10. Nick Hedley, 'Steinhoff deal to take Pep stores to Europe', 'Steinhoff deal to take Pep stores to Europe,' *Business Day*, 26 November 2014.

11. Andrew Cuffe, interview with author.

12. Cautionary announcement, Brait, 19 September 2014.

13. Anonymous email, sent to author, December 2014.

14. Rob Rose, 'Will Wiese run rings around the FSB's probe?', *Business Times*, 28 June 2015.

15. Mervyn King, interview with author.

16. Craig Butters, interview with author.

17. Johann van Rooyen, interview with author.

CHAPTER 10

1. BusinessDay TV interview with Markus Jooste, 8 December 2015.
2. Barry Norris, interview with author.
3. Andreas Dörnfelder and Peter Köhler, 'Wo waren Sie beim Börsengang, Herr Jooste?', *Handelsblatt*, 8 December 2015.
4. BusinessDay TV interview with Jooste.
5. Christo Wiese, interview with author.
6. BusinessDay TV interview with Jooste.
7. Alec Hogg, 'Markus Jooste: On losing bids, building Steinhoff and drawing inspiration', *BizNews*, 3 June 2016.
8. Ibid.
9. Ashley Armstrong and Jon Yeomans, 'Poundland bought by South African group Steinhoff for £597m, *Daily Telegraph*, 13 July 2016.
10. Ciara Linnane, 'Analysts stunned by 115% premium in Mattress Firm takeover bid', *MarketWatch.com*, 9 August 2016, https://www.marketwatch.com/story/analysts-stunned-by-115-premium-in-mattress-firm-takeover-bid-2016-08-08.
11. Steinhoff non-executive director, interview with author.
12. Steinhoff stock exchange news service announcement, 8 August 2016, 'Steinhoff International to acquire Mattress Firm Corporation for $64.00 per share'.
13. Steinhoff, acquisition of Mattress Firm analyst presentation, 7 August 2016.
14. Case number 2017-73196, *Mattress Firm v Bruce Levy, Alexander Deitch, Ryan Vinson and Others* in the District Court of Harris County, Texas. Plaintiff's original petition, in possession of author.
15. Jarred Schenke, 'Fired Colliers broker says Mattress firm execs weaponized real estate, encouraged insider deals', *Bisnow Atlanta*, 22 March 2018.
16. Mattress Firm report to investors for the quarter ending 2 August 2016, form 10-Q, p. 26.
17. Jessica Kuruthukulangara, 'Tempur Sealy scraps contract with biggest customer Mattress Firm', *Reuters*, 30 January 2017.
18. Austen Hufford, 'Tempur Sealy shares drop after Mattress Firm contracts terminated', *Wall Street Journal*, 30 January 2017.
19. David Perry, 'Industry analysts reflect on Tempur Sealy, Mattress Firm split', *Furniture Today*, 30 January 2017.
20. Nathan Bomey, 'There's a fierce battle over your bed: Industry goes to the mattresses', *USA Today*, 7 August 2018.
21. Barry Norris, interview with author.
22. Greg Bennett, interview with author.
23. Barry Norris, 'Stinky Steinhoff and the secret sauce of Stellenbosch', Argonautica Blog, 8 December 2017, https://blog.argonautcapital.co.uk/articles/2017/12/08/stinky-steinhoff-and-the-secret-sauce-of-stellenbosch/.
24. 'Why secretive UK hedge fund shorted Steinhoff International', *Australian Financial Review*, 5 January 2018.
25. Sebastian Mallaby, 'Go for the jugular', *The Atlantic*, 4 June 2010.
26. Stanley Druckenmiller, interview with CNBC's Kelly Evans, 12 December 2017.

27. 'Fairtree Assegai wins fund of the year', *HedgeNews Africa*, 23 February 2018.
28. JP Verster, interview with author.
29. Author's discussion with former Kaizen Asset Management employee.
30. Portsea Asset Management, 'The empire builder has no clothes', June 2017, in possession of author.
31. Ursula Schwarzer and Sven Clausen, 'Einstürzende Neubauten, *Manager Magazin*, 25 August 2017.
32. Christo Wiese, interview with author.

CHAPTER 12
1. Karen Breytenbach, 'Hundreds gather for Rupert's funeral', Independent Newspapers, 26 January 2006.
2. Ebbe Dommisse, *Anton Rupert: A Biography* (Tafelberg: Cape Town, 2009).
3. New World Wealth, 'AfrAsia Bank South Africa Wealth Report', April 2018.
4. Piet Mouton, interview with author.
5. Johann Rupert, interview with author.
6. Ibid.
7. Jannie Mouton, Deloitte presentation to CNBC in Green Point, Cape Town, 6 June 2012, https://www.youtube.com/watch?v=SaWMgJMoEF4.
8. Jannie Mouton, 'Dear colleagues, shareholders and friends ...', 2 May 2018, http://psggroup.co.za/sens-content/?id=201805020038A.
9. Piet Mouton, interview with author.
10. David Meades, interview with author.
11. 'How Shoprite chairman Christo Wiese made his billions', *CNBC*, 19 October 2015, https://www.youtube.com/watch?v=kyQD-bSGJYs.
12. David Meades, interview with author.
13. Christo Wiese, interview with author.
14. GT Ferreira, discussion with author.
15. 'Tokara named one of the top 50 most admired wine brands', www.wine.co.za, 21 March 2018.
16. Jancis Robinson, 'South African overview 2003', 6 July 2003, https://www.jancisrobinson.com/articles/south-african-overview-2003.
17. Founding affidavit, *Gerritt Thomas Ferreira and Tokara v Steinhoff International*, High Court of South Africa Western Cape.
18. Jannie Mouton, discussion with author, January 2018.
19. Founding affidavit, *Gerritt Thomas Ferreira and Tokara v Steinhoff International*, High Court of South Africa Western Cape.
20. Thys du Toit, interview with author.
21. Founding affidavit, *Gerritt Thomas Ferreira and Tokara v Steinhoff International*, High Court of South Africa Western Cape.
22. Piet Mouton, interview with author.
23. GT Ferreira, interview with author.
24. Thys du Toit, interview with author.
25. Anonymous Stellenbosch University alumnus, interview with author.

26. Angelique Serrao and Pieter du Toit, 'Markus Jooste, the blonde polo player, and the room with a view', *News24*, 13 December 2017, https://www.news24.com/SouthAfrica/News/exclusive-markus-jooste-the-blonde-polo-player-and-a-room-with-a-view-20171213.
27. Carlu Swart, interview with author.
28. Berdine Odendaal, Deeds Office records of purchases and sales, www.windeed.com.
29. Christo Wiese, interview with author.
30. Janice Kew, 'Steinhoff's angry hometown erases traces of its fallen star', *Bloomberg*, 2 February 2018.
31. Frikkie Nel, interview with author.
32. Steinhoff annual report 2014 and 2015, calculations by author.
33. Ibid.

CHAPTER 14
1. Heather Sonn, interview with author.
2. Steve Booysen, interview with author.
3. Heather Sonn, interview with author.
4. Steve Booysen, interview with author.
5. Ben la Grange, testimony to the South African Parliament, 29 August 2018.
6. Tony Gouveia, interview with author.
7. *Absa Bank v Mayfair Holdings and Mayfair Speculators*, Western Cape High Court, 14 December 2017, case number 23195/17.
8. *Investec Bank v Mayfair Speculators and Ruby Street Investments*, Western Cape High Court, 14 December 2017, case number 22973/17.
9. Tony Gouveia, interview with author.
10. Panel discussions: ethics versus legality in South Africa at Bain & Co., attended by author.
11. University of Stellenbosch Business School, 'The Steinhoff saga', June 2018, https://www.usb.ac.za/usb_reports/steinhoff-saga/.
12. Dr Johan van Zyl, interview with author.
13. Heather Sonn, interview with author.
14. University of Stellenbosch, Business School, 'The Steinhoff saga'.
15. Professor Nick Binedell, interview with author.
16. Nicky Newton-King, interview with author.
17. Steve Booysen, interview with author.

CHAPTER 15
1. "Summons to appear before standing committee on finance", 22 August 2018, obtained by author from court papers.
2. *MJ Jooste v The Acting Secretary to Parliament*, Western Cape High Court, case number 15811/18, 24 August 2018.
3. Bernard Agulhas, interview with author.
4. David Maynier, interview with author.
5. Dr Dennis George, Fedusa, interview with author.

CHAPTER 16

1. Thembinkosi Sobazile, interview with author.

2. Deeds Office search, Erf 12257 Hermanus, Transfer document T6219/2016.

3. Lourens Theron, interview with author.

4. Rossouw Theron, interview with author.

5. Debora Wynn, interview with author.

6. Jobre Stassen, interview with author.

7. Bernard Mostert, interview with author.

8. Braam van Huyssteen, interview with author.

9. Rian du Plessis, interview with author.

10. Author's calculation of Markus Jooste's salary and bonuses, based on Steinhoff annual reports, 1998 to 2016.

11. Eugene Soltes, 'Why they do it: Inside the mind of the white-collar criminal', *Public Affairs*, 2016.

12. Ibid.

13. Ibid.

14. Dr Giada Del Fabbro, interview with author.

15. Paul Babiak and Robert D. Hare, *Snakes in Suits: When Psychopaths Go to Work* (HarperCollins: New York, 2006).

16. Robert D. Hare, *Without Conscience: The Disturbing World of the Psychopaths among Us* (Guildford Press: New York, 1999).

17. Jack Abbott, *In the Belly of the Beast: Letters from Prison* (Random House: New York, 1981).

18. Julie Bindel, 'The high price of robbing the rich', *The Guardian*, 17 September 2005, https://www.theguardian.com/theguardian/2005/sep/17/weekend7. weekend.

19. 'De-Laurey's letters to God', *BBC News*, 20 April 2004, http://news.bbc.co.uk/2/hi/uk_news/england/london/3642573.stm.

About the Author

Award-winning journalist Rob Rose is editor of the *Financial Mail*. After earning a law degree, Rose took on the financial-fraud and corporate-governance beats at *Business Day* before moving to the *Financial Mail* in 2007, where he exposed the Barry Tannenbaum Ponzi scheme. He has since worked at the *Sunday Times* as editor of *Business Times* and won numerous awards, including the Sanlam Financial Journalist of the Year. His first book was *The Grand Scam: How Barry Tannenbaum Conned South Africa's Business Elite*.